CHANGING LVN

Seven Life Stages in the Twenty-First Century

Michael Moynagh and Richard Worsley

A & C BLACK • LONDON

First published in Great Britain 2009

A & C Black Publishers Ltd
36 Soho Square, London W1D 3QY
www.acblack.com

Copyright © Michael Moynagh and Richard Worsley, 2009

A CIP record for this book is available from the British Library.

ISBN: 9-781-4081-0847-5

This book is produced using paper that is made from wood grown in managed, sustainable forests. It is natural, renewable and recyclable. The logging and manufacturing processes conform to the environmental regulations of the country of origin.

Design by Fiona Pike, Pike Design, Winchester
Typeset by RefineCatch Limited, Bungay, Suffolk
Printed in the United Kingdom by Caligraving

CONTENTS

Changing Lives, Changing Business has been produced as one element of a partnership agreement between the Economic and Social Research Council and The Tomorrow Project, designed to aid the transfer of academic knowledge to business and other audiences.

The Economic and Social Research Council is the UK's leading research, training and knowledge exchange agency addressing economic and social concerns. It aims to provide high-quality research on issues of importance to business, government, the public and third sectors. The issues considered include economic competitiveness, the effectiveness of public services and policy, and quality of life. The ESRC is an independent organisation, established by Royal Charter in 1965, and funded mainly by government.

The Tomorrow Project is an independent charity undertaking a programme of research, consultation and communication about people's lives in Britain in the next 20 years. Its aims are to help individuals and organisations to think and learn about the future of people's lives in order to gain a better understanding of the present and to learn about the choices which will influence the future. (For more information, see **www.tomorrowproject.net**)

ACKNOWLEDGEMENTS

We would like to express our thanks to the many people who have in different ways contributed to this book:

to the Economic and Social Research Council (ESRC) for their support and partnership, and particularly to Dr. David Guy;

to the Centre for Longitudinal Studies at the Institute of Education who worked in partnership with us;

to the Chartered Institute of Personnel and Development (CIPD) and Right Management for their support for the project and for their sponsorship of one of its consultative events;

to the following, who helped us in various ways, including taking part in interviews, reviewing our texts and serving as members of a steering group for the project: Heather Alderson of BBH, Professor James Banks of University College London, Richard Bartholomew of the Department for Children, Schools and Families, Professor John Bond of Newcastle University, Vivienne Brown of Skills Development Scotland, Professor Ann Buchanan of Oxford University, Professor John Bynner of the Institute of Education, Professor David Coleman of Oxford University, Mick Fletcher, Professor Emily Grundy of the London School of Hygiene and Tropical Medicine, Dr. David Guy of ESRC, Dr. Paul Higgs of University College London, Liz Macham of Right Management, Mary MacLeod of the Family and Parenting Institute, Ken Mayhew of the ESRC Centre on Skills, Knowledge and Organisational Performance (SKOPE), Professor Stephen McNair of the National Institute for Adult and Continuing Education, Jill Mortimer of Local Government Analysis and Research, Kathy Murphy of the Department for Innovation, Universities and Skills, Professor Mike Murphy of the London School of Economics, David Passey of Hewitts, John Philpott of CIPD, Ingrid Schoon of the Institute of Education, Peter Shepherd of the Centre for Longitudinal Studies at the Institute of Education, Adam Steventon of the Pensions Policy Institute and Professor Alan Walker of Sheffield University;

to Louise Miller for her invaluable support as both content and copy-editor and for undertaking much of the electronic handling of our material;

to Samantha Parsons of the Centre for Longitudinal Studies at the Institute of Education who supported our research;

to A & C Black, our publisher, and particularly to Lisa Carden, our editor; to all those who took part in the consultations that so helpfully informed our work, and

to our Tomorrow Project Trustees, under the wise chairmanship of Patrick Coldstream, for their encouragement and guidance.

The book owes much to all these people, while its shortcomings are, of course, our own.

Michael Moynagh and Richard Worsley

JOIN THE TOMORROW NETWORK— *for individuals with an interest in futures – free of charge. Members receive invitations to The Tomorrow Project's Network events involving distinguished speakers. To join the Network simply email* **richard.worsley2@btinternet.com.**

PHOTO CREDITS

Photographs on pages 4, 22, 38, 42, 75, 82, 86, 100, 115, 143, 149, 173 and 192 © Getty Images

Photographs on pages 32 and 221 © Photofusion Picture Library

Photograph on page 218 © Corbis

Photograph on page 225 © John Birdsall Social Issues Photo Library

CHAPTER 1
PEOPLE'S CHANGING LIVES

- People's lives are increasingly diverse
- Their lives are progressively more fluid
- They have a stronger business focus
- They have a future as well as a past

People's lives are changing in all sorts of ways. These changes are endlessly fascinating and are the subject of research, media speculation, debate in business planning meetings and everyday conversation.

They can be viewed from many different angles. The approach we take is to look at seven stages of life: not quite the 'seven ages' described by Shakespeare in *As You Like It*, but pretty close – birth, childhood, becoming an adult, personal relationships between roughly age 25 and 45, the middle years, retirement and being very old.

- How has life been changing at each of these stages?
- What will influence the future?
- What should we think about?

In asking these questions, it is important to remember four things – threads that run throughout the book.

Firstly, people's lives are increasingly diverse. The story here is not that everyone was much the same in the past and now they are very different. There have always been differences – between the aristocracy, merchants and the 'common people' of the late 1700s, for example.

But what is new is that these differences have multiplied, particularly since the Second World War. The journey of life – in technical language 'the life course' – has fractured into growing numbers of groups.

Rich, white women may have one journey, farmers a different one, Somali immigrants a third, while the

> 'The life journey has fractured into growing numbers of groups'

experience of white, working-class men in Tower Hamlets, London will vary again.

Rather than society having atomised with everyone travelling a unique journey, there are more distinct groups of people: each group shares a similar journey through life, with themes that are common for that group.

If we keep this fragmentation in mind, however, it is still possible to generalise about the stages of life. Each stage has certain characteristics that are shared across different groups.

The tendency for well-educated people to delay having children would be one example. The increase in cohabitation would be another. A third would be the later onset of middle age.

We can discuss what is typical in a life stage if we remember there will always be exceptions. Broad statements about the life course are fine so long as we don't squeeze everyone into the same mould.

Secondly, people's lives are progressively more fluid – in two ways.

One of these is that there is frequent change within each stage.

Again, we mustn't pit too strongly the idea of predictable lives in the past against constant flux today. Previous generations had their lives disrupted by death, wars and economic depressions.

There *were* changes, while today there is considerable stability – in where people live, for instance: in the year 2000, 40% of the population had lived in the same house for 20 years or more.[1]

> '40% of people live in the same house for 20 years or more'

Perhaps the big difference is that today we expect change. Fashions change all the time. Technology advances at a rapid pace. One reorganisation follows another at work.

Our lives are lived within this swirling rush of change, and so we expect our own journey through life to keep changing as well.

In many cases it does, despite elements of stability. For example, becoming an adult may involve leaving school, going to university, a gap year, some further training, a first job, then another and perhaps another, before gaining a sense of having finally arrived as an adult and settling down with a partner. There was far less change in the past.

Lives are fluid in a second way. One stage of life increasingly flows into the next. People's lives used to be divided 'horizontally', on the basis of age. Individuals moved sequentially from education to work, to marriage, to parenthood, to middle age and to retirement.

But nowadays, as shown in the illustration below, the divisions are becoming more vertical than horizontal. Transitions occur more flexibly (and frequently) throughout people's lives:

Horizontal lives   Vertical lives

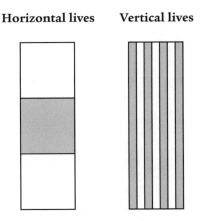

- from full-time education into a mixture of full- and part-time work and lifelong learning;
- from cohabitation to marriage, possibly to marital breakdown, then to cohabitation and remarriage;
- from becoming a parent to children growing up, maybe to starting parenthood again with another partner;
- from young adulthood to 'eternal youth', as people try to stay young in their middle and older years;
- from work to retirement, as more people begin to stay in employment after their normal retirement age, a trend that is blurring the age of retirement.

People experience 'liquid lives',[2] with greater fluidity between each stage of life and more change within each stage than before.

Thirdly, people's lives have a stronger business focus. Again, this focus has also been present in the past. The industrial revolution uprooted whole communities and reconfigured their lives round the factory or the mine.

But now the influence of business is much greater. Privatisation has cut back the size of the public sector (to about a fifth of all workers[3]), so that today individuals have a greater chance of being employed by business than at any time since 1945.

Perhaps more important has been the growing influence of business on other aspects of life. The emergence of the consumer society (and more recently new forms of media) means that lives are increasingly fashioned by advertising and consumer opportunities.

Business now penetrates spheres of activity that were once mainly free of corporate influence. Much of education policy, for example, is designed to help British companies thrive in a highly competitive world.

The result is that life journeys are increasingly shaped by business: either directly, or indirectly through values that emerge from what companies do.

- Whether you are born at all may be the outcome of a consumerist trade-off, as couples balance their desire for a child with the implications for their consumer lifestyle and careers.
- Advertising for and consumer spending by children has commercialised significant aspects of childhood.
- Transitions to adulthood follow paths laid down largely by the skill needs of business.
- Adult relationships are influenced by consumerist values, such as it-must-fit-me expectations, that are slowly changing the nature of commitment.
- Middle years (and old age) increasingly involve the search for eternal youth, a by-product of the consumer society's elevation of youthfulness.
- The sharp transition from work to retirement for most people – you are at work on Friday and are then retired on Monday – reflects work arrangements that suit employers.

- Business is transforming the experience of being very old through the development of new medical and healthcare products.

To understand how life stages are evolving, you have to see them in their economic context. That is why this is a book about 'changing lives, changing business'.

The book highlights the business context within a broad view of each stage of the life journey, including non-economic aspects.

It complements our previous book, *Going Global*,[4] which tackled big issues facing the world: in this book, we address some of the issues that face people in their everyday lives.

The aim is to illuminate influences on each stage of life, to help business people (as well as caring professionals) to make more informed decisions, and to increase awareness among companies of how they affect individuals.

Finally, life journeys have a future as well as a past. This may seem obvious, but most studies of how people live have a backward-looking emphasis ('how did we get here?') or concentrate on the here-and-now.

Our approach is a threefold framework, asking for each stage of the life journey:

- Where have we come from?
- Where are we going?
- What do we need to think about?

Though there are other ways to arrange your thoughts, these questions have a strong intuitive appeal: they are what most people want to know. They encourage you to look backwards and forwards, and to take stock.

Accordingly, for each stage of life we have examined some of the best academic and other research. To provide a fuller picture than if you stop with the present, we have put this research into the same outline shape:

- 'The story so far' – describing recent and current trends.
- 'What will shape the next 20 years?' – drivers that will mould the future.
- 'What might be the implications?' – the all-important 'so what?' question.

Individuals and organisations all make some assumptions about the future – that it will be much the same as today, perhaps. Systematically thinking about the future can help you to test these assumptions. Are they valid?

Sociologists often hesitate to speculate about the future. They prefer to rely on solid evidence – 'We can't collect evidence about the future like we can about the present and the past.'

Yet in fact it *is* possible to have an evidence-based approach to the future. You can collect evidence about recent trends (the birth rate, for example) and about what has caused those trends. From this you can build a model of what influences the birth rate, and then infer what will drive birth rates in future.

These inferences won't be complete. You may have underestimated some factors, while new drivers may emerge. As you peer further into the future, it becomes harder to know how much weight to put on each influence.

But at least you will have a better idea of what is probable and what is uncertain. To allow for uncertainties, you may have to talk about possible futures ('scenarios') rather than one set future.

Uncertainty is typical of knowledge, whatever the field. In history, for instance, events may be recorded by only one person, with a slanted view. Conversations and the like, which if we knew about them would change our take on what happened, may not have been recorded at all.

Yet, though our understanding of the past is limited, we still see it as valid. Likewise, our limited knowledge of the future is valid, too.

> 'Videoconferencing could abolish loneliness in old age'

It is better than no knowledge and can provide us with a wider perspective on the present. To take just one example: the likelihood that videoconferencing, using flat, wall-mounted TV screens, could abolish loneliness in old age gives a whole new slant to these emerging technologies. They could radically change people's lives.

If you want to understand today, you need some sense of tomorrow.

---

1 Melissa Coulthard, Alison Walker and Antony Walker, *People's Perceptions of their Neighbourhood and Community Involvement*, London: The Stationery Office, 2002, p. 90.

2 See Zygmunt Bauman, *Liquid Modernity*, London: Polity Press, 2000.

3 ONS, *Labour Market Statistics: First Release,* July 2008.

4 Michael Moynagh and Richard Worsley, *Going Global: Key Questions for the 21st Century*, London: A & C Black, 2008.

CHAPTER 2

WILL WE PRODUCE ENOUGH BABIES?
THE STORY SO FAR

- The birth rate began to fall in the late nineteenth century
- There was an exceptional baby boom from 1945 to 1970
- The birth rate has been below replacement level since 1970
- The number of births has risen significantly in recent years
- Nearly all developed countries have a birth rate below replacement level

Today's low birth rate is a big talking point. Though the rate has always bobbed up and down, for the last 40 years it has remained well below the replacement level – too few babies are being born to replace their parents' generation. Does this matter? The answer is highly contentious.

Some would say that we have too many babies. The Optimum Population Trust, for example, claims that Britain's population is already growing too fast.

If the number of people continues to rise by 0.6% a year – its current rate – the UK will have over 100 million people by the end of the century (compared to just over 60 million today) and a colossal 200 million by 2206.[1]

The Trust recommends adopting policies that would stabilise the population and then slowly reduce it by 5 million, such as encouraging parents to 'stop at two' children.

> 'The UK could have over 100 million people by the end of the century'

If the population did fall, the implications for business would be profound. In the short term, the highly important market for children's products would shrink.

In the long term, fewer people would enter the workforce. Employers would face mounting skill shortages. Would they relocate to countries where labour was more abundant, or would they use their existing workers more efficiently?

Others would say that not enough babies are being born. In 2006 the Institute of Public Policy Research, a left-leaning think tank, published a book calling for government measures to increase the birth rate. Older women often don't have as many children as they want, and are left disappointed, the authors argued.

In time, a higher birth rate would swell the working population, making it easier to support the expected growth of the retired age group.[2]

Policies to raise the birth rate would have implications for business – either directly (more generous parental leave, for instance) or indirectly: taxes might have to rise to pay for financial and other incentives to have children.

A third view is that we have about the right number of babies. Britain's birth rate is one of the highest in Europe. Raising the birth rate further to boost the population would be difficult to achieve; the effects would be 20 or more years away; and other measures, such as encouraging more immigration, might be more effective.

With this debate as a background, we look at trends in the country's birth rate and put them into a wider European context.

The birth rate began to fall in the late nineteenth century, as shown in the chart below.[3] The chart shows long-term trends in the general fertility rate (roughly the birth rate).

The general fertility rate is the estimated average number of children per woman of childbearing age, which is usually 16 to 44. Anything below 2.1 (known as the replacement level) is too low to replace the childbearing generation when it dies.

The general fertility rate fell from around 3.2 in the 1880s to about 1.7 in the 1930s, and remained at that level till the mid 1940s.

The long-term evolution of the general fertility rate (GFR)

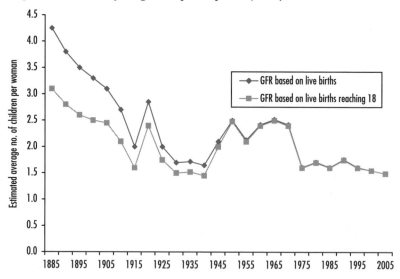

Source: adapted from *Pension: Challenges and Choices. The First Report of the Pensions Commission,* London: The Stationery Office, 2004, p. 129.

What's striking is that birth rates below replacement level are nothing new. They have been the norm since the early 1920s.

From 1945 to 1970 there was an exceptional baby boom, which in reality was two booms – a short one after the Second World War with a peak in 1947, just as there had been after the First World War; this reflected the catch-up effect of soldiers returning home.

Another longer boom occurred from the mid 1950s to 1970, peaking in 1964, when (as in 1947) births exceeded one million.

This second boom was an aberration in terms of the general trend. The short catch-up boom could be expected because of the war. But the second one was less predictable. It interrupted the long-running decline in birth rates that began during the late nineteenth century.

The coming together of the red and grey lines in the chart above reflects a drop in infant mortality, which contributed to the second boom. Probably more important, however, was rising affluence after a lengthy period of austerity.

One possible factor is that greater affluence allowed people to buy new domestic appliances. Washing machines, gas fires (you no longer had to clean out a coal fire) and other products freed up women's time, making it easier for growing numbers to have larger families.[4]

The effect of the second baby boom has been to delay the ageing of the population. Until the early 1980s, the population had been ageing steadily.

Lower birth rates earlier in the twentieth century helped to push up the old-age dependency ratio – the ratio of people over 65 to the rest of the adult population (18- to 64-year-olds). The ratio climbed by almost half between the early 1950s and the early 1980s. Working people were having to support a larger retired population.

Since 1983, however, the old-age dependency ratio has remained roughly stable – mainly because the pre-1970 baby boom led to an expansion of the working age adult population 18 or more years later. The dependency ratio is not expected to rise again (and only slightly) till 2011.

In other words, Britain has already had one period of population ageing (due partly to lower birth rates), from 1953 to 1983, and is in a lull before the next period, due to begin in 2011. Recent immigration, rather than the birth rate, is now having a big impact, and will ensure that the next period of ageing is modest.[5]

Since 1970 the birth rate has been below the replacement level – not enough children are being born to replace their parents' generation.

The 1970s 'baby bust' saw the number of live births hit a record low of about 660,000 in the middle of the decade, after which the number recovered modestly to reach a mini peak of 792,300 in 1991 – the 'baby blip'. The number of births subsequently declined, before stabilising at the start of the century.

But since 2002 the number of births has risen significantly (see chart below). The 'total period' fertility rate – the number of children that would be born to a woman if current patterns of fertility persisted throughout her childbearing life – has followed a similar pattern.

Scotland has tended to have a lower birth rate than other parts of the UK, though the trend up and down has been broadly similar. Northern Ireland's above-average rate has been converging with the rest of Britain.[6]

Recently, the number of births has grown significantly, reversing the previous trend. At nearly 749,000 per year, live births in 2006 were almost 12% higher than in 2001 (see chart below). The total fertility rate looks set to reach 1.9 in 2007, its highest for more than a quarter of a century.[9] Several factors lie behind this latest trend.

Number of births and fertility rate in the UK, 1976–2006

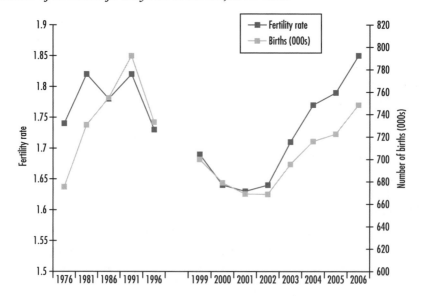

Sources: *Population Trends,* 118, 2004, Table 2.2; *Population Trends,* 128, 2007, Tables 2.1 and 2.2, **http://www.statistics.gov.uk**.

What lies behind the low birth rates of the past 40 years?

■ *An increase in childlessness has been the main driving force.* The chart below shows that 10% of women born in 1945 had no children by age 40. For those born in 1960, the proportion was nearly double.

■ *Linked with this has been later parenting.* The average age of mothers giving birth for the first time in England and Wales in 1971 was a touch under 24; in 2005, it was just over 27.[7]

If lots of women delay having children in any given year, obviously the number of children born in that year will be correspondingly less. Starting your family later also means there is less time to have children. This has shown up particularly in the increase in childlessness.

■ *But having one child has not become significantly more common* in Britain, unlike in several other European countries. Indeed, as a proportion of all family sizes it has actually fallen. The UK is also special in having more three- and four-child families than almost any other nation in Western Europe. They are most common among mothers with either low or very high incomes.[8]

Most important has been the increase in immigration since the late 1990s. Proportionately more immigrants than UK-born citizens are of childbearing age, and they tend to have larger families.[10]

Both characteristics have pushed up the number of births to mothers born outside the UK. The total leapt by 77% between 1996 and 2006 – from just over 83,000 per year to nearly 147,000. In 2006, more than a fifth of births were to mothers who had migrated to Britain.[11]

Achieved family size at age 40 for selected birth cohorts

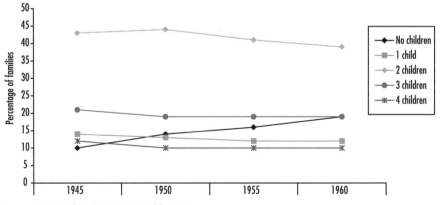

Source: *ONS Birth Statistics*, 2002, Table 10.5.

More older women are having children. The table below shows that the proportion of 35- to 39-year-olds having children increased by around 6% between 1996 and 2006, while that for mothers aged 40 and over almost doubled. Women who postponed motherhood in earlier years have been deciding to start a family.

This catch-up has been anticipated by demographers for quite a while, and now seems to be having a significant effect on the birth rate. If postponing children reduces the number of births in a given year, having them later must increase the total number subsequently.

There has also been a noticeable growth in younger mothers. Live births to mothers aged 20 to 24 in England and Wales went up from 108,800 in 2001 to 127,800 in 2006.[12] Only women born in the UK seem to have been responsible for this. Foreign-born mothers have tended to be older.[13]

Births to mothers aged 25 to 29 fell by about 7% between 1996 and 2006, while those to 30- to 34-year-olds also declined, but only slightly (by about 0.5%). This has created a U-shaped curve: births among younger and older mothers have risen, while those in the middle have dropped.

How significant is this recent trend to higher births? If it continues, it will have quite a dramatic effect on the long-term size of the population. This is reflected in Britain's official population projections.

Because of the recent rise in fertility rates, for the first time since the 1960s estimates now assume an increase in the average family size. The latest 2006-based

Percentage of live births by age of mother in England & Wales, 1996–2006

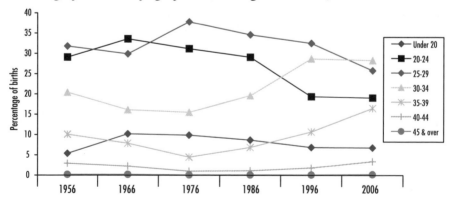

Source: ONS, Birth Statistics 1837–1983 – Historical Series FM1, Table 3.1; ONS, Birth Statistics 2006 – Series FM1, Table 3.1

projections presume a completed family of 1.84 children per woman, compared to 1.74 in the 2004 projections.

Along with higher immigration and longer life expectancy, this assumption shoves up the population projection for 2031 from 67 million to 71.1 million. (The estimated population in 2006 was nearly 61 million.) On current trends, the population would reach a staggering 85 million by 2081.[14]

Yet movements up and down in birth rates are quite common. Birth rates rose in the 1980s, for example, before declining in the 1990s. So we should not automatically assume either that today's trend will continue or that birth rates will level off.

Birth rates would decrease if:

- immigration declined;
- fewer older women had children;
- younger mothers had the same-sized families as women who had them later. At present, women who start families early tend to have slightly larger families because they have more years in which to have additional children.

Perhaps the most important point is that, even at current birth rates, not enough children are being born to replace their parents. The population will grow only because of immigration and longer life expectancy.

Nearly all developed countries have fertility rates below the replacement level. This is particularly true of Europe (see chart below).

Among the EU 15 (the pre-2004 EU), three 'low' countries had rates between 1.32 and 1.4 in 2006, three 'middling' ones had rates between 1.65 and 1.7 and six 'high' ones had rates from 1.83 to 2.0, *all* below the replacement level. The UK was in the high group, having been in the middle group previously.

However, of the countries newly admitted to the EU, with the exception of Estonia (1.55), all have a fertility rate below 1.5. The only countries within Europe as a whole with a rate above 2.0 are Turkey (2.20 in 2004) and Iceland (2.05 in 2005).

Fertility in the European Union

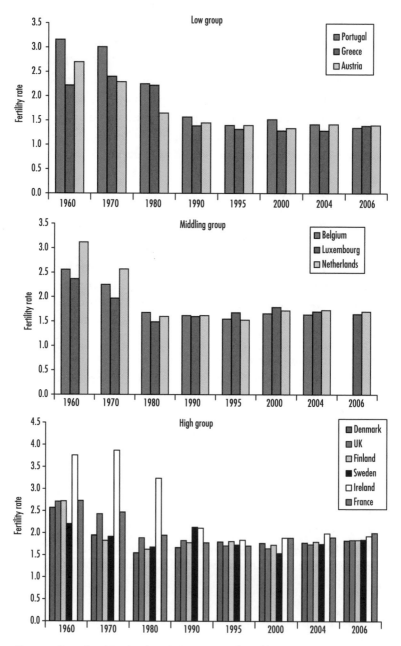

Source: Eurostat General and Regional Statistics, Datasets, **http://epp.eurostat.cec.eu.int**

Notes:

1. The UK figure does not match exactly with that in the tables above due to a difference in calculation methods.
2. 2006 figures for Belgium were not available.
3. Italy and Spain figures in the 2006 column are from 2005.

1   http://www.optimumpopulation.org

2   Mike Dixon & Julia Margo, *Population Politics*, London: IPPR, 2006.

3   This section is largely based on Appendix E, 'An Explanation of Past and Future Trends in the Old-Age Dependency Ratio', in *Pension: Challenges and Choice: The First Report of the Pensions Commission*, London: The Stationery Office, pp. 123–135.

4   Jeremy Greenwood, Ananth Seshadri & Guillaume Vandenbroucke, 'The Baby Boom and Baby Bust', in *The American Economic Review*, 95(1), 2005, pp. 183–207.

5   The proportion of pensioners to the working-age population (who are in this case defined as people aged between 16 and their pension age) is expected to rise from 3.2 in 2011 to 3.23 in 2016, and to stay at that figure till 2021, after which it will fall. See *2006-Based National Population Projections for the UK and Constituent Countries*, London: ONS, 2007.

6   Karen Dunnell, 'The Changing Demographic Picture of the UK: National Statistician's Annual Article on the Population', in *Population Trends*, 130, 2007, p. 16.

7   *Social Trends*, 37, 2007, p. 21.

8   Didier Breton & France Prioux, 'Two Children or Three? Influence of Family Policy and Sociodemographic Factors', *Populations*, 60 (4), 2005, p. 419.

9   We are grateful to Dr. David Coleman for pointing this out to us.

10 While white ethnic groups had an average age of 40 in the 2001 census, the averages for black and Asian groups were 31 and 29 years old respectively. 'Fertility rate is highest for 26 years', ONS news release, 7 June 2007.

11 'Both UK and foreign-born women contribute to rise in fertility', National Statistics news release, 11 December 2007.

12 *Population Trends*, 128, 2007, table 3.1.

13 'Both UK and foreign-born women contribute to rise in birth rate', National Statistics news release, 11 December 2007.

14 Karen Dunnell, 'The Changing Demographic Picture of the UK: National Statisticians' Annual Article on the Population', in *Population Trends*, 130, 2007, p. 13 & p. 17; 'Forecasters say UK population may grow to 108 million by 2081', *Guardian*, 28 November 2007.

WILL WE PRODUCE ENOUGH BABIES?
WHAT WILL SHAPE THE NEXT 20 YEARS?

- Attitudes to having children will change
- The cost of children will put off some potential parents
- Consumer expectations will add to these perceived costs
- The balance between work and family will be another trade-off
- Sharing roles more evenly at home could raise the birth rate
- Will the government encourage couples to have children?
- A high percentage of children will still be born into poverty

Attitudes to having children are likely to change gradually, as has been happening in recent years. There are two aspects to this.

The first factor is the ideal family size. There is some evidence that in many European countries the perceived ideal family size among people younger than 35 is lower than for those who are older.[1]

Are younger generations adapting their ideals to the experience of the generation above them? Many in this older generation may have hoped for several children, but ended up with just two.

Younger people see this as reality and scale down their hopes accordingly. Could fertility spiral downwards as successive generations lower their expectations?

The other is the increase in child-free couples. Though most young adults still expect to have children, the minority that does not has been growing. For example, among women in England and Wales:

- Only 6% of 24- to 26-year-olds did not expect to have any children in 1979–81. By 1998–2000, the proportion had risen to 10%.
- The increase in expected childlessness among 33- to 35-year-olds was more substantial – from 7% to 13%.
- The figure for 36- to 38-year-olds rose from 8% to 15%.[2]

The growing numbers expecting to be child-free reflect shifting attitudes that are likely to continue. Individuals feel less bound by social conventions and freer to make choices that bring personal fulfilment.

'The whole idea of the child-free lifestyle is beginning to be recognised by the media', sociologist Dr. Catherine Hakim commented in a BBC interview. 'Private feelings are being legitimised and people are beginning to feel that they are not being deviant in some way. Very consciously, people are more confident in saying they have a different lifestyle.'[3]

More child-free couples could pose a problem for employers wanting to introduce family-friendly policies, and for governments wanting to encourage companies to do so.

Might childless couples increasingly ask, as some have begun to, 'Why should parents have the right to request flexible working hours, but not me? I've chosen to use my time differently. Why should they be favoured?'

The cost of having children will reinforce these emerging attitudes. Research based on a nationally representative sample of British children found that in 1997, raising children to their 17th birthday cost a total of about £50,000 per child (excluding paid childcare).[4] A poll of 500 parents for the online bank Egg produced roughly the same figure in 2004.[5]

Children have become an expensive business – even more so when paid childcare is taken into account. This situation is very different to the past, when children were an economic asset.

In eighteenth-century Britain, for example, children were an important source of family labour from a young age, and this remained largely the case in the early stages of industrialisation. Children's earnings from factory work supplemented the household income.

But as the economy developed, children spent longer in education and the economic equation changed. Children brought less money into the home, but the costs of feeding, clothing and looking after them did not go away. Children shifted from being an economic plus to a cost.

This coincided with a decline in child mortality. Traditionally, parents in effect insured against the likelihood that some children would die by having a large number of them. If one or two children passed away, there would still be others to love, who could also help on the farm, supplement the family income, look after their ageing parents and – hopefully – carry on the family name.

> 'Children have shifted from being an economic plus to being a cost'

But as deaths in childhood fell, the need for this 'insurance' dropped away. At the same time, once children became more of an expense than a source of income, the cost of such an insurance rose substantially. The economic equation shifted in favour of smaller families.

With parents now expecting to give their offspring an expanding range of consumer products – from game consoles to holidays abroad – modern consumerism has pushed up the expense of having a family further still. More and more couples are weighing the cost carefully before deciding whether to commit to this extra expenditure.

Rising consumer expectations will add to the cost of having children. One result of the post-war consumer revolution has been to elevate choice as a value. Consumers now take choice for granted.

At the heart of consumer choice are trade-offs – 'If we take the family to the cinema, we'll have less to spend on eating out'. Since trade-offs come naturally to modern consumers, it is hardly surprising that couples think about starting a family in the same way – and this will carry on. Couples will weigh up the joys of having children against their existing standard of living.

Will greater affluence make the trade-off easier? If trends over the past two decades persist, average living standards could double in the next 28 years. There will be more money for parents *and* their children.

But equally, might the trade-off become more difficult? In the consumer society, parents' love is often expressed through shopping. Good parenting, it is thought, involves buying things that give children pleasure and enable them to walk tall among their friends.[6]

Greater affluence will bring more consumer possibilities, enticingly sold. As affluence grows, children's expectations will rise and parents will want to satisfy them, further raising the cost of having a family.

At the same time, adults' hopes for their own living standards will escalate. There will be so many more consumer products – from kitchenware to entertainment – for them to enjoy! The trade-off between having children and maintaining a particular lifestyle could become even tougher.

Young adults will face mounting financial pressures, which will complicate the trade-off.

- *Student debt will increase,* as the £3,000 cap on university fees is raised and possibly abolished, and as more school leavers go to university. Young adults are likely to delay buying a home while they pay off their debts.
- *House prices will stay high in the long term.* Supply constraints – worsened by the current downturn – will face ballooning demand, fuelled by

immigration (in all likelihood) and more single-person households. Compared to today, middle-class parents may be less able to help their children on to the housing ladder because they will be saving more heavily for retirement. Buying your first home will be delayed further.

■ *When people do buy, they may purchase smaller properties* – one-bedroom flats instead of two and accommodation with smaller rooms, leaving less space for a family.

All this could make the decision to have children more difficult. Many couples will think, 'We can't start a family yet. We haven't bought our own place.' Or, 'Our flat's too small for children.'

Already couples are tending to buy smaller properties. If this continues, will more parents – in a very new development for Britain – have just one child? Or will the housing market change instead, with renting a more acceptable option as in parts of Europe?

Most likely is that more women will delay starting their families. This will reduce the time available for having children. Though people are ageing later, the timing of the menopause has remained stubbornly fixed. There may be fewer families with three or more children because there is less time to fit them all in.

As now, some women who want to start a family in their mid or late 30s will have difficulty conceiving, but will be helped by continuing advances in medicine. On the other hand, while some of these advances will be free on the NHS, others will require patients to contribute to their costs, as already happens today.

For couples who are feeling the financial pinch and for whom the costs and benefits of starting a family are finely balanced, this may be enough to tilt the scales against children.

The balance between work and family will be another trade-off. The easier it is for mothers to combine employment with having children, the more attractive starting a family will be.

British mothers combine work and family with fairly traditional expectations. They have a traditional view of their domestic responsibilities – they should do most of the housework and childcare. But they also want a job.

Being able to do both has made it reasonably attractive to have children, which helps to explain why Britain's birth rate is relatively high by European standards.

Certain features of the British labour market encourage this traditional motherhood-plus-work combination. For example:

- *Men's wages are significantly higher than women's.* So if parents want to take time out from work to look after young children, it makes economic sense for *mothers* to do so. The household will lose less income. Just over half of mothers with children born in 2000 were not employed when their children were nine to 10 months old. (The proportion drops as children get older.)[7] The figure for fathers was a fraction of this.
- *Of mothers who do work, a significant proportion have part-time jobs.* The study just quoted found that three out of five mothers who were employed when their babies were nine to 10 months old worked less than 30 hours a week, leading them to shoulder more of the childcare than their husbands.[8]
- *Parents of children under six now have the right to request flexible work,* and employers are obliged to consider such requests seriously. In a 2007 survey, 43% of workplaces had received such a request from at least one employee in the previous month, and only 9% had turned it down.[9] Where the father is the main earner, mothers are most likely to request flexible work, reinforcing the traditional division of roles.

All this has made traditional motherhood reasonably compatible with a job. By contrast, in some European countries where traditional approaches to motherhood persist but labour markets are less flexible, women have faced a starker choice. Larger numbers have delayed having children, or chosen not to, in order to protect their careers.[10]

A big difficulty with the UK model is the cost of childcare. Juggling work and children can be a nightmare for mothers who assume most of the responsibility.

Some rely on grandparents, but in future older workers (especially women) will be increasingly likely to stay in employment up to age 65 and sometimes beyond (see Chapter 7, 'Will "retirement" disappear?').[11] Fewer grandparents may be available to care.

For many couples, paid childcare is not an alternative. It is too expensive. Nursery fees, for example, have been rising at an inflation-beating 5% a year. In 2008 a full-time place in an English day nursery for children aged two and over averaged nearly £150 a week, compared to just over £110 in 2002.[12]

Recruiting more nursery workers from abroad might temper the rising costs. On the other hand, Britain's ageing population will increase the demand for care at the other end of the life cycle. Greater competition for care workers will keep childcare expensive.

More help from government is on the way. At present, all three- and four-year-olds are entitled to 15 hours of free pre-school education per week during term-time, and the government plans to extend this to 20 hours. For school children, 'wrap-around' care will eventually be available at either end of the school day (from 8am to 6pm) and in the holidays.

These aspirations will take a number of years to realise, and even then parents will face considerable difficulties:

- What will happen to childcare for children aged two, where care is particularly expensive because of high staff-to-child ratios? The government has announced plans to extend free nursery care to this age group, but in stages which won't be completed until 2018!
- For three- to four-year-olds, what provision will be available after their four hours of free nursery a day?
- For school-age children, how much will parents have to pay for 'wrap-around' care?

Might governments increase parents' entitlement to paid leave? Instead of paying for childcare, parents – mainly mothers – would have more time to do it themselves.

Though plans are in the pipeline to extend paid leave, dramatic steps in this direction are unlikely. As now, a government priority will be to increase the number of women at work, in order to accelerate economic growth and boost tax revenues. Governments won't want to encourage these women to leave employment for longer periods.

It could well become harder for mothers to combine their quite traditional parenting roles with employment. Might couples find it less attractive to have children?

What it means to be a good parent may be seen differently, piling still more pressure on the traditional mother-plus-work approach.

There is some evidence that if mothers are employed when children are under two, the child is more likely to experience at least one sort of problem later on. The child's ability to get good qualifications may also be slightly damaged.[13]

If this evidence mounts, concerns could grow about the effect of low-quality, non-parental care on children in their first two years, when attachment to the mother is most important.

Parenting guru Steve Biddulph used to think that paid childcare was not damaging to young children. He has changed his mind, and now believes that putting children under the age of three in nurseries risks damaging their development.[14]

His view is based on growing evidence of increased aggression, antisocial behaviour and other problems among children who have spent a large part of their infancy being cared for away from home. He argues that such children may have problems developing close relationships later in life.[15]

'Might being a good mother mean giving up work for your child's first two years?'

Instead of notions of good parenting evolving in a Scandinavian direction ('you can be a good mother and work full time'), might the idea spread that to be a good mother means giving up work for the child's first two years? 'That's too much to ask', some women may think, as they decide not to have children (or only one).

Sharing roles more evenly at home could raise the birth rate. There is some evidence that greater gender equality at home can increase the willingness of women to have children.

Sharing the housework seems to be crucial. One study found that Spanish couples tend to have fewer children on average than their Swedish counterparts. Spanish women are more traditional in their general approach to family, so why aren't they more traditional when comes to having large families?

The answer appears to be that Spanish couples have fewer children precisely *because* they are more traditional, particularly when it comes to doing the housework.

When Spanish women get a job, they continue to do most of the domestic chores. Their partners don't provide much extra help, so the pressure on women's time becomes quite acute. Working women solve the time pressures by having fewer children.[16]

Letizia Mencarini, a professor of demography at the University of Florence, interviewed more than 3,000 mothers from five cities across Italy. She found that the more involved the father became in household tasks, the more likely his wife was to want a second baby.

'A lot of Italian men do nothing around the house,' she told the BBC. 'There is sufficient evidence to show that many women here are frightened of taking on the added work and responsibility that comes with a second child.'[17]

So will domestic chores in Britain be shared more evenly? It is likely that this will happen slowly, as the economic status of men and women grows gradually more equal. There is some evidence that men take on more of the childcare when their partners' earnings are relatively high.[18]

Several factors will gradually increase the opportunities for women at work, not least:

- *Women's educational attainment* – girls are outperforming boys at every level.
- *Skill shortages,* which will encourage employers to recruit women into jobs formerly occupied by men.
- *Some improvements to parental leave.* The government intends to make paid maternity leave, which is to be extended gradually from six months to a year, transferable to fathers. Though payments will remain low, this may encourage some parents to share work and childcare more evenly.

As women become more equal in the workplace, they will make a bigger financial contribution to the home. It will not necessarily make economic sense to see men as the main breadwinners, with mothers making the employment sacrifice to have children. Sharing the childcare more equally will help women to keep working and maximise their income.

In addition, as more young mothers work full time, a larger number of couples may be able to afford paid childcare. Motherhood could be more attractive. 'We can start a family without having to put my career on hold', more women may think, 'and also without me feeling totally knackered in the evening.'

Survey data from Britain, Germany and the United States suggests that employed women reduce their quantity of housework substantially. At first only a small amount is picked up by their partner. Conventional expectations limit the willingness of couples to re-adjust their roles.

Over the course of a relationship, however, these expectations weaken and a move to greater equality begins. After four or five years, the man gradually does more of the chores.[19] This supports the expectation that as women become more equal at work, roles at home will adjust, too, albeit after some delay.

Rather than the labour market reinforcing traditional motherhood, eventually it may create circumstances that challenge conventional roles at home and so increase the appeal of having children.

Might a future government try to raise the birth rate? Since the mid 1970s a growing number of industrialised countries have introduced incentives to have babies.[20]

In Italy, where the population could shrink by as much as one-third by 2050, one town has started to offer couples 10,000 euros for each newborn baby they have.[21] The Polish parliament has introduced legislation to pay women for each new child. Germany has started to give tax breaks to families, and its government has floated the idea of eliminating fees for kindergarten.

France has gone furthest in this direction. Over a number of years it has introduced a series of cash and tax incentives for those having babies. In 2005 the Government promised to offer cash incentives to mothers who have a third child.

Might pro-natalist policies become the flavour of the month in Britain? Alongside the need to raise the birth rate for economic reasons is the difficulty some older women have conceiving. Helping women to afford to start a family when they are younger might enable couples to have the number of children they want.[22]

But trying to raise the birth rate would have disadvantages:

- *Financial incentives would be expensive.* To really bite, they would have to be quite large. The think tank IPPR (Institute of Public Policy Research) has proposed a number of incentives, but the package would cost 1-2% of GDP.[23] This would require several pence on income tax!
- *It is not clear how effective pro-natalist policies are.* France has the highest birth rate in Europe, but even so, fewer children are being born than are needed

to replace their parents' generation. Nor is it clear which policies work best. Money could easily be spent on measures that don't make a big difference.

■ *The economic benefits would be very long term.* Increasing the birth rate today would not enlarge the workforce for 20 years or so. Meanwhile, the costs of a pro-natalist policy would have to be borne now.

■ *Might there be better ways of increasing the UK workforce,* such as encouraging more older workers to stay in employment and promoting modest levels of immigration? These might be easier to achieve and the impact would be more immediate.

A large proportion of children will continue to be born into poverty, despite recent encouraging trends: the teenage pregnancy rate has fallen,[24] while the number of children in poor households dropped by almost 15% between 1998 and 2007, reducing the proportion of children in poverty from 26% to 22%.[25]

However, the number of children in poverty went up between 2004 and 2007, and the government remains far from achieving its target of halving the total by 2010. Hitting this target and then going beyond it will be increasingly difficult – for several reasons:

■ *The incomes of the poor would have to rise faster than those in the middle,* which will be far from easy. This is because poverty is understood mainly in relative terms, as a proportion of median earnings. So to reduce poverty, it would not be enough for poor households to keep pace with middling incomes. Their earnings would have to rise more steeply, eating into pay differentials.

■ *Poverty is strongly linked to low pay.* Half the children in poverty in 2005–06 were in households where someone was doing paid work.[26] Earnings were insufficient to prevent the family being poor. To reduce childhood poverty, you would have to transform the business models of employers at the bottom end.

For years, these employers have made profits by relying on low skills, low pay and cheap methods of production. Their approach is deeply entrenched. What would persuade them to adopt methods based on higher productivity, higher skills and higher salaries instead?

■ *State benefits would have to be raised substantially.* Most of the recent reduction in child poverty has come through higher welfare payments. With many other calls on government funds, are sharp increases really likely in future?

A high proportion – perhaps around a quarter – of children will continue to be born into poor households because reducing poverty will remain so difficult.

Climbing out of poverty is a tough challenge. For example, poor mothers are more likely to have their children when they are younger than women who are more affluent. This then compounds their poverty because having a child makes it harder to get a job.[27]

There is also evidence that mothers who have children early tend to have slightly larger families, which increases the general proportion of children who are poor.[28]

Large families, with four or more dependent children, make up less than 5% of all families but more than 20% of poor families. Not only are there more mouths to feed (which adds to poverty), but their fathers are less likely to be employed than in smaller families.[29]

Poor children will continue to have a very different experience of growing up than those who are better off.

1   Wolfgang Lutz, 'Alternative Paths for Future European Fertility: Will the Birth Rate Recover or Continue to Decline?' in Wolfgang Lutz, Rudolph Richter and Chris Wilson, *The New Generations of Europeans*, London: Earthscan, 2006, pp. 96–97.

2   Steve Smallwood & Julie Jeffries, 'Family-Building Intentions in England and Wales: Trends, Outcomes and Interpretations', *Population Trends*, 112, 2003, p. 17.

3   'The rise of the "childfree" ', 31 March 2006, **http://news.bbc.co.uk.**

4   Sue Middleton, Karl Ashworth & Ian Braithwaite, 'Expenditure on Children in Great Britain', *Findings*, York: Joseph Rowntree Foundation, 1997.

5   **http://news.bbc.co.uk** (downloaded 14 December 2004).

6   See, for example, Daniel Miller, *A Theory of Shopping*, Cambridge: Polity Press, 1998, pp. 15–36.

7   Shirley Dex & Heather Joshi (eds.), *Millennium Cohort Study First Survey: A User's Guide to Initial Findings*, London: Institute of Education Centre for Longitudinal Studies, 2004, p. 160.

8   Shirley Dex & Heather Joshi (eds.), *Millennium Cohort Study First Survey: A User's Guide to Initial Findings*, London: Institute of Education Centre for Longitudinal Studies, 2004, p. 160.

9   Bruce Hayward, Barry Fong & Alex Thornton, 'The Third Work–Life Balance Employer Survey', *Employment Relations Research Series No. 86*, London: BERR, 2007, p. 6.

10 Wolfgang Lutz, 'Alternative Paths for Future European Fertility: Will the Birth Rate Recover or Continue to Decline?' in Wolfgang Lutz, Rudolph Richter and Chris Wilson, *The New Generations of Europeans*, London: Earthscan, 2006, p. 94.

11 In the Millennium Cohort Study, 42.2% of mothers who were employed or studying used grandparents to look after their 9- to ten-month-old babies, by far the most common form of childcare. 24.7% used nurseries, paid childcare or nannies/au pairs, while 20.5% relied on partners. Shirley Dex & Heather Joshi (eds.), *Millennium Cohort Study First Survey: A User's Guide to Initial Findings*, London: Institute of Education Centre for Longitudinal Studies, 2004, p. 220.

12 *Daycare Trust Childcare Costs Survey 2008*, London: Daycare Trust, 2008.

13 For example, Heather Joshi & Georgia Verropoulou, *Maternal Employment and Child Outcomes. Analysis of Two Birth Cohort Studies*, London: The Smith Institute, 2000, p. 25.

14 Steve Biddulph is the author of best-selling books such as (with Sharon Biddulph) *The Complete Secrets of Happy Children*, London: HarperCollins, 2003.

15 *Sunday Times*, 12 February 2006.

16 Joost de Laat & Almudena Seville Sanz, 'Working Women, Men's Home Time and Lowest-Low Fertility', *ISER Working Paper 2006–23*, Colchester: University of Essex, 2006.

17 'Italian women shun "mamma" role', **http://news.bbc.co.uk** (downloaded 27 March 2006).

18 'Parenting', *CLS Briefings*, November 2005.

19 J. Gershuny, M. Bittman & J. Brice, 'Exit, Voice and Suffering: Do Couples Adapt to Changing Employment Patterns?', *Journal of Marriage and Family*, 67, 2005, pp. 656–665.

20 Mike Dixon & Julia Margo, *Population Politics*, London: IPPR, 2006, p. 31.

21 'The EU's baby blues', **http://news.bbc.co.uk** (downloaded 27 March 2006).

22 Surveys repeatedly show that the desired number of children is higher than the actual number of children. Juan Antonio Fernandez Cordon, 'Low Fertility and the Scope for Social Policy: Understanding the Context', in Wolfgang Lutz, Rudolph Richter and Chris Wilson, *The New Generations of Europeans*, London: Earthscan, 2006, p. 52.

23 Mike Dixon & Julia Margo, *Population Politics*, London: IPPR, 2006, p. 88.

24 The pregnancy rate per 1,000 females aged 15 to 17 in England fell from 46.6 in 1998 to 41.3 in 2005. ONS and Teenage Pregnancy Unit, November 2007.

25 Nick Adams et al. (eds.), *Households Below Average Income: An Analysis of the Income Distribution 1994/5 – 2006/07*, London: DWP, 2008. See Tables 4.1tr & 4.3tr. Figures are for households below 60% of median earnings before housing costs.

26 'Monitoring Poverty and Social Exclusion in the UK 2007', *Findings*, York: Joseph Rowntree Foundation, December 2007.

27 Denise Hawkes, Heather Joshi & Kelly Ward, 'Unequal Entry to Motherhood and Unequal Starts in Life: Evidence from the First Survey of the UK Millennium Cohort', *CLS Cohort Studies Working Paper 6*, London: Centre for Longitudinal Studies, 2004, p. 29.

28 Heather Joshi, 'Production, Reproduction and Education: Women, Children and Work in a British Perspective', Professorial Lecture, Institute of Education, Revised March 2002, p. 21; Heather E. Joshi & Robert E. Wright, 'Population replacement and the reproduction of disadvantage', 2004, pp. 41–45, **http://www.fraser.strath.ac.uk**.

29 'The Economic Position of Large Families', *Taking the Long View: The ISER Report 2006/7*, Colchester: University of Essex, 2007, pp. 6–7.

WILL WE PRODUCE ENOUGH BABIES?
WHAT MIGHT BE THE IMPLICATIONS?

- The overall trends
- More child-free couples are likely
- Might there be more one-child families?
- Couples are likely to start families at an older age
- High teenage pregnancy rates will remain a concern

Firstly, what will be the overall trends? Annual births are likely to rise slightly in the short term because of immigration, but in the long term the birth rate is likely to fall back a little.

There will certainly be no return to the large families of the past.

- *The expectation of having around two children* is now deeply entrenched, and a growing minority of women don't expect to have any children.
- *Graduates will experience greater financial pressures* as student debts rise and house prices go up once again. This will encourage them to postpone having children, giving them less time to have more than two.
- *The increasing cost of childcare* will make it difficult to combine work with raising children.

Equally, the birth rate is unlikely to fall to a very low level as it has in Japan, Korea and Eastern Europe, for example.

- There will continue to be a catch-up effect, as women who have delayed having children start their families.
- The government will continue to take steps to improve the balance between work and life. Though the measures are unlikely to make a radical difference, they will give women some extra help in combining having children and a job.
- Gender roles at home are likely to become gradually more equal, as women gain ground in the workplace. This could make having children more attractive to women – mothers won't have to shoulder all the hard work.

Annual births will increase and then gently decline. The Government Actuary's Department (GAD) projects an increase in UK births from 780,000 a year in

2006–11 to 805,000 in 2016–21. This will be largely due to immigration. The number is then expected to tail off to 788,000 in 2026–31 (see table below).

Components of population change in the UK, 2006–2031 (by five-year period)

	2006–11	**2011–16**	**2016–21**	**2021–26**	**2026–31**
Population at start of period	60,587	62,761	64,975	67,191	69,260
Births	780	799	805	796	788
Deaths	565	549	552	573	610
Natural change	**215**	**250**	**253**	**224**	**178**
Migration	220	193	190	190	190
Total change	**435**	**443**	**443**	**414**	**368**
Population at end of period	62,761	64,975	67,191	69,260	71,100

Source: 'Projection Database', Government Actuary's Department, **http://www.gad.gov.uk**.
Note: The 2006-based principal projection is used.
The figures for births, deaths and migration are annual averages, which explains why they don't completely add up.

Whereas women born in 1960 had 1.98 children, the GAD's 2006-based projection expects the average to level off at 1.84 (see table below).

The projection is slightly higher than two years earlier because of the recent rise in twentysomethings giving birth. If you start a family early, you have more time to have a large one. But this is offset to a great extent by the greater number of women putting off their first child, so the net effect is small.

Projected completed family size for women born after 1990

	Projected average number of children per woman
England and Wales	1.85
Northern Ireland	1.95
Scotland	1.65
UK	1.84

Source: 'Projection Database', Government Actuary's Department, **http://www.gad.gov.uk**.
Note: 'Projected average number of children per woman' refers to the total number of children born to women who have completed their childbearing years.

The number of child-free couples is likely to grow. Though the GAD doesn't make a projection for such couples, this is a reasonable inference from likely influences on the future and from recent trends.

As discussed in 'The story so far', the proportion of women born in 1960 without children by their 40th birthday was almost twice that of women born in 1945. *Further increases are likely* as:

- more couples feel comfortable about deciding not to have children;
- the cost of having children rises;
- graduates face mounting financial pressures;
- a larger number of women give higher priority to pursuing their careers;
- more women delay having children and then find it difficult to conceive. Though medical advances should reduce the latter problem, might they increase the risk by encouraging women to be over-confident about conceiving?

An increase in child-free couples could be significant for employers. Though they will boost the labour supply by not taking time off to have children, childless couples will be more able to fund periods of unpaid leave, for example to travel. Along with single people, might these couples demand the same rights to paid leave as parents have?

Despite changing values, being child-free is not always what childless women want. Couples may delay having children, only to find that they can't have them at all. Might this present an opportunity for business? Companies' human resource policies could make it easier for couples to start a family earlier, giving the employer an edge in recruitment. Policies might include:

- *Generous parental leave,* an obvious example.
- *Making work more flexible,* so that mothers with young children can return to full-time employment more quickly. The number of people working from home, for instance, has risen significantly.[1] With continuing advances in technology, home-based work should be a viable option for a growing number of young parents.
- *Providing financial support for more workplace nurseries,* either on their own premises or nearby, as is common in the NHS, for example.
- *Helping younger workers to save for their first home.* From 2012, all employees and employers will contribute to a pension scheme unless the individual

opts out. In these cases, might employers provide a 'home deposit' scheme instead? (See Chapter 7, 'Will "retirement" disappear?')

Young workers and the employer would pay into this scheme rather than a pension, helping individuals to get onto the housing ladder more rapidly.

Not having their own home is one reason why couples postpone parenthood.

Child-free couples will continue to be a growing market for business. In terms of income to spend on themselves, they will be better off than couples who have to support children and people living alone, who can't share their household costs. Child-free couples will be able to eat out more often, spend more on holidays and invest more heavily in their homes.

Could there be a rise in the proportion of one-child families? This might happen if more women delayed having a family till their late 30s or beyond. The time and energy required for their baby might encourage them to have just one.

One child might also be a compromise between the desire to have a family on the one hand, and the attractions of being child-free on the other.

An increase in one-child families would be a new development for Britain. Parents would have more time and money to lavish on their only child. Children themselves would be far wealthier. This could have implications for businesses that market products to children.

Children's attitudes might change. Would there be a boom in 'little emperors', as more children grew up expecting to be the centre of attention? When they became adults, how would they interact with others in the workplace?

Couples are likely to start families at an older age, despite the recent increase in younger women having children.

The GAD projects a rise in the average age of motherhood in the UK from 27.8 years for women born in 1960 (the most recent group to have reached the end of their childbearing years) to 29 years for those born after 1972.[2]

But might the average age rise even higher as more young people go to university, encouraging twentysomethings to delay starting a family, and also as thirtysomethings feel the strain of larger mortgages? (See Chapter 4, Will becoming an adult be more difficult?)

Postponing children could reduce the number of couples with more than two offspring, making Britain more like the rest of Europe in this respect.

Older parents could be at a financial disadvantage in later life. Couples who delay starting a family till their mid or late 30s will incur the costs of children, perhaps including support through university, till their late 50s. This could have serious repercussions for their ability to save.

To what extent would parents be able to repay their mortgages while meeting the costs of children, and how much would they be able to put aside for a pension? Couples would have relatively little time after their children left home – perhaps 10 years or fewer – to increase their savings for retirement. Might they have to keep working till they are 70 or even beyond?

As future generations observe these long-term trends, might the idea of *not* raising children have a stronger appeal?

The high rate of teenage pregnancies will remain a concern. Despite reducing teenage conceptions to their lowest level in 20 years, Britain has more teenage births than any other country in Western Europe and the third-highest rate in the industrialised world.

A teenage mother is more likely to drop out of school, have low qualifications, be unemployed or low paid, live in poor housing conditions, have depression or be on welfare. Children brought up with these influences have a high chance of being poor as adults and repeating the cycle all over again.[3]

A young girl who is mistreated at home, has achieved little at school and has only a low-paid job to look forward to may think that having a baby to love and be loved by, plus a small income from benefits and a home of her own, is more attractive than the alternatives.

There are no easy answers to this, but some companies may be in a position to support government efforts to reduce teenage pregnancies. For example:

- *They could offer apprenticeships* (and work experience) to girls most at risk.
- *They could support local schools* in disadvantaged areas. Why not sponsor scholarships for youngsters with the potential to learn music, play sport or develop some other skill? Scholarships would boost the confidence of teenagers who feel failures at school and perhaps offer some of them an escape from poverty.
- *They could help to sponsor local initiatives* to cut teenage pregnancies, as part of their corporate social responsibility.

---

1 Michael Moynagh & Richard Worsley, *Working in the Twenty-First Century*, Leeds: ESRC Future of Work Programme, 2005, p. 102.

2 'Projection Database', Government Actuary's Department, **http://www.gad.gov.uk**.

3 'British Cohort Study Report 2003', Institute of Social and Economic Research, **http://www.esds.ac.uk**.

CHAPTER 3

HOW WILL WE BRING UP OUR CHILDREN? THE STORY SO FAR

- Children have become important in economic competition
- The quality of parenting has improved
- Schools have been transformed
- Childhood has been commercialised
- Disadvantaged children are being left behind

Children have become important in global economic competition. Modern economies increasingly require workers who are skilled both technically and in their ability to form good working relationships. The foundations for these skills are laid in childhood – roughly the first 16 years of a person's life – through formal education and, more generally, in how children are brought up.

Countries can create a platform for long-term success in the global economy by raising children to be assured and motivated and equipping them with skills in literacy, numeracy, science, IT and 'emotional intelligence'. Around the world, the quality of the childhood experience has become a pressing *economic* question.

Of course, children are not just a means to an economic end. They are individuals with rights who are entitled to respect. Valuing the wellbeing of children is important for its own sake – and secure, happy children are more likely to help society to flourish economically when they become adults!

Children have also become important as consumers. It is said that the average child in the US, UK and Australia sees between 20,000 and 40,000 TV adverts a year.[1]

'Children influence 67% of US car purchases'

As avid TV watchers, children pass on marketing messages to parents and so influence everything the family buys, not just the kids' products. Children influence 67% of US car purchases, for example.[2]

The effects of this commercialisation of childhood are fiercely debated. Are children being pressured by companies to eat unhealthy food? Is their addiction to modern media damaging their emotional and physical health? Are advertisers forcing children to grow up too quickly? Business is being asked to justify itself.

The number of children under age 15 in the UK, 1986–2006 (000s)

Year	Under 1	1–4	5–14	Total under 15
1986	748	2,886	7,143	**10,777**
1996	719	3,019	7,544	**11,282**
2006	732	2,765	7,241	**10,738**

Source: *Population Trends*, 132, 2008, Table 1.4.

By children, we shall be thinking mainly of the 16s and under. But official statistics are not helpful here. They give age breakdowns only for children up to 14 and then from 15 to 19.

For this reason, in the table above we provide figures for children under 15, and in Chapter 4, 'Will becoming an adult be more difficult?', we include totals for 15- to 19-year olds. In 2006, the UK had 10.7 million children who were under 15.

Three groups of adults have the most impact on children's lives – parents, schools and business, the latter through the products it develops and sells. How has the effect of these groups been changing in recent years?

Has the quality of parenting improved? Though generalisations have to be taken with a pinch of salt, we discuss three important indicators.

More children are being raised in unstable households. The chart below shows that between 1996 and 2006 the proportion of 'married couple families' continued its long-term decline.

Lone parents remained at a high level – nearly a quarter of all families – while cohabiting couples with children increased substantially, from 9% to 14%. Approaching two-fifths of children are now born to cohabiting parents.[3]

Proportion of families by family type, 1996 and 2006 (%)

Family type	1996	2006
Married couple families	76	71
Cohabiting couple families	9	14
Lone parent families	15	16

Source: National Statistics, 'Overview of families', 4 October 2007, **http://www.statistics.gov.uk**.

Cohabiting couples tend to be less stable than married ones (see 'What will shape the next 20 years?' on p. 47). So although the divorce rate has fallen slightly in recent years, this is more than offset by the growing number of cohabiting couples who break up.

Reflecting the greater instability of couples overall, stepfamilies have become the fastest growing family type. A 2004 estimate put the proportion of dads aged 34 who were stepfathers at slightly under 20%. This was nearly double the figure for men born just 12 years earlier.[4]

Research shows that stable couples are most beneficial for children. So the increasing numbers of parents breaking up must be damaging for many children. But that need not be true in all cases.[5]

- *The amount of conflict matters.* A lot of conflict between parents can cause children considerable pain. Sometimes it can be better for children if the parents separate.
- *How parents separate is vital.* Children may weather the process well if they are shielded from the worst of parental strife and continue to have regular access to the non-custodial parent.
- *Single parents and step-parents can do a brilliant job.* Children can be wonderfully resilient and often bounce back from the effects of separation. This is most likely if they continue to be parented in a warm, supportive and consistent way by at least one of their parents, without this being undermined by the other.

Parents are spending more time with children, which may come as a surprise to many people. How can this be so in our 'long hours' culture where more mothers work full-time than ever before?

Time-use diaries from 16 industrialised countries, including the UK, reveal that twenty-first-century parents devote more time to interacting with their children than mothers and fathers in the 1960s. In a number of countries, fathers are beginning to close the gap with mothers in the amount of time they give.

Parents are spending longer with their children by cutting back on their own leisure and personal activities. This is especially true of mothers who combine caring for their children with part-time employment.[6]

Fast food and mod cons round the home may also be helping. Instead of mum slaving away in the kitchen and doing the washing while little Jonny plays in the next room, she can put the clothes in the washing machine and the food in the microwave. She has time to read her son a story.

A 2002 Future Foundation study reported that almost a fifth of families sat down to a home-cooked dinner every night of the week, compared to a mere 12% of families in the 1960s.[7]

Devoting time to playing, chatting and reading with children is good for them. But might some parents be overdoing it? After a busy day at school followed by an after-school club and homework, children need time to 'chill' and do activities of their own choosing. Could some parents be taking this space away from them?

> 'In the US, stress management workshops exist for children in kindergarten'

American children tell marketers that they want less pressure, less overload and more time to relax. Stress management workshops now exist in the US for children in kindergarten![8]

The general pattern of parenting seems to be improving. Experts sometimes refer to four types of parenting style:[9]

- *Authoritative parenting* involves high levels of warmth combined with high levels of control. The degree of control lessens as the child gets older. Children brought up in this way tend to do better at school and have fewer emotional problems than those who experience other styles of parenting.
- *Authoritarian parenting* consists of high control and low warmth. Children achieve less academically and have lower social competence. They tend to be more aggressive.
- *Permissive parenting* puts control and warmth the other way round. Parents have high warmth and low control. Their children tend to be more aggressive, more impulsive and more prone to drug-related problems.
- *Disengaged parenting* occurs where control and warmth are both low. Children are more likely to be overly impulsive, drop out of school, become dependent on drugs or turn to crime.

There seems to be no research showing how widespread these different parenting styles are. However, an Australian study (albeit using a small sample) compared parents' reports of their own parenting behaviours with their accounts of how they themselves had been brought up.

The study looked for changes between the generations in permissive, authoritarian and authoritative parenting styles. It didn't test for disengaged parenting.[10]

The results showed little change between the generations in the proportion of parents who were permissive. The biggest change was a shift from

authoritarian to authoritative parenting, which had become the most frequent parenting style.

The sample was largely middle class and better educated than the previous generation. This was in line with other studies showing that well-educated parents are more likely to adopt an authoritative approach.

With growing numbers staying on in education since the 1960s, it seems reasonable to believe that authoritative parenting has become more widespread in Britain, too.

If this is the good news, the bad news is the evidence from teachers and other professionals. They come across many children whose parents either seem to have disengaged or are too permissive, and whose behaviour reflects this. Improvements in parenting still have a long way to go.

Adults in schools are a second group to have a big effect on children. Schools have been transformed over the past 25 years. Given the amount of time children spend at school, these changes have had a profound effect on their lives. We focus on England, recognising that experiences in Northern Ireland, Scotland and Wales have sometimes been different.

The school system has been extended vertically and horizontally. Vertically, the system has stretched its reach upward with a steady increase in education and training opportunities for school leavers. The government intends to make education or training for 16- to 18-year-olds compulsory by 2015.

The school system has also reached down to younger ages with the expansion of nursery and early years provision (such as children's centres). These developments have been seen primarily as *education* initiatives.

Schools have also extended horizontally by providing 'wrap-around' care at both ends of the day – from breakfast before school to clubs afterwards.

In 2005, approaching half a million children were in breakfast, after-school and holiday clubs registered with Ofsted.[11] Some after-school activities or childcare were provided by 87% of primary schools and 95% of secondary schools.[12] 'School' has been encroaching more and more on children's lives.

School policy has been driven increasingly by Whitehall. The 1988 Education Reform Act introduced the National Curriculum and national testing at four Key Stages – ages 7, 11, 14 and 16.

Testing made possible the introduction of league tables in 1992 which – along with Ofsted inspections – were seen as a vehicle to drive up standards. The government began to address 'failing' schools the following year.

Before leaving office, the Conservatives set in motion the introduction of a daily 'literacy hour' in primary schools to improve teaching standards. New Labour introduced a daily 'numeracy hour' as a natural next step.

Labour took the standards theme much further with Tony Blair's promise in 1997 that education reform would be about 'standards, not structures'. Targets – to improve literacy and numeracy, for example – became central to policy. Failing schools were re-opened as 'Fresh Start' schools, often with new staff and management.

These and other initiatives led to a massive transfer of power from local authorities, who previously had been mainly responsible for education, to central government. Standards, targets and school performance came to dominate the education debate.

> 'In 2000, the government launched an incredible 106 education initiatives in July alone'

Head teachers have often felt swamped by central government initiatives. In July 2000, for instance, the 'Monthly Listing of Official Publications Relating to the Department for Education and Employment' contained 106 items. For just one month of the year. Imagine being a head teacher and dealing with 106 initiatives in four weeks![13]

Governments have tried to increase competition between schools. League tables were designed to help parents choose between competing schools. To help head teachers respond to this market, the Conservative government gave them greater financial and management autonomy.

Expanding the diversity of school types to increase competition (and choice) has become a major theme. Developments have included:

- *Foundation schools,* which are successors to grant-maintained schools and are now becoming 'trust' schools. The governing body or a charitable foundation owns the school buildings and land, and employs the staff.
- *Academy schools* – state-maintained independent schools set up with the help of sponsors. Funders originally had to put up £2 million, but this requirement has now been waived for universities, high-performing colleges or other schools that become sponsors. By September 2010 it is expected that 230 academies will have been established.[14]
- *Specialist schools.* In partnership with private sector sponsors and with extra government money, these schools have developed distinctive identities since 1994 by offering a specialism in languages, music or art, for instance. By early 2006, 75% of England's state-maintained secondary schools had specialist status.[15]

Making schools more responsive to the market has been a vital government objective. Borrowing ideas from business, this has entailed schools becoming more 'customer'-focused, partly in the hope of pushing up standards. The most effective schools would experience strong public demand. Two sets of customers have been involved.

The most important customers have been parents. Their ability to choose has been aided by the publication of league tables, which have helped them to compare schools. Widening the diversity of available schools has given them more choice. The voice of parents has been strengthened by increasing their role in school governance and giving them more information about their child's progress.

Pupils have been the other set of customers. In the public sector, the concept of 'customisation', an idea frequently used by the marketing industry, has been translated into 'personalisation'.

For schools, according to an official press release, this has come to mean 'reshaping the education system around the individual pupil and ensuring that no school adopts a "one-size-fits-all" approach to teaching'.[16]

Personalisation in schools has been powered by research into pupils' different learning styles, which teachers are expected to take into account, and by the promise of technology. IT-based learning should make it easier for pupils to proceed at their own pace within a class context.[17] Personalisation also includes more help for children falling behind.

Improving the capacity of the school workforce has been another priority. This has involved:

- *Improving leadership* – by creating institutions such as the National College for School Leadership in 2000.
- *Encouraging collaboration and partnership* – for example, establishing federations of schools that work together to raise standards and find new ways of teaching.
- *Remodelling teachers* – by encouraging greater use of teaching assistants, for instance, with their own national professional standards.

These developments have affected children in a number of ways. Firstly, standards have risen. In 1984 a little under 25% of 16-year-olds attained five or more GCEs. In 2004–05, 20 years later, the proportion had more than doubled: 62% of girls and 52% of boys attained five GCSEs at grades A-C, roughly the equivalent of the old GCE.[18]

Though critics complain that GCSEs have become easier, that teachers 'teach to the test', that papers are marked more leniently and that some pupils may cheat in their coursework, there can be little doubt that standards – as measured by exams taken in the last compulsory year of school – have gone up.

Secondly, there are some signs that the school experience has improved. Between 1984 and 1999 there was a clear upward trend in the proportion of young people who commented favourably on their last two years of compulsory education.

They reported that these years had helped to give them confidence in making decisions and taught them things that would be useful in a job. There was a reduction in the proportion who said that school had done little to prepare them for life afterwards.[19]

Yet this is not the whole story. School has become more stressful for many pupils, especially younger ones, who are now assessed more frequently and experience stronger pressure to perform well from an early age. Children are on the receiving end of more parental anxiety about their performance.

Research in the early 2000s found that 60-70 % of 15-year-old girls in England felt pressured by their schoolwork, compared to fewer than 40% in France, Germany and the Netherlands.[20]

Thirdly, not enough teenagers are taking 'STEM' subjects nowadays – science, technology, engineering and maths – at A-level or university. Though Britain is not the only rich country where this is the case, skill shortages in these subjects are a growing concern.

There is a shortage of maths teachers in schools, and this is damaging the teaching of that subject. With maths increasingly a foundation skill for the knowledge economy, how seriously might Britain's competitiveness suffer in the years ahead?

Finally, the school culture has become more business-like, with a stress on competition, responding to customers (parents in this case), measuring performance and improving it.

These emphases are some of the key market assumptions that dominate today's world, and children are being brought up to embrace them. Many professionals wonder whether this 'hidden curriculum' contains too narrow a set of values.

Childhood has been commercialised in a more general sense, too. Teenagers emerged as a distinct youth market in the 1950s. The media responded to young people's growing spending power to create a distinct youth culture, which challenged the values and institutions cherished by adults. A 'generation gap' emerged in the 1960s.

Younger children have now been brought into this youth market, a phenomenon that began in the late 1980s.

- *Global media have played a central role.* For example, 85% of Britain's five- to 16-year-olds regularly accessed the Internet in 2007. As many as 72% of the age group had visited a social networking site and over half had set up their own profile. Some of the latter group were as young as eight years old.[21]
- *Youth culture is being marketed to an ever-younger age.* Marketers have adopted a 'Kids Are Getting Older Younger' strategy, selling teenage notions of cool to pre-teens (known as 'tweenies'). According to one retail marketing executive, 'Tweens aspire to look like older teenagers, so our assortment for them encompasses the look of the average 15-year-old.'[22]
- *The market for youth culture is now incredibly broad.* According to the World Youth Report 2005:

  'In their shared enthusiasm for certain kinds of music, sportswear or video games, for example, both 10- and 40-year-olds may be seen as members of a "youth" market that is quite self-consciously distinct from the "family" market.'[23]

  Children are growing up earlier than in previous generations.
- *Pre-teens inhabit their own world of consumption.* Eight in 10 children aged five to 16 have their own TV.[24] According to ChildWise, one in three primary school children had their own PC in 2005–06.[25] Pre-teens are increasingly exposed to marketing messages in their bedrooms, free from parental control.
- *The 1960s 'generation gap' has changed profoundly.* Though marketers encourage children to be independent of adults and sometimes present adults as their enemy, they also enlist children in their sales pitch to parents. Children increasingly influence what their parents buy – shaping what they choose to wear, for instance.[26]

  So while at times children seek to be different from their parents, on other occasions they try to bring parents round to their view of good taste – to close the generation gap.

In a sense, the global media are bringing up children. The media's extensive influence on children makes them a third party in the 'parenting' process, alongside parents and schools.

This has raised all sorts of issues such as the sexualisation of young girls' clothing, children's exposure to pornography and violence, and marketing pressure to over- or under-eat.

On top of all this, children are suffering from tiredness at school because they watch TV, play computer games or surf the Internet till late at night. It is also said that the consumerisation of childhood exacerbates other behavioural issues such as problems with self-restraint.

The industry claims these problems arise largely because parents don't supervise their children while they are watching TV or using the Internet.

New media, it says, are actually giving children more opportunities. Teenagers are learning to create music, manipulate images and edit video to a high standard. Homework is being enriched as children surf the net and collaborate together.

There are gains as well as problems. But these gains are not universally shared.

Children from disadvantaged families are being left behind. More than a fifth of all children in the UK are brought up in poverty, one of the highest figures in the industrialised world.

The total fell by 500,000 between 1998–99 and 2006–07, reducing the proportion of children in poverty from 26% to 22%. But with numbers rising since 2004–05, the government's target of halving child poverty by 2010 is still a long way off.[27]

Average rank in test scores at age 22, 42, 60 and 120 months by social class of parents and early rank position in tests

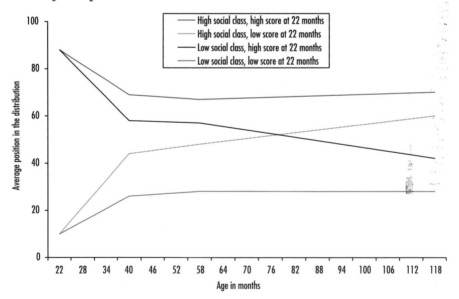

Source: Stephen Aldridge, 'Life chances and social mobility: An Overview of the Evidence', Prime Minister's Strategy Unit, 30 March 2004, p. 19.

Children's chances of doing well later in life are largely determined by their social background. If you are born into a family with a low income, you are highly likely to earn a low income as an adult.[28]

The chart above uses data about people born in 1970. Someone from a 'high social class', whose IQ ranked in the bottom tenth when 22 months old, climbed comfortably into the top half by their tenth birthday. But a child from a 'low social class' with an IQ score near the top at 22 months had dropped to the bottom two-fifths by age 10.

A study of children born in 2000 found that those from the richest households who scored poorly in cognitive tests at age three were gaining ground by age five. Children from the poorest backgrounds who scored well at age three were losing ground by their fifth birthday.[29] Social disadvantage remains deeply entrenched.

Sue Palmer, *Toxic Childhood*, London: Orion, 2007, p. 230.

Juliet B. Schor, *Born to Buy*, New York: Scribner, 2004, p. 24.

3 In 2006 nearly 44% of all births were to unmarried mothers, 85% of which were registered by both mother and father, assumed to be cohabiting. See tables 2.1 and 3.2 in *Health Statistics Quarterly*, 37, London: ONS, 2008.
'Complex Christmases of Britain's growing number of stepfamilies',
http://www.esrcsocietytoday.ac.uk, December 2004

See, for example, Bryan Rogers & Jan Pryor, *Divorce and Separation: The Outcomes for Children*, York: Joseph Rowntree Foundation, 1998; T. David et al, 'Birth to Three Matters: A Review of the Literature', *Research Paper No. 444*, DfES, 2003, p. 130; Susie Burke, Jennifer McIntosh & Heather Gridley, 'Parenting after Separation: A Position Statement Prepared for the Australian Psychological Society', unpublished, August 2007.

6 Anne H. Gauthier, Timothy M. Smeedeng & Frank F. Furstenberg, Jr., 'Are Parents Investing Less Time in Children? Trends in Selected Industrialized Countries', *Population and Development Review*, 30(4), 2004, pp. 647–671.

7 Quoted by the BBC in 'Living alone is the norm', 11 January 2002 http://news.bbc.co.uk.

Juliet B. Schor, *Born to Buy*, New York: Scribner, 2004, p. 31.

Melissa Wake et al, 'Preschooler Obesity and Parenting Styles of Mothers and Fathers: Australian National Population Study', *Pediatrics*, 120, 2007, p.1521.

10 Sophie Zervides & Ann Knowles, 'Generational Changes in Parenting Styles and the Effect of Culture', *E-Journal of Applied Psychology*, 3(1), 2007, pp. 65–75.

11 Abigail Self & Linda Zealey (eds.), *Social Trends*, 37, 2007, p. 26.

12 'Contribution of Schools to Every Child Matters Outcomes: Evidence to Support Education Productivity Measures', Department for Children, Schools and Families, 4 September 2007.

13 Stephen J. Ball, *The Education Debate: Policy and Politics in the Twenty-First Century*, Bristol: Policy Press, 2008, p. 3. Our summary of changes in school policy draws heavily on Ball.

14 Anthea Lipsett, 'What are Academy Schools?', 13 November 2007, http://education.guardian.co.uk.

15 Stephen J. Ball, *The Education Debate: Policy and Politics in the Twenty-first Century*, Bristol: Policy Press, 2008, p. 123.

16 'More catch-up and stretch as experts promote lessons catering to individual pupils' needs', DfES Press Release, 13 March 2006.

17 *Ibid.*

18 Linda Croxford et al, 'Trends in Education and Youth Transitions across Britain 1984–2002', *Working Paper 17*, ESRC, 2006, p. 9 (This paper forms part of the ESRC research project 'Education and Youth Transitions in England, Wales and Scotland', 1984–2002. These are figures for England, Scotland and Wales and include the equivalents of GCEs and GCSEs); Abigail Self & Linda Zealey (eds.), *Social Trends*, 37, London: National Statistics, 2007, p. 33. (These figures are for the whole of the UK and refer to GCSE passes at A*-C, or their equivalent.)

19 Linda Croxford et al, 'Trends in Education and Youth Transitions across Britain 1984–2002', *Working Paper 17*, ESRC, 2006, p. 12.

20 'Social pressures on children and risk-taking behaviour', *ESRC Seminar Series: Mapping the Public Policy Landscape*, Swindon: ESRC, p. 9.

21 'Life through a lens: how Britain's children eat, breathe and sleep TV', **http://www.guardian.co.uk**, 16 January 2008.

22 *Consuming Kids*, New York: New Press, 2004, p. 132, quoted by Susan Linn.

23 Department of Economic and Social Affairs, *World Youth Report 2005*, New York: UN, 2005, p. 95.

24 *The Monitor Trends Report*, 2007, **http://www.childwise.co.uk/trends.htm**.

25 Cited by Rosemary Duff in 'Primary-Aged Children: Interests and Aptitudes', **http://www.projectsetc.org**.

26 'New Consumers? Children, Fashion and Consumption', Culture as Consumption Findings, 2005, **http://www.consume.bbk.ac.uk**.

27 Nick Adams et al (eds.), *Households Below Average Income: An Analysis of the Income Distribution 1994/95 – 2006/07*, London: DWP, 2008, tables 4.1tr & 4.3tr. Figures are for households below 60% of median earnings before housing costs.

28 There appears to be a significant correlation between parents' position in the earnings distribution and the position of their children. Stephen Aldridge, *Life Chances and Social Mobility: An Overview of the Evidence*, Prime Minister's Strategy Unit, 30 March 2004, p. 26.

29 Jo Blanden & Stephen Machin, *Recent Changes in Intergenerational Mobility in Britain*, Report for Sutton Trust, 2007, p. 23.

HOW WILL WE BRING UP OUR CHILDREN?
WHAT WILL SHAPE THE NEXT 20 YEARS?

- The number of children in the UK will reach record levels
- What will influence the quality of parenting?
- What will happen to schools?
- Will the commercialisation of childhood be checked?
- A large number of children will still be disadvantaged

The number of children in the UK will reach record levels. As in 'The story so far', by children we mean primarily 16-year-olds and under, but because the official statistics do not break down the figures in this way, the table below provides projections for the under-15 age group only (those aged 15–19 are included in Chapter 4, 'Will becoming an adult be more difficult?').

The table shows that the number of under-15s in the UK is expected to grow substantially by 2026 and remain fairly stable thereafter. The total will increase rapidly between 2006 and 2016, reaching a record 11.4 million, and will continue rising to over 12 million 10 years later. This will put significant pressure on the government's schools budget.

Projected number of children aged under 15 in the UK, 2006–2036 (000s)

	Under 1 yr old	1–4 yrs old	5–14 yrs old	Total under 15
2006	732	2,765	7,241	**10,738**
2016	799	3,191	7,438	**11,428**
2026	790	3,188	8,048	**12,026**
2036	Included in next column	3,981*	7,956	**11,937**

Source: ONS, Population Estimates Unit, June 2008; *National Population Projections: 2006-Based*, London: ONS, 2008, pp. 64–5.
Note: 1. The 'principal projection' is used.
　　2. *The figure of 3,981 is the projected number of children aged 0–4 years old in 2036.

The business concern will be whether all these children are being equipped to seize the opportunities of the global economy. Will they be able to compete when they are grown up? Other people, stressing children's rights, will be more concerned about child welfare.

These two emphases complement each other – adults are more likely to flourish economically if they were respected as children. But in practice the two may rub shoulders uncomfortably.

Even now, for example, government pressure to raise educational standards meets strong resistance from professionals who fear that children are becoming too stressed. Resolving tensions between competitiveness and children's wellbeing will remain a key issue for government.

Parents, schools and new media will continue to bring up children for the most part. The role of each will remain under the spotlight.

What will influence the quality of parenting? We pick up the themes from 'The story so far' – the stability of households, the amount of time parents spend with their children, and parenting styles.

More children are likely to be brought up in unstable homes. Though trends in the divorce rate have been falling – the rate in 2007 was the lowest since 1981[1] – and births to teenage mothers have dropped, too,[2] this is more than offset by the growing number of cohabiting couples with children. These couples are more likely to break up than married ones.

In 2006 nearly 44% of all births were to unmarried mothers, the great majority of whom were cohabiting – 85% of these births were registered by both mother and father. Thirty years earlier unmarried mothers had less than 10% of all babies.[3]

The proportion of births outside marriage is likely to keep escalating for at least two reasons:

- *The trend will reinforce itself.* Couples will think, 'Our friends are having children before they are married, so why shouldn't we?'
- *The costs of a wedding ceremony* – and rising expectations about what the ceremony should comprise – will compete with mounting student debt and the higher cost of housing (once the current downturn is past). Even more couples will postpone marriage and have children first, or have children without getting married at all.

Traditionally, cohabiting couples have been less stable than married ones. According to one source, by a child's fifth birthday fewer than one in twelve married couples (8%) have split up compared to almost one in two cohabiting couples (43%).[4] This has probably been because less stable couples have been most inclined to cohabit.

But as cohabiting couples with children become more widespread, they will include a growing number of stable unions.

Some couples will marry later – in 2006, 56% of cohabiting partners had gone on to marry. Others will remain together, seeing cohabitation as an alternative to marriage. Significantly, couples who don't marry are staying together for longer than they used to.[5]

An optimistic view is that growing numbers of people are having children later (and marrying later), once they are confident that their relationship will last. Having been together for some time, they are less likely to encounter a nasty surprise in the behaviour and character of their spouse. If this is the case and it continues, fewer couples with children will split up.

On the other hand, there is a risk that rising expectations will undermine the stability of parenting couples. With self-fulfilment near the top of people's wish lists, partners may well expect more from each other. If their expectations are unmet, dissatisfaction will grow.

In a climate where separation is widely accepted, this discontent would fuel demands to part. There would be a continuing, if gradual, rise in the proportion of parents who go their separate ways.

A future government may well do more to encourage couples with children to stay together. The Conservatives are considering measures to promote relationship education and remove a perceived bias toward single parents in the tax and benefit system. For example, they are looking at increasing the Working Tax Credit by an average of just over £32 a week for 1.8 million couples.[6]

At present, a couple with children get the same level of Working Tax Credit as a single parent. It is hoped that increasing the benefits couples receive would give them a stronger incentive not to separate.

But the idea would be expensive – about £3 billion, equal to almost 1p on income tax.[7] Will the proposal be watered down to make it more affordable? And if so, will the incentive be big enough to make a difference?

Parents are likely to spend more time with their children. In 'The story so far', we saw that parents have been devoting more and more time to their children. This is set to continue.

■ *Mod cons will further automate household chores,* freeing up parents' time. Researchers have found that American middle-class city-dwellers now have so many gadgets that they can cram into a total of 24 hours all the tasks that would have taken them 31 hours 10 years ago.[8]

Advances in robotics will free up even more time. You can now order online robot pet care, robot floor cleaners, robot vacuum cleaners and robot lawn mowers.[9]

- *The flexible hours culture will take a firmer hold on workplace life.* Currently parents of children under six have the right to request flexible work and employers are obliged to consider such requests seriously. A 2007 survey found that 43% of workplaces had received such a request from at least one employee in the previous month. Of these, only 9% had turned the request down.[10]

  There have been calls to extend the right to request flexible working to all parents. As these calls are heeded, flexible work will become still more acceptable, allowing parents to spend longer with their children.

- *Couples will want to do the best for their children.* Children's centres, schools, parenting gurus and other professionals will encourage parents to spend time with their offspring, on activities such as reading to them when they are young and supporting their homework.

- *Fathers in particular will give more time to their children.* This upward trend is set to resume and perhaps accelerate for the reasons described in Chapter 2, 'Will we produce enough babies?' As more women achieve equal pay, their financial contribution to the household will increase. Fathers will want to share childcare so that mothers can earn their full potential.

Overall, the quality of parenting is likely to improve. In 'The story so far', we saw that an 'authoritative' style of parenting, combining warmth with appropriate control, was the healthiest approach.

We found some evidence that this style of parenting has become more widespread, while 'authoritarian' approaches – with their over-reliance on control – seem less common nowadays. Claims by professionals that 'permissive' and 'disengaged' parenting are not infrequent, however, suggested that there was plenty of room for parenting to get better.

'Authoritative' parenting is likely to spread as higher proportions of young people stay on at school and enter university. This is because this style of parenting seems to be especially associated with people who have spent longer in education.

Reinforcing this positive change will be greater support for parents. In the push to raise educational standards, growing attention is now being paid to what happens in the family.

According to the Department for Education and Skills (as it was), research shows that parenting in the home has a far more significant impact on children's achievement than parents' social class or level of education. It has a bigger effect on the achievement and adjustment of primary-school-age children than school itself.[13]

With government encouragement, some schools are beginning to set up parenting groups to help fathers and mothers better support their child's education. Parenting skills are taught in a school context, using high-quality material that is increasingly available.

> 'Parents have a bigger effect on children's achievement than schools'

This is set to become a growing trend, backed with significant government funds. Over the next two decades, parenting groups focusing on key transitions – perhaps entry to nursery, primary and secondary school, and post-16 level – will become part of the education scene.

Finding enough skilled facilitators will be a constraint. So will encouraging those parents who most need support to attend. The results, therefore, will be mixed. Yet overall, support groups could well do much to raise parenting skills.

In particular, they could boost parents' confidence. 'Paranoid parents' have been blamed for being over-protective. Obsessively frightened about children's safety, parents don't give their offspring enough space to play on their own and make mistakes. The potential joy of parenting is undermined by excessive worry.[14]

Being with other parents, sharing fears and receiving encouragement is a strong antidote to anxiety. Support groups could help parents to feel reassured.

What will happen to schools? There will be developments in the curriculum, in classroom practice and in the market model of education.

The global economy will largely drive the curriculum, as it does now. The international race up the skills ladder will accelerate as China, India and other developing countries churn out more sophisticated products, adopt more complex methods of production and expand their universities to enlarge their pools of talent.

These countries will increasingly compete in the high-end manufacturing industry, and in financial and other services. With the 'Asian tigers' biting at their heels, countries like Britain that specialise in high-value-added products will be forced further up the value chain. The UK's workforce will need to become ever more skilled.

In 2006, the influential Leitch Report called for a doubling of attainment at most skill levels by 2020, to ensure that Britain's skills remain in the top quartile of the industrialised world. This would require 95% of adults to attain the basic skills of both functional literacy and numeracy, up from 85% and 79% respectively in 2005. To help achieve this, schools would have to raise their game.[15]

Besides literacy and numeracy, schools will continue to prioritise IT and – as now – government will invest more heavily in the teaching of science, where there are acute shortages of skills.

Will there be a change in the content of 'communication', another priority skill? Until now, communication as a skill has been understood mainly in a cognitive sense – such as your ability to summarise, evaluate and apply information.

> ## 'Emotional skills are very important for 65% of jobs'

While these abilities will remain important, social skills, or 'emotional literacy', have emerged as perhaps even more vital. In a 2006 study, emotional skills were rated as 'very important' for 65% of jobs. In 52% of jobs, 'aesthetic skills' – which include how you present yourself to other people – were also 'very important'.[16]

Interpersonal skills will become steadily more crucial as customer-focused jobs increase and technology advances. Technology allows more complex tasks to be done – think of how today's supply chains are managed! Increasingly these tasks are beyond the skills of any one person, which puts a premium on relating well to other people.

Interpersonal skills include not just written and oral communication, but dialogue skills, negotiating capacity, self-awareness, empathy, personal presentation and the ability to regulate one's feelings.

Will 'communication' evolve into 'emotional literacy'? And if so, building on what already happens in the classroom and the government's growing interest in this area, what new methodologies will be developed to teach and assess social skills?

'Life skills', ranging from citizenship to financial ability to personal health, will compete for space with the rest of the curriculum. But how much room will these topics have? Their position will be squeezed by the priority given to skills that directly contribute to the economy and also by a desire to make the curriculum less prescriptive and give more scope for teacher initiative.

Education practice will continue to evolve, especially under the influence of advances in science and technology:

- *Smart drugs will improve cognitive performance.* Drugs like Modafinil, which improves short-term memory, attention span and reaction time, are already widely used by American university students, who currently buy them on the black market.[17] As brain-boosting drugs are developed, and bought by middle-class parents for their children at school, what will happen to equality of opportunity?
- *Brain sciences will advance our understanding of dyslexia* and other conditions, making possible more effective support for children with special needs.

Will 'dyslexia' eventually become an umbrella term like 'cancer', covering a number of quite distinct conditions?

■ *Differential learning* – taking account of pupils' varied learning styles – will become easier. Visual learners will benefit from virtual reality, for instance, which is advancing rapidly. By the 2020s, history lessons may include studying famous battles in 3D. Haptic technologies, which provide vibrations and movement to the computer user, will benefit children who learn best by feeling things. Online audio effects will aid audio learners.

■ *Learning will be more self-paced.* Even now, learners can use a computer-based program to work through a series of maths problems at their own pace, getting feedback as they go. In future continuous assessment will be built into the core structure of curriculum material. Learners will have to complete tasks successfully at each stage before progressing to the next one.[18] Online tests will be supervised in class to avoid cheating. Faster pupils could support slower ones.

■ *Will new forms of assessment emerge?* Continuous assessment may eventually replace formal tests at a particular time. Computerised records would then keep track of what stage each pupil had reached and their scores. Children would have ongoing records of achievement.

■ *Might this hasten the demise of GCSEs* and make SATs in their current form a thing of the past? Everyone might take just one formal test – at around 18 years old, which is to become the age for leaving compulsory education and training. Employers and universities would use the results of this test, alongside continuous assessment records, as a measure of a person's school achievement.

Children's achievement records could be used to produce league tables of school performance at earlier ages, with a growing emphasis on value-added measurements (which are increasingly used by teachers now) – for example, how many 14-year-old pupils in a particular school have reached such-and-such a stage in maths, and how does this compare to other schools whose pupils started out at roughly the same level when they were 11?

■ *Collaborative learning will spread.* Instead of doing assignments on their own when they get home, more and more pupils will work together online (as many already do today). Collaborative educational games may feature more often as 'edutainment' becomes mainstream.

The technology to support these developments is either here or in the pipeline, but how rapidly it transforms classroom practice will depend especially on:

■ *Teachers' willingness to embrace change.* Over the years, teachers have proved remarkably adaptable. They have taken on board a vast number of changes in a relatively short time. Over the next 20 years, older teachers, who have sometimes struggled with new technology, will be replaced by a more technologically savvy generation.

■ *The availability of resources.* This will include pupils' access to laptops at school and broadband at home. In particular, how much support will be given to teachers who have the technical abilities to develop good quality computer-based courseware and new methods of teaching? Will they be given the time and resources to do so? What incentives will they have to spread good practice?

■ *Economies of scale.* Because developing course material, updating it and providing online support can be costly, economies of scale will be vital. This could require the standardisation of course content across the examining boards, so that there are enough learners to warrant the costs involved. Encouraging the right amount of innovation will be difficult: too many innovators could fragment the market and make high-quality material uneconomic; too few might leave too little competition.

How will the market model of education develop, particularly in England? Notions of competition and choice are so deeply entrenched that it is hard to envisage the model being abandoned. Indeed, parents' determination to get their children into good schools may actually strengthen the market approach.

Might popular state schools be allowed to opt for independent status, for example, and might they be given the freedom to expand and borrow for this purpose? (If schools were independent, their loans wouldn't appear on the government's books, which would remove a technical constraint on borrowing.) Parents could choose their school knowing the state would pay up to a certain amount – a logical extension of academies, which are government-funded independent schools.[19]

On the other hand, the market model may be strained by two tensions within it. The first concerns the customer. Who are schools' consumers – parents or children? The government would say both, but in practice gives most weight to parents.

However, if governments want the market model to work most effectively, there is a strong argument for paying more attention to children. After all, they are the direct consumers of education – in the classroom.

In theory, if children had market power, they could put pressure on teachers to improve the quality of service. They might go to another provider. Or they could buy an online GCSE package instead of attending incompetently taught French classes. They could vote with their feet.

Children don't have market power in that sense, of course. But an alternative way to strengthen their position might be to give them more of a voice in school, particularly in giving feedback on lessons and through involvement in course reviews. Leading-edge schools have begun to do this in ways appropriate to different age groups.

Might there be a stronger move in this direction, driven by the market approach to education? Giving children something akin to market power would be a way to drive up standards further.

This would also draw support from advocates of children's rights, who believe that children have a right to be heard (in a way that is appropriate to their age). The 'economics' and 'wellbeing' approaches to children would join hands.

The second tension is between inter-school competition and the need to collaborate. Teachers are increasingly expected to research good practice, and to share what they discover so that standards across the system go up. But local schools have little incentive to share their knowledge and experience if they are competing with one other.

Might the emphasis shift from sharing good practice at a local level to communicating it on a national scale? Teachers could form various national networks to exchange good practice online and face-to-face. If several networks existed for each discipline, teachers from locally competing schools could avoid joining the same one.

Such networks have started to emerge already. Using them effectively will be a growing priority – and part of Ofsted inspections – as learning networks generally become more and more central to the knowledge economy.[20]

Spreading good practice could be the single biggest contribution to raising school standards.

Will the commercialisation of childhood be checked? The key factor will be the continued growth of the children's retail market, which is worth about £30 billion a year in the UK.[21]

If Britain's economy continues to expand at the same rate as it has for the past 25 years, average incomes per head will nearly double over the next quarter of a century. Families will have much more to spend than they do now. As part of this, children will be drawn even deeper into the consumer society, and at an ever-younger age.

Concerns about this will continue to mount. Among other things, they will focus on:

- *Health*. Marketing encourages children to eat unhealthy food by associating the food with 'fun' – through the colourful packaging and the use of pictures, cartoons and characters from TV or films.[22] In England, 10% of children are now obese, with a further 20% to 25% overweight. According to the government's Foresight team, by 2050 Britain could be a mainly obese society.[23]

- *Security*. Use of the Internet by paedophiles has caught media attention, and so, too, has the online bullying of children: the rapid spread of a defamatory story on a social networking site can trash a child's reputation. More insidious has been the escalation of gratuitous violence. Psychologists believe that much of what children under 10 view and hear through the media is frightening and emotionally destabilising.[24] Protecting children from this will remain a worry.

- *The sexualisation of young children*. In March 2007, the *Sunday Times* reported that women's groups were beginning to picket retail chains that were selling goods unsuitable for children, such as thongs for young girls emblazoned with the phrase 'eye candy'. Protestors complained that these and other products were costing younger children their innocence and dignity, and that children were being made to grow up too quickly.[25]

- *Performance at school*. With the great majority of schoolchildren now having a TV and games console in their bedroom, lateness to bed is producing sleepy children in class. A 2003 survey estimated that as many as two-thirds of British children were not getting enough sleep.[26]

What action will be taken? Companies can't be relied on to take the lead. They will reduce some of the worst excesses, no doubt. But they won't want to do more because children are so important commercially – as consumers themselves and as an influence on what their parents buy.

Companies will be reluctant to rein in a large source of income unless compelled to do so by strong public demand. So, expect companies to be followers of concerned public opinion rather than leaders in checking the commercialisation of childhood.

There will be more government regulation in response to public fears about the media's influence on children. For example, if Internet companies fail to take greater responsibility for the content of their sites and to promote what society thinks is acceptable behaviour, regulation is likely. Tighter controls on advertising to very young children are on the cards.

But there are limits to what regulation can do. You might stop a company advertising junk food on TV, for instance, only to find that its products are promoted through viral marketing (spreading the word), or as prizes in magazine competitions. Inventive marketers can always find a way round regulation.

Creating a culture of responsible consumerism could emerge as the most effective way forward. Parents and schools would seek to raise children to resist the worst forms of consumer behaviour.[27]

Parents would be strongly encouraged to use 'safe search', which blocks access to undesirable websites, and other tools to manage their children's access to the net. Might school-based parenting support groups encourage members to stand together in setting boundaries on TV watching and Internet use?

Might schools challenge consumerist values through the curriculum? Heston Blumenthal, chef-proprietor of the much-lauded Fat Duck restaurant at Bray, has written *Kitchen Chemistry* to help schools and colleges teach chemistry using examples from food. Might chemistry, as well as biology, become an opportunity to learn about healthy eating? Might maths problems include examples of using wealth to benefit other people rather than just oneself?

> 'Is the curriculum being fully harnessed to promote positive values?'

No curriculum is value-neutral. Could curriculum values climb up the policy agenda? What sort of values is the current curriculum passing on to our children? Is it being fully harnessed to promote positive values?

Business could play a key role in encouraging responsible behaviour among its young consumers, and would be likely to do so if responsible consumerism became a public priority.

A brand like Nike, employing hero messages, might include an anti-bullying story in its online adverts. A successful sportsman might be shown saying, 'I am where I am today because I was bullied at school. This made me determined to succeed. Who's heard of the kid that bullied me?'

Brands might take greater responsibility for the flipside of their products. Might McDonald's open gyms and encourage people who eat its burgers to take exercise? Might Johnnie Walker sell a version of its whisky which is non-alcoholic but carries the same brand values?

The number of disadvantaged children will remain stubbornly high. The government aims to halve the child poverty levels of 1997 by 2010 and to put an end to child poverty completely by 2020. But as we saw in 'The story so far' (see p. 34, it is still a long way from meeting these targets.

One reason is that the middle classes have so many resources to draw on, which leaves the poor at a disadvantage. These include:

- *Material resources.* They can afford to move house to be near better schools and to pay for extra help if their children fall behind;
- *Cultural resources.* Middle-class parents are more inclined to read to their children (which encourages children in their turn to read), to take their teenagers to the theatre when they are studying GCSE Shakespeare and to pass on to their offspring an expectation of doing well.
- *Social resources.* Middle-class families tend to know people who can help them work the system. 'Not doing well at maths? I know an excellent tutor who can help.' 'Want some work experience? I'll talk to my colleagues.'

The middle classes are well able to protect their position using these resources. What is more, when governments try to provide disadvantaged families with extra support, it is often the middle classes who benefit most.

In some areas, for example, the middle classes are heavy users of Sure Start children's centres, which were set up mainly to support families from poor backgrounds. Disadvantaged parents stay away because they feel uncomfortable and see that the people going are not their type.[28]

Unless there is a lot more room at the top, poorer children can only move up the social ladder if children from more fortunate families drop down and create space for them. But there is little evidence that this is happening on a large scale.

In fact, there was far less mobility from low-occupation backgrounds to better-paid occupations among people born in 1970 than in the generation born in 1958.[29] Given the middle classes' ability to protect their position, how might this worrying trend be reversed?

One approach will be to build on research into the resilience of children. Some disadvantaged children do better than expected of people from their background because they get extra support from parents, schools or some other adult who is significant in their lives.[30]

Understanding what helps children to be resilient may aid the design of measures to help other children overcome their disadvantages and equip parents and schools to provide better support.

The government is investing more heavily in one-to-one support and other forms of help to make it harder for young children fall behind at school. Might this and the development of other initiatives in the same vein be a fruitful way forward?

1 'Divorces: England and Wales rate at 26-year low', **http://www.statistics.gov.uk** (accessed 3 September 2008).

2 The number of births per thousand mothers under age 20 fell from 30.9 in 1999 to 26.6 in 2006. See Table 3.1, *Health Statistics Quarterly*, 37, 2008.

3 See Tables 2.1 and 3.2, *Health Statistics Quarterly*, 37, London: ONS, 2008.

4 *Breakthrough Britain: Ending the Costs of Social Breakdown: Policy Recommendations to the Conservative Party*, London: Social Justice Policy Group, 2007, p. 69.

5 Anne Barlow et al, 'Cohabitation and the Law: Myths, Money and the Media' in Alison Park et al (eds.), *British Social Attitudes: The 24th Report*, London: Sage, 2008, p. 33.

6 *Breakthrough Britain: Ending the Costs of Social Breakdown: Policy Recommendations to the Conservative Party*, London: Social Justice Policy Group, 2007, pp. 73–4.

7 *Breakthrough Britain: Ending the Costs of Social Breakdown: Policy Recommendations to the Conservative Party*, London: Social Justice Policy Group, 2007, p. 74.

8 Research by Patrick Moriarty of think-tank OTX, cited in *Management Today*, 14 April 2008.

9 See, for example, **http://www.robotshop.ca**.

10 Bruce Hayward, Barry Fong & Alex Thornton, 'The Third Work-Life Balance Employer Survey', *Employment Relations Research Series No. 86*, London: BERR, 2007, p. 6.

11 'Who does what?' **http://www.sociology.org.uk**.

12 Rosemary Crompton & Clare Lyonette, 'Who Does the Housework? The Division of Labour within the Home', in Alison Park et al (eds), *British Social Attitudes: The 24th Report*, London: Sage, 2008, p. 55.

13 *Parenting Support*, London: DfES, 2006, p. 1.

14 This has been argued particularly by Frank Furedi in *Paranoid Parenting*, London: Penguin, 2001.

15 *Prosperity for All in the Global Economy – World-Class Skills: Final Report*, Norwich: HMSO, 2006, p. 3.

16 Alan Felstead et al., *Skills at Work: 1996–2006*, Cardiff/Oxford: ESRC, 2007, p. 47.

17 *The Times*, 14 May 2007.

18 In its 'Children's Plan', the government has promised new 'stage not age' tests, which children will take when they are ready, and which – if current trials are successful – will replace Key Stage tests at ages 11 and 14. *The Children's Plan. Building brighter futures – Summary*, London: DCSF, 2007, p. 10.

19 The objection has always been that government would have to subsidise the fees of the 8% of children who attend today's private schools, which would be prohibitively expensive. If state schools became private, it would be hard to justify treating existing private schools differently. But this might be overcome by giving the new independent schools a distinct legal status (a bit like grant-maintained schools). Where the old private schools offered a superior education, parents could still opt out of the state-subsidised system. If they didn't offer value for money, these schools would be under pressure to raise their game, which would help to drive up standards overall. Weaker public schools would find it hard to abandon their existing charitable status in favour of the new category of school, since under charity law their assets would still have to be employed for their original charitable purpose.

20 'Futures and Educational Research', *NERF Working Paper 6.5*, London: DfES, 2006.

21 Estimate provided to the Children's Society, as part of their enquiry into childhood in Britain. Quoted by the BBC, **http://news.bbc.co.uk** (accessed 26 February 2008).

22 Sue Palmer, *Toxic Childhood*, London: Orion, 2006, p. 24.

23 Foresight, *Tackling Obesities: Future Choices – Project Report*, London: Department of Innovation, Universities & Skills, 2007, p. 6.

24 Sue Palmer, *Toxic Childhood*, London: Orion, 2006, p. 260.

25 *Sunday Times*, 4 March 2007.

26 Sue Palmer, *Toxic Childhood*, London: Orion, 2006, p. 89.

27 This was the thrust of the Byron Review on e-safety, *Safer Children in a Digital World: The Report of the Byron Review*, London: DCSF, 2008.

28 Rosie Bennett, 'Poor turned off Sure Start by middle-class mothers', *The Times,* 6 October 2006.

29 Jo Blanden, Paul Gregg & Stephen Machin, *Intergenerational Mobility in Europe and North America: A Report Supported by the Sutton Trust*, London: LSE Centre for Economic Performance, 2005.

30 Ingrid Schoon et al, 'The Influence of Context, Timing, and Duration of Risk Experiences for the Passage from Childhood to Midadulthood', *Child Development*, 73(5), 2002, pp. 1486–1504.

HOW WILL WE BRING UP OUR CHILDREN? WHAT MIGHT BE THE IMPLICATIONS?

- All is not well for children
- Will there be improvements in the next 20 years?
- Better parenting will be a government priority
- This focus on parenting will be important for business

All is not well for children. Though anxieties are often exaggerated, concerns are mounting about the childhood experience in Britain.

Concerns include the level of children's performance at school, which is vital for the skills of tomorrow's workforce.

Every three years, the OECD's Programme for International Student Assessment (PISA) conducts tests on a sample of 15-year-olds from 57 countries. When compared to results in the year 2000, those from 2006 show the UK sliding from eighth to 24th place in maths, from seventh to 17th in literacy and from fourth to 11th in science.

From above average scores, the UK slipped to average in maths and literacy, though it stayed above the norm in science. It was the only country to drop from a top to a lower-performing group.[1] The wide national gap between top and bottom schools contributed to Britain's lower ranking.

Were the results a statistical freak,[2] or are schools in other countries improving faster than those in the UK? If the latter, and the trend were to continue, how well would British children compete in tomorrow's world?

Another big concern is children's wellbeing in the UK compared to other countries. A sense of wellbeing and feeling happy in oneself is a prerequisite for flourishing at work and in other contexts as an adult.

A 2007 report for the United Nation's Children's Fund found the UK ranked bottom of 21 rich countries on its average score across six aspects of wellbeing. The United States was next bottom with an average score of 18.0, while the Netherlands was top with 4.2, followed by Sweden with 5.0.

Britain did best in the category 'health and safety', in 12th position, and worst on both 'family and peer relationships' and 'behaviours and risks', where it came bottom.

More specifically, within the category 'family and peer relationships' the UK had the second-lowest score when it came to the amount of time parents spent

UK's ranking among rich countries on six dimensions of wellbeing

Dimension	Ranking out of 21 countries
Material wellbeing	18
Health and safety	12
Educational wellbeing	17
Family and peer relationships	21
Behaviours and risks	21
Subjective wellbeing	20
Average (for all six dimensions)	18.2

Source: *Child Poverty in Perspective: An Overview of Child Wellbeing in Rich Countries,*
Florence: UNICEF, 2007, p. 2.

with their children (even though this was higher than in the past), and was bottom
in terms of the proportion of 11-, 13- and 15-year-olds who found their peers 'kind
and helpful'.

In 'behaviours and risks', the UK was near the bottom, having the highest
proportion of 13- and 15-year-olds who reported being overweight and who
smoked cigarettes at least once a week. It was bottom by a long way for 11-,
13- and 15-year-olds who said they were drunk two or more times per week, and for
15-year-olds who claimed to have had sexual intercourse.[3]

Can we hope for improvements over the next 20 years in children's educational
performance and their wellbeing?
There are some grounds for optimism:

■ *Parenting is likely to get better,* with mothers and fathers spending more time
with their children and more parents combining warmth with appropriate
control.

It is far from certain that substantially more parents will separate. Even
if they do: divorce has lost much of its stigma for children, society is more
aware of how to protect children from the harmful effects of separation,
and more support for separating couples and their children is slowly
becoming available (though much remains to be done). Recently, children
seem to have been reacting less negatively when their parents divorce than
previously.[4]

- *Schools will almost certainly improve.* The monitoring of children's performance will continue to be refined, and will be used increasingly for educational purposes – such as judging whether a child is ready to move on to the next stage – rather than just for league tables. Though imperfect, value-added measurements (which show the progress made by each child) will help to identify good practice.

  Technology will gradually make it easier for learning to be self-paced, collaborative and able to take account of different learning styles. Paying more attention to pupil feedback will help to drive up standards, while the spread of learning networks will make it easier for teachers to share good practice.

But there are also reasons to be concerned:

- *Will schools improve as fast as our main competitors?* The 2006 PISA survey mentioned above suggests that other countries could race ahead.
- *Can the worst effects of consumerism be checked?* Though children benefit immensely from many aspects of modern consumer society, they can also be severely damaged by it. Especially worrying are the effects of the media on children's health, security, innocence and school performance. Voluntary restraint by business and government regulation may not be enough.
- *Britain's 'long tail' of underachievement seems likely to persist.* Over a quarter of British children live in poverty, a major reason why the UK is ranked bottom in UNICEF's report on child wellbeing.

  In particular, pupils from lower social classes tend to do least well at school, which damages their chance of getting a good job later. This link between social background and prospects in life is strongly established and deep seated. Breaking it will be a formidable challenge.

Policy will focus increasingly on parenting as one of the key ways, though by no means the only one, to address these concerns.

What happens at home – from the discipline-plus-warmth approach to encouragement with homework – has a huge impact on children's performance at school. For younger children especially it can be more important than what happens in the classroom.

Parents can play a large role in helping children acquire a balanced attitude to consumer culture – welcoming the benefits, but keeping a distance from the downsides.

Parental behaviour (including parenting style) has a big influence on children's eating practices, for example, and can help counter many of the damaging food messages conveyed by advertising.[5]

Good parenting can head off the damage that might be done to children by poverty. By shielding children from the worst effects of being poor, parents can help them to do better at school and, later, as adults than would be expected from their background.

Policy-makers are now focusing on changing the culture associated with poverty rather than just topping up the incomes of those involved. How would the culture of poor families have to change for children to escape poverty? Key to this seems to be the behaviour of parents.

Improving the quality of parenting will become a priority, therefore. Research shows that parenting programmes (such as courses, support groups and helplines) can be highly effective in improving the behaviour of children with conduct disorders, especially when combined with training children in social skills.

Time and again it has been shown that parents gain confidence and skills from these programmes.[6] The Australian-based company Triple P, or the 'Positive Parenting Program', has gained international recognition for its work in this field.

Backed with extensive research, it trains people to facilitate and teach parenting groups, and provides them with high-quality resources. Triple P is being rolled out in a number of countries, including Britain.

Might the UK 'ad hoc' its way to a four-level approach? This would involve:

- *The use of TV to raise awareness in the whole population.* Programmes such as *Supernanny, The House of Tiny Tearaways, Brat Camp* and *Honey We're Killing the Kids* have attracted large audiences. A 2006 survey found that most parents with children under 16 had watched at least one TV programme about parenting, and more than three-quarters of them said they had discovered a helpful parenting technique as a result.[7]

  Building on this, might TV parenting programmes provide material – supported by helplines – containing further activities for families to work through while watching the series, such as video diaries for families to record?

  A 2005 experiment in Manchester involved 500 families carrying out activities like this while watching *Driving Mum and Dad Mad,* a TV programme in which five families were shown attending a Triple P group. Follow-up questionnaires revealed that for most of the 500 families, child behaviour improved and remained better six months after the series.[8]

■ *Parenting programmes at key stages of a child's life* might provide support at birth, entry to nursery school, the start of primary school, age seven, the start of secondary school, age 14 and just before leaving school.

Developing these 'key stage' programmes would take time and require high-quality instructors, of course. But Triple P experience suggests that parenting skills can be taught to large groups of 50 or 60 parents, using video material combined with small-group discussion. This cuts the number of instructors required.

Might Sure Start centres and schools become responsible for running these programmes? Might courses be run in a pub or cafe to help attract parents who feel uncomfortable visiting their child's school? And one day, when the programmes are universally available, might child benefit be paid on condition that parents attend?

■ *Parenting programmes in smaller groups* for families with a particular need might be run in conjunction with the 'key stage' courses mentioned above, which would be designed to whet parents' appetite for more.

■ *A national network of 'family nurses'* is being piloted by the government. These nurses would support disadvantaged mothers from pregnancy until their baby was two years old in matters of health, parenting skills and even continuing education. Might the concept evolve so that parents had access to an 'accompanier' through the whole of parenthood, till their children left home?

This focus on parenting will be important for business. It will create a number of business opportunities – from sponsorship of TV-based parenting programmes to providing family coaches as part of an employee's remuneration package.

Some City companies already offer their workers lunch-time seminars and one-to-one counselling on childcare. These initiatives are said to have a high impact for a relatively low cost and apparently help to cut staff turnover. Might the practice spread to other sectors of the economy?

Companies have not traditionally taken an interest in parenting, but they might benefit from getting more involved. Alongside flexible working hours, support for parents could help employers to develop a family-friendly brand.

Assisting people to be more confident and skilled as parents would raise children's social skills and strengthen their performance at school. This would improve the long-term quality of the human capital available to business.

Might adults who are more confident parents be more confident in other aspects of their lives, including work? Some of the skills learnt in parenting programmes, such as a greater understanding of the feelings of oneself and others, might rub off in the workplace, too.

Better parenting would not be a magic recipe – many other ingredients are also needed to make a healthy childhood. Even so, is it time for business to press for an effective national strategy to support parents?

1 'UK schools slip down global table', **http://news.bbc.co.uk**; 'Launch of PISA 2006', PISA PowerPoint presentation, **http://www.oecd.org** (both downloaded 4 December 2007).

2 For example, in reading, only seven countries had mean scores significantly higher than the UK's. The difference between the next group of countries, including the UK, were statistically insignificant. Likewise, in maths 18 countries had mean scores significantly higher than Britain's. Fewer questions were asked about literacy and maths than science. The UK's sample size was substantially larger than in previous years. 'Programme for International Student Assessment (PISA 2006)', Research Brief, Department for Children, Schools and Families, December 2007, **http://www.dfes.gov.uk**.

3 *Child Poverty in Perspective: An Overview of Child Well-Being in Rich Countries*, Florence: UNICEF, 2007, pp. 23–33.

4 For example, 1997 research found that compared to 20 years earlier, children of divorcees were 50% less likely to get divorced themselves. Cited by Jeff Wood in 'The Effects of Divorce on Children', **http://jeffwood.bol.ucla.edu**.

5 Kyung Rhee, 'Childhood Overweight and the Relationship between Parent Behaviours, Parenting Style, and Family Functioning', *The ANNALS of the American Academy of Political and Social Science*, 615, 2008, pp. 12–37.

6 See, for example, Stephen Scott, 'Effective treatment for conduct disorder', in Rajinder M. Gupta & Deepa S. Parry-Gupta (eds.), *Children and Parents: Clinical Issues for Psychologists and Psychiatrists*, London: Whurr, 2003, pp. 49–79.

7 Fiona Millar, 'For the sake of the children', *British Journalism Review*, 18(1), 2007, pp. 45–49.

8 'The Great Parenting Experiment 1', **http://www.greatparentingexperiment.net**.

CHAPTER 4

WILL BECOMING AN ADULT BE MORE DIFFICULT?
THE STORY SO FAR

- Moving from youth to adulthood is now very different
- There were two traditional pathways
- Routes today are far more varied
- They have changed fundamentally the journey to adulthood
- Government policy is set to bring in further changes

The journey from youth to adulthood has been transformed. In the 1950s and '60s most young people moved fairly quickly from adolescence to adulthood: finding a job, leaving home, settling down and starting a family.

Today, the transition takes longer. It starts at around age 16 and often continues till a person's late 20s or early 30s. In this stage of life, as in the others, circumstances vary immensely – from teenagers who drop out of school to those who complete their PhDs.

The table below gives some indication of the size of the age groups involved. We have included 30- to 34-year-olds because thirtysomethings, especially those with a postgraduate qualification, could still be repaying their student loans. Clearly individuals' experiences will vary greatly, and young people will see themselves as completing the journey to adulthood at different ages. Not everyone takes till they are 34 to arrive! The table needs to be read with those caveats.

Estimated number of 15- to 34-year-olds in the UK, 1981–2006 (000s)

Age	1986	1996	2006
15–19	4,457	3,479	3,996
20–24	4,744	3,752	4,024
25–29	4,223	4,470	3,856
30–34	3,783	4,661	4,040
Total 15–29	**13,424**	**11,701**	**11,876**
Total 15–34	**17,207**	**16,362**	**15,916**

Source: ONS, Population Estimates Unit, June 2008.

The figures challenge the view sometimes heard that it has become harder to fill vacancies because of demographic factors – specifically, that fewer young people are coming into the labour force. In fact, the big drop occurred some time ago – between 1986 and 1996, after which the total rose slightly.

More important for the supply of young workers have been the growing numbers staying on at school and going to university. Instead of being available for permanent full-time employment, this group only has time for casual and part-time jobs.

Becoming an adult is now a stage of life in its own right (sometimes known as 'emerging adulthood') which involves various transitions:

- from education to work (possibly via unemployment);
- from economic dependence to financial independence;
- from living in the parental home to living independently;
- from being single to finding a partner;
- from being childless to becoming a parent;
- from being focused on home and school to taking your place in the wider community.

Behind these transitions is a process of firming up your identity – developing, hopefully, a strong sense of your 'self' and the contribution you can make to your family, friends and the wider society.

Peers, parents and significant adults such as youth workers, teachers or mentors at work all play a role in helping individuals to develop their sense of self. Encouragement, advice and inspiration from a mature adult and role model can be particularly valuable.

We focus on the move from education to work (and the role of government policy in this) because the shift from full-time learning to work greatly influences the other transitions and is especially important for the economy. With education and training playing an ever-more central part in the journey to adulthood, how well will young people be equipped for employment?

Over the next 20 years, graduates will face unprecedented levels of student debt and, by global standards, high house prices. How they respond could transform the housing market, reduce their savings for a pension or lower the birth rate. Any one of these would affect consumer demand – and business as a result.

Traditionally, journeys to adulthood were rooted in Britain's class structure. The educational elite had a prolonged transition through sixth form and university, often followed by postgraduate training in law, accountancy or one of the other professions.

Despite the expansion of higher education in the 1960s, less than a sixth of those born in 1958 went on to get a degree or the equivalent.[1] Universities functioned as a cultural finishing school – mainly for the professional classes.

> 'Universities were a cultural finishing school for the professional classes'

In the 1950s nearly two-thirds of young people left school at 15 (the school leaving age was raised to 16 in 1972). The cream entered apprenticeships, which were mainly in the skilled trades and for boys only, but less than a quarter of all entrants (about 120,000 a year[2]) completed them. Most young people found jobs of varying quality, only some of which provided training.

Many school leavers played the job market, trying one occupation and then another till they found their niche. This lengthened the journey to adulthood, but not by very much. Most young people experienced a relatively brief transition from school to work, where they were helped to adapt to the adult world.

The contrasting pathways of the elite and the majority may help to explain the law's confusion over the age of maturity. Sixteen-year-olds have the right to give consent for medical treatment and to have sex, for example. But until the age of 17 young people can't drive a car or be interviewed by the police without an adult (an over-18) present; and they can't vote till they are 18.

With two strata of society leaving adolescence behind at a very different pace, uncertainty about exactly when young people had grown up was perhaps inevitable!

This twofold approach to becoming an adult gave way to a more complex set of transitions from the 1970s onwards.

- *The restructuring of the British economy* in the 1980s led to the collapse of the youth labour market. Apprenticeships and other established ladders to the world of work disappeared as the service sector replaced much of manufacturing. New pathways to employment became necessary. Prominent among them were a succession of youth training schemes.

■ *The emergence of the high-skills economy* in the 1980s and '90s increased the demand for technical skills to take advantage of new technology, social skills to cope with teamwork and customer relationships, and 'identity' skills such as being adaptable, presenting yourself well and being creative. In response, more young people have stayed on in education or done vocational training.

■ *Globalisation* intensified the pressure to improve education and training at all levels so that British companies could remain competitive.

In the 1980s and '90s more varied routes to adulthood emerged, creating the picture we see today.

Just over 40% of the 18-plus age group now enter higher education. In a burst of expansion, the proportion of over-18s in higher education in England and Wales doubled from around 14% in the late 1980s to 30% in the early 1990s. A decade later the figure had reached 43%.[3]

The proportion has more or less plateaued since then, which means government is likely to miss its goal of half of 18- to 30-year-olds 'benefiting from higher education by 2010'.

About three-quarters of 16- to 18-year-olds now remain in full-time education or receive some form of training. The table below shows how the proportion in England staying on in full-time education has nearly doubled since 1986 – to over 60%. Most of the increase occurred between 1986 and 1996.

Work-based learning and employer-funded training have tailed off significantly, despite the introduction of new apprenticeships, and account for just over 16% of the 16–18 age group.

As more teenagers continue to study at 16-plus, their options have widened. Apart from AS and A-levels they can, for example, do Vocational A-levels (previously known as Advanced GNVQs), Vocational GCSEs if they want to add to their GCSE tally (previously Intermediate GNVQs), a BTEC, an OCR National or a work-based apprenticeship.

The remaining quarter of 16- to 18-year-olds get a job or drop out of education, training or work. As the table below shows, the number in this category in England has almost halved since 1986 – from 39.1% to 22.7%.

The biggest fall has been among those in employment, but not in training or education. Teenagers not in employment, education or training (the so-called NEETs) have remained about 10%.

Participation in education and training of 16- to 18-year-olds in England, 1986 onwards (%).

Type of education or training	1986	1996	2006 (provisional)
Full-time education	32.2	57.7	61.1
Work-based learning (1)	13.5	10.2	6.9
Employer-funded training	10.8	5.3	4.6
Other education & training (2)	5.2	5.1	4.9
In employment, but not education or training	27.3	13.4	12.4
Not in education, training or employment (NEET)	11.8	8.9	10.3

Source: *http://www.dfes.gov.uk/*
Notes:
1. Includes part- or full-time education.
2. For example, part-time training not funded by employers.

But there is a fair amount of flux between the two groups. Those in employment tend to have casual or insecure jobs. Many are constantly moving in and out of work – from casual employment to NEET status and back again.

The demonisation of youth in parts of the media, with its scares about 'hoodies' and youth crime, arise mainly from the difficulties some of these young people have in entering adulthood.

The journey to adulthood now looks very different because of the developments mentioned above.

For most people the transition has become longer. In 1986, about two-thirds of 16- to 18-year-olds in England had already left school. If they were not unemployed, they were in some kind of job. They became adults through their experience of work.

By 2006, the statistics had almost reversed. Approaching two-thirds of the 16 to 18 age group now stay on at school.

■ *Many remain at school or college for a year or two,* and then look for work (rather than continuing to higher education). Their journey to employment has lengthened by up to two years.

■ *Roughly 40% of those aged 18 plus go to university.* The once small university-bound elite, who had a long transition between school and work, has now almost tripled in number to become a sizable chunk of the population. With more young people taking gap years before or after university and then studying for a professional qualification, starting a full-time job can be delayed by at least five or six years. Even then, individuals may try several jobs before settling down into one career.

Lengthier transitions to work mean that leaving home now takes more time, too. This applies to those who stay on at school, those who go to university or college but remain at home, and 'boomerang children', who go away to university but come home afterwards.

58% of men and 39% of women aged between 20 and 24 were living at home with their parents in 2006, a rise of 8% since 1991.

Adults living with their parents: by sex and age (%)

Sex & age group	1991 (%)	2006 (%)
Men		
20–24	50	58
25–29	19	22
30–34	9	9
Women		
20–24	32	39
25–29	9	11
30–34	5	3

Source: *Social Trends*, 37, 2007, Table 2:8.

Not surprisingly, delays in leaving home lengthen the time taken before young people become financially independent of their parents and settle down.

They move in with a partner later than in the past. In the 1960s and '70s, 45% of women cohabited with a partner for the first time before they were 19, whereas the proportion had fallen to 34% in the 1990s.[4] In 1971, the average age at first marriage for women in England and Wales was 23; in 2005 it was 29.[5]

Settling down later has led to delays in starting a family. As noted in Chapter 2, 'Will we produce enough babies?', in 1971 the average age of mothers giving birth for the first time in England and Wales was a little under 24: by 2005, it had risen to just over 27.

Political and social engagement by young people has also seen a marked decline. Samples of people born in 1946, 1958 and 1970 show a steady fall in the numbers of young people belonging to voluntary or community associations, or taking the trouble to vote.[6]

While this doubtless reflects changing attitudes in society at large, might it also result from the extension of youthfulness? The delay in becoming a fully-fledged adult leads to delays in assuming adult responsibilities.

Though transitions have lengthened for most people, for some they remain short. This is especially true of those who leave school and go rapidly into the workplace. It is also true of teenage women who start a family as a way of attaining adult status.

Whereas in the past a small group had a prolonged journey to adulthood and most people a short one, today it is the other way round. The great majority experience an extended transition, while relatively few have a short one. To be in the small group was once a sign of privilege; today, it is a sign of disadvantage.

Choice now plays a bigger part. In the 1950s, for example, most young people assumed the adult roles their families expected of them. The type of job they did and how they lived their lives were both shaped largely by their background.

But this began to break down in the 1960s and '70s. Increasingly, individuals have to decide for themselves nowadays what their lives will be like. They have to 'produce, stage and cobble together their biographies of themselves'.[7]

- *Young people are faced with more alternatives than in the past.* Rather than go straight into a job, a 16-year-old can first choose whether to do vocational or academic A-levels, and which ones; next, whether to go to university, and if so which university and what subject to study; and also whether to take a gap year. The choices are endless: in the vocational route alone some 3,500 exams exist, with 123 awarding bodies![8]
- *University exposes young people to a wider range of values and lifestyles* than they will have witnessed previously. This extends their horizons further. They can find friends with different backgrounds and interests to the ones they had at school or college. Their career opportunities widen. Instead of their identities being given to them by their background, each person – to an extent – moulds their own identity in an intentional way.
- *Those not going to university have a choice mentality, too.* Increasingly, young people are making pragmatic decisions not just about which subjects to study, but which lessons to attend, when to leave school and whether to take time out from education.[9]

Choice is risky, of course. What will your friends think? What happens if you make the wrong choice? By making a decision, are you closing down options that you might later regret? Choice can be full of anxiety.

This has been recognised by policy-makers, who have increased the advice and support available to young people. The government expects children's trusts, which bring together local authorities, schools, colleges and training providers, to make available high-quality information, advice and guidance to support 14- to 19-year-olds in the decisions they make.[10]

Despite the growing importance of choice, however, background remains crucial.[11] Individuals may think they choose freely, but in reality their decisions are significantly influenced by their social class, ethnic group, where they were brought up and, sometimes, their gender.

Being brought up in a middle-class home, for example, confers all sorts of material, social and cultural advantages, as we saw in Chapter 3, 'How will we bring up our children?' Families use these advantages to access options not available to a poorer household.

Background interacts with choice to shape each young person's journey into adult life.

Flexible options are arranged in a linear way. Flexibility is one of the hallmarks of the British system, and has all sorts of advantages:[12]

- individuals can leave secondary education at different points, rather than a single 'graduation' as in the USA;
- the same qualifications can be obtained in a variety of institutions and by different modes of study;
- vocational and academic routes can be combined;
- individuals can move between education or training and the labour market, which overlap;
- there is an emphasis on student and provider choice rather than central prescription.

But options tend to be put together in a linear way – from GCSEs to an Apprenticeship to a skilled job, for example; or from GCSEs to a Vocational A-level to employment; or the academic route (the idea of 'route' being itself a linear metaphor), which leads from A-levels to a degree to a well-paid occupation.

Compared to some other countries, individuals have more scope to move from one pathway (another linear metaphor) to another, but it is not always easy. If you don't complete a university course and start again somewhere else, for instance, your previous learning may not be recognised.

A national system of transferable credits – where each part of a university course would earn a credit that could be combined with credits from another course or institution – is still a long way off. The concept is bedevilled by the difficulty of deciding how far one bit of a course is equivalent to another.

The main rigidity, however, is in the long-standing distinction between the vocational and the academic routes. The academic path is widely seen as superior. It usually leads to better-paying jobs and has been the traditional preserve of the upper middle class. The 'old' universities and professional parents tend to resist any dilution of the gold-star status of academic qualifications.

Vocational training has long been seen as the poor relation. Despite efforts to bridge the two, individuals tend to opt for one or the other. Relatively few switch between them.

How consistent is this linear approach with young people's increasingly fluid lives? How does committing themselves to a pathway fit with today's reluctance to foreclose options?

Routes to adulthood will be significantly modified by government plans for education and training. The latter are devolved responsibilities in Northern Ireland, Scotland and Wales, so we focus on England, where emerging policies will affect the most people in Britain.

The government remains committed to expanding higher education. One way it is seeking to do this is by making two-year foundation degrees more widely available to students who might not cope with a full honours course, or as a step to a three-year degree. Foundation courses accounted for 3% of acceptances to degree study in 2005.[13]

Government wants further education (FE) colleges to collaborate with the new universities (mostly former polytechnics) in teaching part or even the whole of a foundation degree – this is known as higher eduction in further eduction, or 'HE in FE'.

Degree courses would be brought closer to students who wouldn't normally go to university. Since most foundation degrees have a vocational focus (like FE learning generally), they could also become a natural progression from other FE courses.

Some believe that one of the problems with the former polytechnics is that they are tempted to ape the academic emphasis of the older universities, in the hope that some of the latter's elite status will rub off on them.

This can draw the new universities away from what they are really good at, which is vocational education up to degree standard. Might 'HE in FE' pull the new universities in a stronger vocational direction?

Taking the vocational theme a step further, companies are to be allowed to run their own exam courses up to postgraduate level, provided the courses are externally validated to ensure quality.

In early 2008 the budget airline Flybe announced plans to award certificates up to the equivalent of degree standard for its cabin and engineering staff. Network Rail intends to introduce track engineering qualifications as high as PhD level.[14]

If the government reaches its target of at least half of 18- to 30-year-olds benefiting from higher education, approaching an extra tenth of the age group would be studying at degree level compared to the 1990s. They will be in education for longer, extending their transition to adulthood.

> **'Getting a degree could become the norm'**

For the first time, getting a degree could become the norm. With more people having degrees, might more able students increasingly differentiate themselves by getting a postgraduate qualification? This would lengthen their journey to adulthood still further.

Staying in education or training till 18 will be made compulsory. The age will be raised to 17 in 2013 and then later to 18 – probably in 2015. Young people will be required to work towards accredited qualifications either full-time, or part-time in combination with a job.[15]

The aim is to keep the education and training system flexible, with pathways that fit the individual. But it will become compulsory for 17- and 18-year-olds to choose one of the paths.

There will be a carrot in the form of Educational Maintenance Allowances for teenagers with parents on modest incomes. Rather than being a reward for studying full-time (as now), these allowances will be paid if you do well.

The government hopes that compulsion with a financial incentive will sharply reduce the 10% or so of teenagers in the NEET (not in education, employment or training) category, who currently have a poor chance of getting a decent job.

The curriculum for 14- to 19-year-olds is being reformed. There will be a wider mix of academic, vocational and work-based learning.

- *At the academic end*, A-levels are being modified to provide more able pupils with a greater challenge. More state schools are introducing the International Baccalaureate.
- *Vocational qualifications* are being radically revamped. With roll-out from September 2008, Diplomas in 17 subjects covering Creative and Media, Engineering, Information Technology and eventually all sectors of the economy will be available from foundation to A-level standard. They will combine practical skills, work placements and classroom learning.

  They are being designed with strong business input so that they will be recognised by employers. They are intended to bridge the academic and vocational divide, with the possibility that A-levels will be brought into the Diploma structure when secondary school qualifications are reviewed in 2013.
- *Apprenticeships* will be expanded. The number of 16- to 18-year-olds training as apprentices (mostly for a year) has more than doubled in the last decade – from 75,000 in 1997 to 160,000 in 2007.[16]

  The aim is to grow the total further, so that apprenticeships cover a fifth of young people.[17] They would become one of the main routes to employment for those not going to university.

It is envisaged that on completion, apprentices will get a skilled job or progress to a two-year Advanced Apprenticeship equivalent to A-level. Training will be integrated with the new Diplomas, making movement between the two easier. These changes have been described as 'a revolution in the making'.[18]

1 Gerry Makepeace et al, 'From School to the Labour Market', in Elsa Ferri, John Bynner & Michael Wadsworth (eds.), *Changing Britain, Changing Lives*, London: Institute of Education, 2003, p. 41.

2 John Bynner, 'British Youth Transitions in Comparative Perspective', *Journal of Youth Studies*, 4(1), 2001, p. 12.

3 Michael Moynagh and Richard Worsley, *Learning from the Future: Scenarios for Post-16 Learning*, London: Learning & Skills Research Centre, 2003, p. 6.

4 **http://www.statistics.gov.uk** (accessed 2 April 2008).

5 *Social Trends*, 37, 2007, p. 18.

6 John Bynner, 'Rethinking the Youth Phase of the Life-Course: The Case for Emerging Adulthood?', *Journal of Youth Studies*, 8(4), 2005, p. 373.

7 Ulrich Beck, 'The Reinvention of Politics: Towards a Theory of Reflexive Modernization', in U. Beck, A. Giddens & S. Lash (eds.), *Reflexive Modernization*, Cambridge: Polity Press, 1994, p. 502.

8 Though it is hoped that the new Diplomas will help to simplify things a bit.

9 Johanna Wyn & Peter Dwyer, 'New Patterns of Youth Transition in Education', *International Social Science Journal*, 164, 2000, pp. 147–159.

10 *Youth Matter: Next Steps*, London: DfES, 2006, p. 22.

11 Craig Jeffrey & Linda McDowell, 'Youth in a Comparative Perspective: Global Change, Local Lives', *Youth & Society*, 36, 2004, p. 133.

12 John Bynner, 'British Youth Transitions in Comparative Perspective', *Journal of Youth Studies*, 4(1), 2001, p. 8.

13 *The Nuffield Review of 14–19 Education and Training: Annual Report, 2005–06*, Oxford: Dept. of Educational Studies, 2006, p. 152.

14 *The Times*, 28 January 2008.

15 *Raising Expectations: Staying in Education and Training Post-16*, Cm 7065, Norwich: The Stationery Office, 2007, pp. 19–22.

16 *Ibid.* p. 26. The total number of apprentices, including people over age 18, was 250,000 in 2007.

17 *World-Class Apprenticeships: Unlocking Talent, Building Skills for All*, London: DCSF, 2008, p. 5.

18 Richard Layard and Iain Vallance, 'Hard Work Ahead to Promote Apprenticeships', *Financial Times*, 11 February 2008.

WILL BECOMING AN ADULT BE MORE DIFFICULT? WHAT WILL SHAPE THE NEXT 20 YEARS?

- The journey to adulthood will change for many people
- University fees will rise
- More teenagers will go to university
- The journey of less academic teenagers will be transformed
- Shortcomings in government plans will complicate the journey
- How might the government respond?

Government plans will change the journey to adulthood for many young people. As we saw in 'The story so far', the government intends to expand higher education (HE), extend compulsory education and training to include 16- to 18-year-olds, and increase the number of apprenticeships. Will the government achieve its aims, and how will this impact upon the process of becoming an adult?

The table below gives some indication of the size of the age groups that could be affected. It should be read remembering the experiences will vary greatly and individuals will complete the journey at different ages.

A headline trend? The number of 15- to 19-year-olds is projected to decline by about 10% between 2006 and 2016, rise by roughly the same amount over the next decade and then increase more gently thereafter.

Estimated and projected number of 15- to 34-year-olds in the UK, 1986–2036 (000s)

Age group	1986	1996	2006	2016	2026	2036
15–19	4,457	3,479	3,996	3,570	3,992	4,113
20–24	4,744	3,752	4,024	4,166	3,932	4,423
25–29	4,223	4,470	3,856	4,722	4,266	4,689
30–34	3,783	4,661	4,040	4,557	4,654	4,424
Total 15–29	13,424	11,701	11,876	12,458	12,190	13,225
Total 15–35	17,207	16,362	15,916	17,015	16,844	17,649

Source: ONS, Population Estimates Unit, June 2008; *National Population Projections: 2006-based*, London: ONS, 2008, pp. 64–65.
Note: The 'principal projection' is used.

Education systems vary slightly across England, Northern Ireland, Scotland and Wales. Due to devolution, differences are becoming more marked as each country develops its own approach. We focus on England, where the numbers of young people are largest, and on developments that will have the most impact on transitions to adulthood.

University fees will rise, partly to fund an expansion of higher education. Current student fees are a relatively small proportion of the cost of a course. The government pays the balance. So if student numbers went up, government HE spending would have to rise significantly, too. Higher student fees could offset some of this additional expense.

Since 2006, almost every HE institution in England has charged students a 'top-up' fee of £3,000 a year. The fee is paid upfront by the government-owned Student Loans Company, which also makes loans to students to cover reasonable living costs. Graduates repay their fees and maintenance loans once they start earning at least £15,000 a year.

Around 60% of students also get means-tested financial support from the government to cover part of their fees, and two-thirds get a means-tested grant to help with their living expenses.[1]

These arrangements will be reviewed in 2009, when it is widely expected that fees will be raised. Besides making it easier to fund a further expansion of HE, higher fees would help to:

- *Achieve the aim of variability.* The government's original idea was that there should be a cap on fees. Universities could set fees below the cap to attract business. A less prestigious institution might charge lower fees to compete for students, or low fees might attract students to an under-subscribed course. More competition would also improve quality.

    But at £3,000 a year, the cap has been too low to work. Nearly every institution has charged the maximum. Substantially raising the cap would put this right. There would be more room for universities to charge different amounts for different courses.[2]

- *Get more funds into the universities.* Universities claim that despite 'top-up' fees they remain seriously under-financed. To maintain its reputation, a prestigious university must be able to recruit academics with international reputations. To do this, its facilities and salaries must compare with the best. Under-funding puts at risk the UK's reputation of having some of the best universities in the world.

This will be of concern to the government, not least because universities are a major source of overseas income. In 2006 foreign students boosted the economy by an estimated £5 billion.[3] Maintaining this income will be difficult if universities lose their competitive edge. Raising the fee cap would bring extra money into the system.

■ *Prevent British undergraduates from being squeezed out.* If the fee cap is set too low, universities will look for other ways to earn the income they need. For example, they may try to recruit more undergraduates from outside the EU, who can be charged the full fee. Places might go to them rather than to students from Britain or Europe. (European rules prevent EU students from being charged more than British ones.)

Some universities might also reduce their undergraduate intake in favour of postgraduate teaching, recruiting heavily from abroad. Postgraduates normally pay substantially more than undergraduates. Again, fewer undergraduate places would be left for British applicants. Raising fees would reduce the risk of either possibility.

■ *Potentially provide more support for poorer students.* Despite 'top-up' fees, the government still funds the bulk of each course taken by British (and EU) students. This support amounts to an annual average of about £5,000 a student.[4]

Were government to push up fees considerably, it could switch resources from subsidising everyone to supporting students most in need. This might help to increase the number of students coming from poorer backgrounds, which looks likely to remain a priority.

However, raising fees will not be easy. Politicians will fear offending middle-class families, who would lose out, and this will put a limit on fee increases. Even so, fees will almost certainly rise after the 2009 review, and continue to go up significantly thereafter.

Graduates will leave university with higher debts. The government reckons that graduate debt will almost double as a result of introducing the £3,000 'top-up' fee – from an average debt of £8,666 in 2002–03 to about £15,000 for those starting university in 2006–07.[5] In future, debts will climb higher still.

Growing numbers of students can be expected to do paid work while they study. In 2006 more than half held down a job for between 11 and 20 hours a week during term-time.[6] The proportion will almost certainly increase, making the British university experience more like America's.

To reduce their living costs and keep down their debt, more students will stay at home rather than go away to university. Among those who leave home, larger numbers will return once they graduate. Living with parents and not having to rent will leave them with more money to pay off their loans.[7]

With many graduates continuing to repay debt into their early 30s, young couples may delay establishing a permanent home and having children because it will take them longer to save up to buy a flat. Becoming independent of parents, settling down and starting a family will be a lengthier process.

A larger proportion of teenagers are likely to go to university, despite the increase in fees. There will be several reasons for this.

More young people will be qualified to do so. According to one expert, in Britain and continental Europe:

> 'The expansion lines for general secondary and higher education run parallel: a doubling between 1980 and 1995 in the numbers completing a baccalaureate programme is followed by a near doubling over the exact same timescale in the numbers of university students.'[8]

The proportion of teenagers in England getting two A-levels, the normal qualification for higher education, increased from 24.6% in 1994 to 34.2% in 2002.

The great majority went on to university, significantly boosting enrolments.[9] Since 2002, however, the percentage of teenagers with two A-levels has levelled off, as has the expansion of higher education.[10]

Does this mean that the proportion of young people qualified for university is reaching a ceiling? This seems unlikely.

- *The number qualified to do A-levels has risen.* The proportion of the population aged 15-plus with five GCSEs at grades A-C, the normal requirement for A-level study, has leapt by a third – from 45% in 1995 to 60% in 2006.[11] This has by no means been matched by a jump in teenagers doing A-levels. Many leave school after GCSE, while others do less academic studies. Considerable potential therefore exists to boost A-level numbers.
- *Making education or training compulsory* till 18 will have a big impact on the staying-on rate at school or college. Though many teenagers will find compulsion irksome, the majority will continue with their studies. For those with the required GCSEs, A-levels will be an obvious option – all the more so if, as is traditionally the case with vocational qualifications, the new Diplomas being rolled out are seen as second-best.
- *Education Maintenance Allowances* (EMAs) will encourage teenagers from less academic backgrounds to do well in their studies, whether A-levels or another course.[12] Financial incentives do seem to make a difference. Once the leaving age has been raised, the government plans to revamp EMAs. They will become an incentive – not to continue in some form of study (which will be compulsory), but to achieve good results. This could help to motivate teenagers who are doing A-levels reluctantly.
- *A-levels will be stretched* to allow weaker students to qualify for university. This seems to have happened in the past. As more people have got their A-levels, top grades have stopped being a badge of excellence. A*s are being introduced to differentiate the most able students. The result will be a wider spread of grades from top to bottom, better reflecting the spread of abilities.

  We can expect this process to continue, with special exam questions and extra project work for candidates who are aiming for the highest grades. But will one exam be able to encompass an ever-wider range of abilities? It is probable that the exam system will fragment, as it is beginning to do, with the most academically able students being entered for more demanding exams such as the International Baccalaureate.

WHAT WILL HAPPEN TO A-LEVELS?

Among the possibilities are:

- *Stretched gold standard* – A-levels will still be the main route to university but for wider ability range.
- *A less academic route* – A-levels become the standard route to university for less able students. More able ones take International Baccalaureate or university-set entrance exams (eg. plans by Imperial College, London).
- *Merged with Diplomas* – Academic routes within new Diplomas replace A-levels to end vocational-academic divide.

More young people will want to do a degree. Most of the extra teenagers doing A-levels will be likely to go on to higher education. Not least, they will be influenced by the expectations of their peers. 84% of teenagers with qualifying A-levels start a degree course.[13] As has happened in the past, peer pressure will counter any expectations at home not to go to university.

The extra pay associated with a degree will be an incentive. Though the evidence is mixed and experiences vary, this pay premium seems to have been holding up well.

A survey in 2002 of 1995 graduates found that seven years after they had left university, there was no sign that employers were valuing higher education less than in the past, despite many more degree-holders looking for jobs.[14]

But this may change. Graduates with an arts degree from a low-ranking university increasingly tend to end up in a non-graduate job five years after they have left university.[15] If more graduates find themselves in this position, will fewer young people want to do a degree considering all the costs involved?

More likely is that as the higher education 'bush fire' spreads from one group of youngsters to another, employers will assume that it is normal for people with average ability to get a degree.

> 'Going to university will be a way of not being left behind'

When sifting job applications, managers will screen out non-graduates. Not having a degree will suggest that you have a below average level of competence. With more and more ordinary jobs being filled by graduates, a degree will be a gateway to avoid the worst jobs.

Your 'average graduate' will complain of course that they can't get a decent graduate-type job. But if it is so hard to get a good job *with* a degree, what hope would they have without one? Going to university will be a way of not being left behind.

Financial arrangements are likely to remain attractive to students. The introduction of fees in 1998 had no noticeable long-term effect on the number of students going to university, and the same will probably be true for the 'top-up' fee introduced in 2006.[16] Though university applications dropped for 2006–07, they show every sign of recovering.

The government has tried hard to prevent fees putting off potential students. Students don't have to pay any up-front costs. Interest on loans is at the rate of inflation – zero in real terms. Repayments don't start till graduates are earning at least £15,000 a year. Students from poor-to-middle-income families receive means-tested support from the government.

Parents are only expected to support students if the latter apply for means-tested assistance (although many well-off parents provide support anyway). Even then, a couple earning £75,000 a year with two children would be expected to contribute only £3,800 a year in 2006–07. This is much less than in the United States, where the equivalent family would expect to pay £14,000.[17]

The quality of degrees will become more variable to accommodate a wider range of abilities. Just as A-levels will be stretched to include students who are less academically able, the same will happen with degrees.[18]

Variations in quality will reflect differences in the reputations of the institutions concerned. Universities with a lower reputation will tend to attract the less able students. Despite quality control (usually by academics from a similar status institution), these universities will award degrees that will be seen as easier to pass.

This already happens to a significant extent now, but there could be larger disparities in future. It is widely expected that the university sector will polarise – between universities with a European or global reach on the one hand, and regional universities with a local focus on the other. Within each group, status variations may become more marked.

As regional universities increase their offerings through further education colleges, might they start to take over the latter, bringing about the eventual merger of the two sectors?

Regional universities might compete with each other through campuses scattered throughout their region. Or a new breed of further education college could emerge: independent, drawing people from their town and relying on a regional university to validate their degrees. They would be a bit like community colleges in the United States.

All this makes it probable that the expansion of higher education will resume. Though the government is unlikely to hit its target of half of 18- to 30-year-olds benefiting from HE by 2010, the target could well be exceeded by the end of the next decade.

The UK will be on track to see two-thirds of this age group benefiting from HE eventually – which is roughly today's level of university and college participation in the US.

This will prolong the transition to adulthood for many who would otherwise have left school after GCSEs. Currently, 40% of young people have a lengthy journey through sixth form, university and the start of employment before settling down – but by the mid 2020s the proportion is likely to be nearer 65%.

How will a much bigger graduate population affect values and attitudes in society at large?

The journey to adulthood of less academic teenagers will be transformed by a combination of factors: an increase in the school-leaving age, the introduction of Diplomas and a big expansion of apprenticeships.

Government expects these initiatives to improve young people's skills. In particular, it intends that:

- *More teenagers will receive training and education.* For youngsters from modest- or low-income families, compulsion will be sweetened by EMAs (the financial incentives to do well just described). The two together, it is thought, should much reduce the 10% or so of 16- to 18-year-olds who are currently not in employment, education or training.
- *Young people will get better training.* The work-based training some teenagers currently receive is haphazard, doesn't lead to recognised skills and fails to address underlying weaknesses in literacy, numeracy and IT skills. By contrast, work-based apprenticeships will require the person to study for roughly one day a week, will normally lead to a qualification certified by the relevant Sector Skills Council and will ensure that apprentices have 'functional' skills in numeracy, literacy and IT. The new Diplomas will also guarantee these functional skills. Both Advanced Apprenticeships and Diplomas will enable people to study up to A-level standard. It is hoped that for some, Diplomas may also be a route to higher education.
- *Training and education will have a strong focus on work.* Each of the new Diplomas will be geared to one sector of the economy, and many apprentices will take a Diploma as their off-the-job training. Employers are being heavily involved in the design of Diplomas to ensure they are relevant to work. Expanding apprenticeships is a response to the view of many white, working-class young people that education in itself is not worthwhile, but a job is; that getting a job is what makes you an adult. Apprenticeships will put education and training firmly in a work context. Instead of 'more school' delaying their entry to employment, teenagers will be able to earn while they train.

But doubts have been raised about whether the government will achieve its aims. Commentators have pointed to a number of potential flaws.

Compulsion may run counter to teenagers' fluid lives. Young people increasingly shun commitment. They don't want to be tied down to anything that leaves them without a choice. As one teenager commented, 'The brilliant thing about texting is that you don't have to arrive on time. You can warn people that you'll be late.'

Of course, teenagers do make commitments – many stay on at school and go to university. But this is because the perceived benefits outweigh the loss of freedom involved.

The reason compulsion is being introduced is to force part of the age group, who have chosen freedom over commitment, to do something they don't want to do.

In particular, the so-called NEETs – young people not in employment, education or training – have made a very clear decision. They have chosen to forego the income they would have got from an EMA, as well as the training and education on offer.

Compulsion will create a group of reluctant learners, whereas motivation is essential for learning. It will further alienate young people from education and training, making lifelong learning – vital now that work changes rapidly – less attractive. Disaffected learners will discourage others who might have been willing to learn.

Increasing the number of apprenticeships will be a tough ask. The government wants to shove up the total from about 250,000 (for all age groups) in 2007 to 400,000 by 2020. It hopes that financial incentives will encourage small- and medium-sized employers especially to offer more places to teenagers.

But if these employers needed apprentices, they would already be recruiting them. A 2007 employers' skills survey commented:

'Those employers not offering apprenticeships most commonly put this down to their staff being fully trained already, to apprenticeships not being relevant to their business and to not needing staff to be trained to the level an apprenticeship provides.'[19]

If employers don't need apprentices, why should they take them on, even with a financial incentive? And if a government grant did persuade them, what is the chance that they would keep that person on when both the grant and the apprenticeship came to an end? The Nuffield Review has noted:

'Financial incentives for employers may not be sufficient to compensate for the effort required to offer apprenticeship places . . . The state seems to want to promote the further growth of apprenticeships for reasons that do not necessarily align with employer demand for apprenticeship training.'[20]

In 2006, just over a tenth of 16- to 18-year-olds were in employment without any additional education and training, roughly the same number who were undergoing work-based learning and training.[21] How many employers offering employment without training will want the bother of turning these jobs into apprenticeships?

When apprenticeships become the only workplace option once compulsion is introduced, might these jobs disappear without enough apprenticeships to replace them?

Many apprenticeships won't involve real jobs. At present there are not enough proper jobs for those who become apprentices.

Many apprenticeships are not like the traditional picture. Apprentices are not working alongside an experienced employee, learning the skills they will need for a job waiting at the end. They are under contract to a training provider, who places them with an employer. On-the-job training feels more like a work placement.

At the end of the year (or sometimes two years), the apprentice finds that the employer has no suitable job to offer. No wonder rates of non-completion are fairly high.[22] People leave halfway through if a job comes up. Will the government's 'World-Class Apprenticeships' become discredited?

Diplomas will suffer from major design flaws, at least to begin with. The word on the street suggests that employers are struggling to articulate a coherent set of learning needs for each Diploma.

Every round of consultation adds more needs to the list. The final list is then too long for the learning time available. Often what is appropriate to learn at each level of the Diploma is not being clearly specified.

Rather than building on a long tradition of dialogue between employers, educationalists and others (as in Germany), Diplomas are emerging from what is often a shallow engagement of different interest groups.

Many employers involved don't understand what works educationally and many educationalists don't understand what employers really want. As a result, serious teething problems are likely, which will damage the learning experience. A significant number of young people may drop out of their course, swelling the NEET population and giving Diplomas a bad name.

Diplomas are unlikely to increase young people's earnings, especially when taken at levels below the A-level equivalent. Diplomas in hair and beauty, travel and tourism, and so on will almost certainly be shunned by pupils seeking more academic qualifications.

Like previous vocational qualifications, they will be seen as suitable for the academically less able and be devalued for that reason. Diplomas could end up like low-level NVQs, whose reputation is so poor that they may have actually decreased individuals' lifetime earnings rather than improved them.

Professor Alison Wolf has summarised the research:

'The returns to NVQ2 awards are effectively non-existent. Spending a year or two taking one on a government training scheme is likely to reduce someone's lifetime earnings, not raise them. The "vocational" qualifications which have clear labour market benefits are BTEC and RSA awards, which are typically taken full-time in colleges ... and can serve as a direct route into higher education.'[23]

If the new Diplomas follow this same pattern and fail to increase young people's earnings, who will want to do them?

These shortcomings in the government's plans could greatly complicate the transition to adulthood. For young people not going to university, enforced education and training could become highly unpopular.

Teenagers trapped by compulsion will be wishing to grow up. They will want to earn a proper income so that they can become more independent, begin to master a job and start making a contribution to society.

Many may feel deeply frustrated by being forced into training and work experience that seem to lead nowhere. More and more teenagers may well drop out. Rather than the NEET population reducing, the total not in employment, education or training may actually grow.

The government's reforms of the youth labour market could actually make it harder for NEETs to settle down and find their feet in employment when they are eventually ready to do so.

Once education and training till 18 becomes compulsory, employers who take on a 16- or 17-year-old will be required to check that the young person has arranged an appropriate course of instruction, give the individual time off for that purpose and continue to give time off till the person either completes the course or turns 19.

How many small- or medium-sized employers, who hire a large proportion of Britain's teenagers, will be bothered with all this? True, government will meet the costs of providing time off. But for the employer, it will still mean extra forms to fill in, another set of inspections – and getting your head round the rules in the first place.

Then, once you have set up the arrangements, who's to know if the teenager won't push off after a couple of weeks? Might not employers prefer to hire young adults instead?

But after a few years these young adults will include 18-year-olds who have never done a real job, whose training may be worth little and who – perhaps in many cases – have a track record of dropping out. Why hire them when migrant workers are available, are more committed, have employment experience and are often more skilled?

In 2008 the House of Lords Select Committee on Economic Affairs warned that immigration may discourage employers from training young people. It could be cheaper to recruit workers from overseas who already have the skills.[24] Will the journey to adulthood for less-educated teenagers become even more fraught than it is today?

How might the government respond? Faced with these difficulties, there seem to be two possibilities.
One is that government will change the system yet again. It might:

- *increase EMAs* to make compulsion more attractive;
- *curb immigration* so that employers, lacking an alternative source of labour, are forced to invest in young people;
- *redesign Diplomas* to make them more attractive and delay raising the leaving age to 18.

This would continue a long tradition of policy-making. If a vocational route doesn't work, governments try to patch it up or develop a different version of the same thing. *But might this approach come under fire?* It is based on the idea that Britain is short of qualified workers. However, the government's skills surveys repeatedly tell a different story. They show that at all levels there are more people with qualifications than there are jobs demanding their level of qualification as an entry requirement.

The number of over-qualified people grew substantially between 1986 and 2006. Workers have become more qualified in a formal sense, but there are not enough jobs to match their levels of attainment.

Qualifications and skills aren't always the same thing. Employers repeatedly complain that many young people have qualifications but don't have the required skills in, for example, communication, literacy and numeracy.

Qualifications can be a device for managers to screen out less able job applicants, rather than a guarantee that workers have the skills employers actually need.[25]

In addition, companies at the bottom end of the labour market are able to make a profit by using low-capital, low-productivity methods of production. These methods require workers who are low-skilled and low-paid. If using low-skilled workers is profitable, why should employers invest in higher skills?[26]
Might a different approach eventually emerge, with a stronger focus on the demand for skills? It could include:

- *Encouraging firms to adopt higher-productivity methods of production* requiring higher skills. Might Regional Development Agencies, for example, seek to expand business people's horizons by arranging visits to companies employing more advanced techniques? Could they also pump-prime research and development in better methods and actively support companies in raising the finance to upgrade their facilities?

- *Encouraging post-16s to find employment* rather than concentrating on raising their skills. Some of the best workplace learning is gained through experience on the job. British firms seem entirely capable of investing in training when it is needed – a survey of nine countries found that British (and German) employers spent more on training than other countries.[27] So why not encourage teenagers to get a job once they have their basic academic qualifications, and rely on employers to provide additional training as required?

- *Spending more on pre-16 education.* Instead of such heavy investment in post-16 vocational training, might the government spend more on improving the basic education of low achievers before they are 16? Heavier investment in one-to-one support and small group learning for children with special needs might be a priority. Ensuring that fewer 16-year-olds lack basic numeracy, literacy and IT would do more to raise skill levels in the long run than anything else.

This would amount to a revolution in received wisdom. At present the government assumes that the key problem is a lack of vocational skills and that it has a responsibility to put this right.

But the bigger problem is a lack of 'academic' skills in numeracy, literacy and IT. Employers keep complaining about young people's lack of these skills at an adequate level. Without a good foundation in 'key skills', further training becomes almost impossible.

Might a future government concentrate on improving key skills within the school system, withdraw largely from vocational training, which it has rarely done well, and rely instead on employers to provide whatever vocational training they and their employees need?

---

1 'DIUS launches new student finance campaign', Dept. of Innovation, Universities & Skills Press Release, 30 October 2007.
2 More-expensive-to-run science and engineering courses could be kept attractive, as now, through government support and/or through cross subsidies from some of the fee revenue from cheaper courses.
3 Tony Blair, 'Why we must attract more students from overseas', in the *Guardian*, 18 April 2006.
4 'Student loans and the question of debt', Department for Education and Skills, **http://www.dfes.gov.uk** (accessed 8 April 2008), p. 3.

5 Ibid. pp. 5–6.

6 *University Lifestyle Survey 2006*, London: Sodexho, 2006, p. 7.

7 85% of students living at home while they were studying did not pay rent in 2006. *University Lifestyle Survey 2006*, Sodexho, 2006, p. 7.

8 Alison Wolf, *Does Education Matter?* London: Penguin, 2002, p. 174.

9 These figures are lower than the proportion of young people in higher education often cited – over 40% in the early 2000s. This is because some people enter HE through non-A-level routes.

10 'Demand for Higher Education to 2020 and beyond', Higher Education Policy Institute, 2007, **http://www.hepi.ac.uk/**, p. 7.

11 Ibid. p. 17.

12 *Diminished Returns: How Raising the Leaving Age to 18 Will Harm Young People and the Economy*, London: Policy Exchange, 2007, p.13.

13 'Demand for Higher Education to 2020 and beyond', Higher Education Policy Institute, 2007, **http://www.hepi.ac.uk/**, p. 12.

14 Kate Purcell & Peter Elias, *Seven Years On: Graduate Careers in a Changing Labour Market*, Manchester: Higher Education Careers Services Unit, 2004.

15 Research by Professor Francis Green, quoted in the *Sunday Times*, 31 August 2008. See also Philip Brown & Anthony Hesketh, *The Mismanagement of Talent: Employability and Jobs in the Knowledge Economy*, Oxford: OUP, 2004, pp. 58–63 and 216–217.

16 Juliet Chester & Bahram Bekhradnia, 'Funding Higher Fees: Some Implications of a Rise in the Fee Cap', Higher Education Policy Institute, April 2008, **http://www.hepi.ac.uk**, p. 2.

17 Juliet Chester & Bahram Bekhradnia, 'Funding Higher Fees: Some Implications of a Rise in the Fee Cap', Higher Education Policy Institute, April 2008, **http://www.hepi.ac.uk**.

18 In a 2008 Greenwich University survey of 300 academics, 90% agreed that funding pressures had led to the admission of weaker students. Academics claimed that universities were lowering pass marks and 'spoon-feeding' students who would otherwise have failed. Reported in the *Sunday Telegraph*, 6 April 2008.

19 *National Employers' Skills Survey 2007: Main Report*, London: Learning & Skills Council, 2008, p. 16.

20 'Apprenticeship 1: Prospects for Growth', Issues Paper 3, 2008, p. 9, and 'Apprenticeship 2: A High-Quality Pathway for Young People?' Issues Paper 4, 2008, p. 15, both from 'The Nuffield Review of 14–19 Education and Training, England and Wales', The Nuffield Foundation.

21 **http://www.dfes.gov.uk/**

22 However, completion rates for all apprenticeship programmes have improved – by nearly 10% between 2005-06 and 2006-07. In the latter academic year, the completion rate was 63%. 'Further Education, Work-Based Learning and Train to Gain: LSC-Funded Learner Outcomes in England 2006-07', Learning and Skills Council Press Release, 22 May 2008.

23 Alison Wolf, *Diminished Returns: How Raising the Leaving Age to 18 Will Harm Young People and the Economy*, London: Policy Exchange, 2007, p. 32.

24 House of Lords Select Committee on Economic Affairs, *The Economic Impact of Immigration. Volume 1: Report*, London: Stationery Office, 2008, p. 31.

25 Alan Felstead et al, *Skills at Work, 1996–2006*, Cardiff/Oxford: ESRC, 2007, p. 169.

26 Ewart Keep, Ken Mayhew & Mark Corney, *Review of the Evidence on the Rate of Return to Employers of Investment in Training and Employer Training Measures*, London: DTI, 2002, pp. 44–47.

27 *Skills Development: Attitudes and Perceptions. Final Report*, London: City & Guilds Centre for Skills Development, 2008, p. 13.

WILL BECOMING AN ADULT BE MORE DIFFICULT? WHAT MIGHT BE THE IMPLICATIONS?

- **What is likely to happen?**
- **The journey for affluent young people will be more complicated**
- **Things will change for those on middle incomes, too**
- **Young people on low incomes will have a difficult time**

What is likely to happen? Today in England (our main focus), over two-fifths of the 18-plus age group enter higher education (HE) and three-quarters of 16- to 18-year-olds are in school or college. A quarter of 16 to 18s get a job or drop out. By the end of the next 20 years things will look very different:

65% of the 18-plus age group may enter higher education, which will be more diverse than it is now. Alongside elite universities with a global or European focus will be universities with stronger regional ties.

As they are beginning to, these regional universities will offer degree courses through further education (FE) colleges, which could be increasingly drawn into the HE sector. In addition, there will be degree courses (or the equivalent) run by companies.

The expansion of HE will be funded by higher fees, with continuing government support for students from households with low or modest incomes.

Such a big increase in the student population will cut substantially the number of young people available for full-time employment. This will reduce the size of the youth labour market – to a greater extent than a fall in the birth rate.

35% of 16- to 18-year-olds will be forced into compulsory education or training, largely comprising the new Diplomas and apprenticeships.

As discussed in 'What will shape the next 20 years?', these will almost certainly prove unattractive to many young people. Diplomas will suffer from serious teething problems and are unlikely to be well regarded in the labour market. Many apprenticeships will not lead to a permanent job.

The likely collapse of the youth labour market in England could encourage employers to turn to migrant labour, making it much harder for young people to find long-term employment.

On past form, a future government will respond to these problems by attempting to patch up the system, perhaps postponing the second stage of raising the leaving age (from 17 to 18). But would a patch-up work?

Young people from more affluent families, say in the top 30% of earnings, will find their journey to adulthood complicated by several factors.

They may find it harder to get into a high-status university. Because of their home advantages – high parental expectations, the ability of parents to get them into good schools and strong parental support for their education in general – many in this group will expect to go to elite 'Russell Group' universities, as they do now.

But they are likely to face growing competition both from the larger number of British teenagers doing A-levels and from overseas students, especially from Europe. The EU's Bologna process, agreed by national governments, is designed to make it easier by 2010 for students to choose courses from across the EU.

The reputation of Britain's universities plus the benefits of studying in English could swell the number of overseas students significantly. Will the elite universities expand to absorb the extra numbers? Or will some British students be squeezed out, forced either to study abroad or to go to a less prestigious university in the UK?

Student debt will rise as 'top-up' fees are increased. As we discussed in 'What will shape the next 20 years?', pressures on the government to raise fees will outweigh resistance from middle-class families who would lose out.

Graduate debt is already set to double as a result of the introduction of top-up fees. The government expects those starting in 2006–07 to leave university with an average debt from all sources of £15,000.[1]

> **'Students starting in 2006–07 will leave university with £15,000 of debt on average'**

But this is an average figure, and includes students who live at home while studying. Many young people from financially better-off families currently study away from home, which pushes up their costs considerably.

As fees rise, students will be faced with mounting costs. Because those from affluent families will want to study at a top university, most will be unable to make savings by staying at home.

So, unless they get extra support from their parents, the great majority will graduate with higher and higher debts. Many will still be paying off student loans in their early 30s.

High debts will combine with high property prices. Though at the time of writing property prices are falling, for the last 40 years the overall trend has been strongly upwards. This long-term trend looks set to continue – for several reasons:

■ *The demand for new homes is likely to grow,* especially in the South East, largely due to immigration and a continuing increase in single-person households. As more couples separate and more older people live for longer, growing numbers are living on their own. To meet the burgeoning demand, the government has set a target of building 3 million new homes in England between 2007 and 2020.

■ *It will be hard to ratchet up the supply of homes,* and this will keep prices high. In 2007, about 185,000 new homes were built. As an annual rate this was substantially below the 223,000 new households forming per year – and the 240,000 new homes a year that the government thinks will be needed both to meet the extra annual demand for housing and clear the current backlog of unsatisfied demand.[2]

Despite financial incentives and other measures to encourage house-building, the government will struggle to reach its 3 million target. Even before the 2008 downturn, bottlenecks within the industry, tough new environmental standards, delays in getting planning permission and opposition to building on greenfield sites were making the target difficult to achieve.

The credit crunch has slashed housing starts and is likely to reduce the building industry's capacity. Demand will continue to outstrip supply for a number of years, forcing up prices.

■ *Property will be kept affordable for first-time buyers,* however, despite the likelihood that prices will rise by more than earnings. Apartments will be smaller, for example. You will be able to afford something, but you'll get less for your money. Mortgages will be for longer periods, as had started to happen before the downturn, allowing home-owners to repay a smaller portion of the loan each year. Keeping repayments down will enable borrowers to afford larger loans. Will 'lifetime' mortgages become popular, as in Japan? These are mortgages that are only repaid when the property is sold, perhaps at the end of your life.

Higher student debts and higher property prices will prolong the transition to adulthood. More 'boomerang children' will live with their parents after university in order to keep down living costs and help pay off their student loans.

Saving enough to buy a home, or – with first homes getting smaller – to move to one large enough for a family, will be a lengthier process. Couples will postpone having children. Leaving parents, settling down and beginning a family will *all* take longer.

Could this be a chance for companies to create an attractive employment package for graduates? In 2012 the government will make it compulsory for employees to be enrolled in a pension scheme unless they specifically opt out.

Many graduates may resent paying into a pension when their priorities are repaying their student loan and saving up for a home. Might employers offer an alternative? 'Pay into a savings account what you would have put into a pension, and we'll add to your savings what we would have paid for your pension. That way, you'll be on the housing ladder more quickly.'

Some parents will provide their children with financial support during the transition to adulthood. This will be nothing new – except for one thing: increasingly, parents will be providing this support at a time when they themselves need to be saving more for a pension and paying off their mortgage.

Until recently, parents whose kids left home for university could look forward to spending less on their children. They might support them through university but not need to support them thereafter. Spending less on the family allowed them to increase their mortgage repayments or put aside more towards a pension.

But as more children return home after university, struggling to repay their loans and get on the housing ladder, will a growing number of parents be tempted to help out? If they do, will they have to postpone repaying their mortgage and paying extra into their pension?

> 'Children's longer transition to adulthood could delay their parents' transition to retirement'

Children's longer transition to adulthood could delay their parents' transition to retirement.

Young people from families with middling incomes can be defined as those whose family income is roughly in the middle 40% of households – between the top and bottom thirds.

They will face a number of the challenges experienced by their contemporaries from more affluent backgrounds, not least higher university fees and rising property prices. In addition, two things stand out for this group.

More people from a middle-income background will go to university, which will lengthen their journey to adulthood. Raising the leaving age will encourage more of them to go on from GCSEs to A-levels or the equivalent, and so qualify for higher education. As more people take degrees, more of their peers will want to do the same to avoid being stuck in the worst jobs.

The financial risks will not seem too great. A good number of students from middle-income backgrounds will be eligible for government financial support to offset some of their costs. As now, student loans will only have to be repaid once graduates get a job with reasonable pay.

The increase in British students in higher education – from just over two-fifths of the 18-plus age group to perhaps two-thirds eventually – will be drawn largely from this middle group of families.

One implication for business is that fewer young adults will be available for full-time, permanent work. There will be more students working part-time and during the holidays, but this will still leave an employment deficit. Part-time, temporary posts won't fill the holes left by more young adults in university.

Many of these extra students will have no family tradition of higher education. But the choices will be greater than ever before. The expansion of HE will lead to an expansion of alternatives. Individuals will wonder whether they should try for a Russell Group university, a regional university some distance away, or an 'HE in FE' option, which will become more widespread.

With most of this group's families new to the university world, high-quality advice will be invaluable. This advice will need to extend beyond the choice of university courses and how to apply. It will have to cover financial matters such as the relative costs of staying at home and going away, possible sources of financial support and perhaps advice on managing a student budget.

What types of course will these students study? One possibility is that regional universities will try to become more academic.

The Russell Group of universities tend to be seen as better. In general, they have more academically able staff, attract more academically able students and receive more funds for research. As can happen now, some regional universities may want to become more like the Russell Group to prove that they are 'proper' universities.

An alternative, as we have noted, is that regional universities will concentrate on providing vocational degrees, their traditional strength. As they develop links with FE colleges, which have a strong vocational remit, regional universities could well be pulled in this direction.

This could open up possibilities for combining vocational qualifications with on-the-job training. For example, companies might offer an apprenticeship to students taking an appropriate degree. This might involve work-based training during a gap year before university (or perhaps afterwards) and in the holidays between university terms.

Students would end up with a degree and a qualification in a recognised trade. They would have a secure source of income while studying and a mentor in the workplace, who would help them adjust to adult life. They would be well placed to get a job at the end of their studies.

Their journey to adulthood would be different to their parents', but could be fairly straightforward.

Young people at the bottom of the income range – whose family incomes are in about the lowest 30% of households – are likely to have a difficult time.

Though some will do A-levels or the equivalent and go on to university, if current trends continue the great majority will not. Lacking the advantages of middle-class families, they will tend to achieve little at school and may often lack basic literacy, numeracy and IT skills.

Many will find compulsory education or training a nightmare. White working-class males in particular frequently disparage education. This attitude has deep cultural roots, stemming from the time when teenagers left school and went straight to employment: getting a job used to mark your entry to adult life.

The persistence of high youth unemployment in some areas has reinforced this low view of education. When work is scarce, people who do well at school may still not get a good job afterwards.

'If even the best-qualified, hardest-working pupils can be seen as "failing" later, what point is there in striving for academic success?'[3]

Especially in areas of high unemployment, many young people will resent compulsory Diplomas which may have little market value, or compulsory apprenticeships which don't lead to a proper job. Both will seem rather pointless.

Even in areas where unemployment is low, young people could face a tougher jobs market when they turn 18. If, as some experts predict, many 18-year-olds find themselves unable to compete with migrant labour, their doubts about the value of education and training will be confirmed.

> 'Young people could face a tougher jobs market when they turn 18'

Guidance and support may help some of these young people: youth workers could play a key role. But the majority will feel disillusioned and powerless – hardly a good foundation for making yourself employable.

Will a growing number of the 16-plus age group drop out, so that the NEET population actually gets larger? If so, will tinkering with the existing system be enough – or will a fundamental rethink be required?

---

1 'Student loans and the question of debt', Department for Education and Skills, **http://www.dfes.gov.uk/** (accessed 8 April 2008), pp. 5–6.

2 *Homes for the Future: More Affordable, Most Sustainable*, Cm 7191, London: The Stationery Office, 2007, p. 6.

3 Robert Macdonald & Jane Marsh, 'Missing School: Educational Engagement, Youth Transitions, and Social Exclusion', *Youth and Society*, 36(143), 2004, p. 156.

CHAPTER 5
HOW WILL ADULT RELATIONSHIPS CHANGE?
THE STORY SO FAR

- Personal relationships feel increasingly important
- More adults have been living on their own
- Couples are more concerned about the quality of their relationship
- The 'beanstalk' family is widespread
- Friendships flourish, especially among higher-income groups
- Family and friendships are blending together

The more society is organised, the more important relationships seem to be.
Personal relationships have always been a key part of human existence, of course,
but it could be argued that they are especially valued today, when an increasing
amount of our life seems to be ordered by social structures and organisational
bureacracy

Organisations have multiplied over the past 50 years and are reaching into the
informal parts of everyday life: pre-school children nowadays are more likely to go
to an organised nursery than be looked after by their parents.

The voluntary sector has become less informal. Organisations themselves feel more organised – they have more regulations, more targets and more accountability.[1] The customer experience can also feel extremely bureaucratic, with its impersonal chain stores and outsourced call centres. The informality of friends and family are a welcome contrast to these highly structured parts of our lives. We can leave the regulated workplace at the end of the day for relationships that feel more relaxed and spontaneous. It can be a relief to be among 'personal communities' where we are known and accepted.

Against this background, being connected is of immense worth. Relationships vary tremendously, of course, so generalising about them may mean glossing over substantial differences. Despite this risk, we focus on the personal communities of people aged between their late twenties and mid forties – and on relationships that are important for love, care, support and friendship.

These relationships are of increasing interest to business – for several reasons:

- *Relationships embody values,* which can inform the tone in which brands speak to their customers. If people are suspicious of hierarchy, for example, brands will need to avoid talking down to them.
- *Relationships influence consumer demand.* For instance, the growth in people living on their own has increased the need for homes – and furniture to fill them. As people travel longer distances to see one another, the purchase of transport-related products has risen.
- *'Wellbeing' is becoming an employer concern.* Research shows that good relationships make a vital contribution to people's wellbeing. They give individuals a sense of security and belonging, are a source of information, provide support in times of need, protect against stress and make a major contribution to health. Employers wanting to promote wellbeing at work will pay close attention to the quality of workplace relationships.[2]

For most people, relationships at home centre on the cohabiting or married couple, and then ripple out to other family members and friends. But this is not true of everyone. We start with the main exception.

There are more single-adult households – in the form of adults living either alone or as the head of a one-parent family.

Solo living has doubled since 1971. In 2007, the proportion of people living alone in Great Britain was 12% (about 7 million people), double the percentage it was in 1971. If we translate this into households, 29% of all households were home to one person in 2007 compared to 18% in 1971. The figure has remained stable since 2001.[3]

About three-quarters of people living alone are over 65. But the fastest-growing group, which doubled between 1986–2007 and 2003–04, comprises people aged 25 to 44. The proportion of this age group living on their own is projected to keep on growing from 12% in 2003–04 to 17% in 2026.[4] Men aged 25 to 44 are twice as likely to live alone as women (see table below).

Proportion (%) of 25- to 44-year-olds in Great Britain living alone: by sex

	1986–7	1996–7	2003–4
Men	7	11	15
Women	4	6	8
All	6	8	12

Source: Jim Bennett & Mike Dixon, *Single Person Households and Social Policy: Looking Forwards,* York: Joseph Rowntree Foundation, 2006, p. 8.

The increase in solo living reflects:

- *Rising prosperity* – more people can afford to be on their own.
- *The longer transition to adulthood* – young people are taking longer to settle down. Larger numbers are living alone before they move in with a partner.
- *The effects of partnership breakdown.* When cohabiting or married couples split up, partners often move into their own accommodation.
- *Higher immigration,* possibly. Some experts think that solo living may be more common among people who have recently arrived in Britain.[5]

One-parent families have also increased substantially since the 1970s, and represented nearly 10% of UK households in 2002.[6] They bring the proportion of 25- to 44-year-olds living alone or as the sole adult living with children to almost a quarter of the age group.[7]

Is the trend to adults living alone a sign that society is becoming more atomised – that individuals are spending more time on their own than with other people?

One study found that:

'The similarity of those who live alone to those who live with others is more striking than their differences. While those living alone tend to report less interaction with family, friends and neighbours, the differences are small.'[8]

As the trend towards 'living apart together', discussed below, illustrates, you can live on your own but still be well connected to other people.

What it means to be a couple is changing. Partners increasingly focus on the quality of their relationships. Over the past 50 years, couples have gradually downplayed the institution of marriage in favour of the relationship itself. The legal shell now counts for less than what is inside it.

This owes much to the 'subjective' turn taken by modern culture. People feel less bound by external roles, duties and obligations. They base their lives on their relationships and subjective experiences. They pay more attention to how they feel and to what *they* think makes sense – to their subjective view of the world.

As part of this, people identify less with marriage as an institution and tend to see their partner as their best friend.

The spread of cohabitation reflects this new emphasis. Cohabitants prioritise their relationship rather than getting married. In 1986, 11% of unmarried men and 13% of women below the age of 60 cohabited in Great Britain. By 2006 these proportions had roughly doubled – to 24% for men and 25% for women.[9]

For many couples, cohabitation is still a prelude to marriage – a 2008 survey of 20- to 35-year-olds found that eight in 10 (79%) of those who were cohabiting wanted to get married.[10]

But for a small and growing minority it seems to have become an alternative. Pointers to this include:

- *The slightly fewer cohabitants who marry their partners.* In 2000, according to the British Social Attitudes survey, 59% of cohabiting relationships ended in marriage; by 2006, this had dropped to 56%. At the same time, the mean average length of cohabiting relationships went up – from 6.5 years in 2000 to 6.9 in 2006.[11]
- *The willingness of cohabiting couples to have children.* Approaching two-fifths of children are now born to cohabiting couples.[12] Where children are involved, cohabiting partnerships now last for an average of 8.5 years (with a median of 7). This is not far short of marriages that end in divorce, which last for 11.5 years.[13]

  The primary carer has less legal protection if the relationship breaks down than in marriage, so – where conception was not a mistake – the willingness to bring up children while remaining unmarried makes quite a strong statement.
- *The attitude of cohabitants.* A 2002 study of 50 parents who cohabited and then separated found that the great majority saw cohabitation as at least equivalent to marriage. Some suggested that the two forms of relationship were indistinguishable, both requiring a commitment.[14]

This seems to be the view of the public generally. A 2008 report found that 48% of respondents agreed that living with a partner shows just as much commitment as getting married, while only 35% disagreed. In addition, 53% thought that a wedding was more about a celebration than a lifelong commitment, with 28% disagreeing.[15]

Might we be at the start of a transformation in the nature of cohabitation? For a minority, cohabitation is starting to become less a stage before marriage than an alternative to marriage.

Factors behind this include:

■ *A negative view of marriage.* For some couples, marriage is associated with a world that is fast disappearing – a world of manufacturing, trade unions, class deference, the church, the male breadwinner and head of household, and the woman at home; cohabitation is part of a new and more modern world. Others, having seen their parents divorce, feel that marriage is discredited.
■ *The cost of weddings.* Some couples have a Hollywood ideal of the perfect wedding, but can't afford it. They keep postponing the 'big day' till they have saved enough, only to find that they never have sufficient savings. They drift into long-term cohabitation. This may help to explain why parents are more likely to cohabit rather than marry if they are poor. In a 2000 survey, 43% of cohabiting parents were reported as living in disadvantaged areas compared to 26% of married parents.[16]
■ *Flexibility* can be a big draw. Despite their hopes that the relationship will last, some cohabitants feel less boxed in than they would in a marriage. If the relationship doesn't work, it is easier to leave.

Does this mean that the ideal of marriage is on the wane? Marriage still remains by far the most popular form of partnership, but the proportion of married people in the population has continued to fall slightly – from 56% in 2000 to 54% in 2006. (This was matched by a small increase in cohabiting couples, from 9 to 11%.)[17]

> 'In the year 2000, 43% of cohabiting parents lived in disadvantaged areas compared to 26% of married parents'

What haven't declined are the ideals traditionally represented by marriage. Just as 85% of people think that extra-marital sex is mostly or always wrong, over 80% of cohabitants think that it would be wrong for them to have an affair with a third party.

Commitment remains important for cohabiting and married couples alike, though personally expressed commitment matters more to most people than a public display of commitment at a wedding. There is an overall consensus that cohabitation and marriage mean much the same in practice.[18]

Although cohabitation may be starting to emerge as an alternative to marriage, the hopes and values surrounding cohabitation remain marriage-like. Couples want their relationship to last and their partners to be committed to them in a sexually exclusive way.

So do people think marriage and cohabitation are the same? Not quite. The majority of the public think that cohabitants should have different legal rights to married couples when they separate.

Financial support for the cohabiting partner should depend on who is bringing up the children, the amount of financial investment both partners have made in the relationship and how long they have been together. Legal rights for cohabitants should reflect differences in circumstance to a greater extent than for married partners.[19]

This legal pliability hints at an underlying appeal of cohabitation – its flexibility. *The meaning of marriage has undergone a subtle shift.* Two big changes occurred during the twentieth century.[20]

Firstly, marriage evolved from an institution into a companionship. There was a growing emphasis on emotional satisfaction and romantic love, continuing developments that had begun in the nineteenth century. Spouses expected to be both friends and lovers.

Secondly, from the 1960s onwards, the 'companionship' marriage developed into the individualised marriage, which included a growing emphasis on:

- *Personal choice.* If the marriage isn't working, partners should be free to leave.
- *Personal growth.* Each partner should develop a fulfilling, independent self instead of merely sacrificing themselves to their spouse.
- *Personal flexibility.* Roles within marriage should be flexible and negotiable.

Because cohabitation is more of an option, getting married increasingly makes a statement. For many people, it is a statement that 'we are committed'. But for some people, getting married is also a statement that they have 'arrived' – 'we're ready to be a family'.

It can even be a statement that the couple have done rather well – 'We've got stable jobs, bought the house and are in a financial position to have a family'. In poorer areas where relationships are unstable, the bride may be saying, 'Aren't I lucky! I've got a stable partner'.[21]

The divorce rate has recently declined. Divorces more than tripled between 1969 and 1993, but the number then fell back, before rising again at the turn of millennium and falling once more since 2004.[22] The divorce *rate* has followed a similar pattern.

Estimated proportion of newly-weds who will divorce

34% of newly-weds in 1979–80
41% of newly-weds in 1993–94
45% of newly-weds in 2005

Source: '45% of marriages will end in divorce', ONS Press Release, 27 March 2008

There has been a long-term rise (see box above), but there are signs that the proportion of married people divorcing each year may be tailing off. In 2007, the proportion fell for the third year in a row, bringing it down to its lowest level for 26 years.[23] Some commentators think that this is because couples are getting married at an older age, after partners have been together for some time. It is the more stable couples who go on to get married and who then stay together. Might the proportion of married couples who divorce have reached a ceiling?

When children are involved, values surrounding divorce are changing. Due partly to the 1989 Children Act, divorce has been redefined as an issue between parents rather than a matter for husbands and wives. Many separating couples seem to be paying more attention to the interests of their children and to maintaining some sort of relationship afterwards for the sake of the children.

Post-divorce relationships – between the former partners, and between each one and the children involved – are being negotiated more carefully and often with considerable skill, in order to meet the needs of all those involved.[24]

Is cohabitation less stable than marriage? Traditionally, this has been the case. Data from the 1990s and early 2000s, for instance, suggests that whereas roughly two-fifths of new marriages were likely to end in divorce, as many as half of cohabiting unions dissolved.[25]

But might this be changing? A decade or so ago, a couple who were serious about their relationship would have got married. Now, they are more likely to cohabit for longer. This has introduced a greater element of stability into cohabitation.

The 2006 survey referred to earlier found that cohabiting relationships were lasting longer. It also revealed that 56% of people who were cohabiting went on to marry their partner. Of the remaining 44%, a small minority continued to cohabit while the rest split up.[26]

New forms of relationship are being recognised. These are long-term relationships that differ from heterosexual couples who live together.[27] In particular, they include:

- *Same-sex partnerships,* which have been legally recognised since 2004. Just 0.3% of couples living together described themselves as being in a same-sex relationship in the 2001 Census. However, some same-sex couples may have been reluctant to label themselves as such, while others will have been living apart together.

  35% of respondents in the 2006 survey said that they had a fairly good friend or a family member with a same-sex orientation. A further 36% said that they were aware of a 'distant' acquaintance who was gay or lesbian, such as someone at work.
- *Couples who 'live apart together'* – so-called 'LAT's. In the 2006 survey, 9% of respondents said they were in a relationship but not living with their partner, compared to 65% who were married or cohabiting and 26% who did not have a current partner.

  Of this 9%, two-fifths said that they were living apart because either they were not ready to live together or it was too early in their relationship. A quarter could not afford to live together, while a fifth had partners working or studying elsewhere.

These alternative forms of intimacy are very much in the public consciousness, and seem to be increasingly accepted.[28]

In the early 1970s cohabitation and divorce were relatively rare. But as larger numbers got involved, it became more acceptable for others to follow suit. The same may be starting to happen with same-sex relationships and living apart together.

Could we be seeing the beginnings of cohabitation as an alternative to marriage, and the early emergence of unconventional relationships as long-term alternatives to (opposite-sex) cohabitation?

Centred on the couple, the 'beanstalk' family has sprung up. Longer life expectancy has kept more grandparents and great-grandparents alive, while low birth rates have reduced the number of siblings and cousins.

The family has grown taller, with more generations involved, and thinner, with fewer brothers and sisters or other immediate relatives.

Perhaps having fewer siblings makes it easier for brothers and sisters to be close to each other. In a 2001 survey, 26% of men and 33% of women who were not living with other members of the family saw an adult sibling at least once a week.[29]

Grandparents feature much more strongly in young people's lives than they did before the mid-twentieth century. The British Social Attitudes survey provides revealing data.

In 2001, just over half of the adult population living separately from their parents saw their mother weekly. Two-fifths saw their father weekly. These figures showed a 7% to 8% drop since 1986, but had remained stable since 1995.[30] The figures were highest for adults with young children. This meant that most grandparents had plenty of opportunity to be involved with their grandchildren.

Children looked after by grandparents (to some extent)

Pre-Second World War : 1 in 3
1960s & 1970s: 3 in 5
1980s & 1990s: 4 in 5

Source: Michael Wilmott & William Nelson, *Complicated Lives,* Chichester: Wiley, 2003, pp. 82–83.

Much has been said about the ageing population. Some fear that a proportionately smaller working population will struggle to produce enough income to support older people adequately. There could be 'generation wars' over scarce resources.

But the growing interdependence of the generations through the beanstalk family makes more extreme versions of this future unlikely. With grandchildren, adult parents and grandparents all involved in each other's lives, younger and older generations have closer relationships and sympathise with one another. Families have become a glue holding the generations together.

Friendships continue to flourish, especially among those on higher incomes.

In the survey just referred to, 56% of 25- to 34-years olds and 58% of those aged 34 to 45 claimed to have 10 or more close friends. Only 5% and 13% of these groups said they had no best friend.

Perhaps surprisingly, women reported having fewer close friends than men, while men were less likely to have a best friend. But the biggest difference was to do with income.

Individuals whose household income was less than £12,000 a year were three times more likely to say they had no best friend than people in households with £35,000 or more – 24% compared to 8%. They also tended to have fewer friends overall.[31]

There is some reason to think that people may have a larger number of friends than in the past, not least because of the Internet.

Early research assumed that the Net would enable people to make more friends. They would meet new people online, and perhaps develop these friendships by meeting up face-to-face. Online would lead to offline contact.

More recent research has highlighted how the Net also helps people to maintain relationships. Face-to-face relationships can be sustained and strengthened online by sending emails, forwarding messages, swapping photographs and using social networking sites. Offline leads to online contact.

A 2006 survey of Michigan State University students using Facebook found that they were using the site to keep in touch with high-school friends after moving to college. Social networking sites were helping users to maintain offline friendships that they had made in the past.[32] The popularity of sites like Friends Reunited suggests that older age groups may be doing the same.

Might individuals be sustaining larger numbers of friends because the Net makes it easier for them to do so? Friendships which might have lapsed can be kept alive through online contact. Rather than making more friends, the Net helps you to *keep* more friends.

Family and friendships are blending together. There has been a blurring of boundaries in how people regard relatives and friends. Friends may be seen as 'honorary' family members, while increasingly family ties take on the character of friendship. *The distinction between chosen and given relationships is not clear cut.* Just as friends are chosen, so individuals may choose to be close to some family members but not others. Relatives become friends. 'My partner is my best friend.' 'My brother is a good friend to me.'

> 'Rather than making more friends, the Net helps you to keep more friends'

Equally, some friendships have a given quality, like family (contrary to the saying which goes 'you can choose your friends, but you can't choose your family'). They are so well established that dropping them would be difficult. Or they are so much part of your life that – like certain relatives – you can't imagine being without them.[33] *Might friends be taking on the family's caring responsibilities?* Most people think that duty and obligation are an essential aspect of family relationships. They are one of the differences between relationships with family and friendships.[34]

In a 2001 survey of people in Britain, only 1% of the sample said they would turn to a friend if they had money difficulties, 6% if they had flu and 21% if they felt depressed.

The great majority would turn to their spouse or partner or to someone else in the family.[35] Respondents were clear that friends and family were different. In terms of care and support, the two are still far from being interchangeable.

However, there is some evidence that family relationships are becoming more like friendships and friends more like family.

Interviews with 53 people in three very different Yorkshire localities revealed that care and support flowed between many of them and their friends, even though they had no recognised ties. They were being family to each other, but were not related in a biological, legal or socially recognised sense.[36]

Families and friends have different degrees of closeness. Ray Pahl and Liz Spenser have described the way personal communities differ according to how close the individual is to relatives and friends. They have distinguished between five broad types of personal community (though further research would be needed to show how widespread these types are):

- partner-based;
- family-based;
- friend-based;
- neighbour-based;
- professional-based – where paid professionals act as closest friends.[37]

Contemporary people live their lives in two spheres: firstly, they engage with organisations (as consumers, for example) and belong to them (not least at work); and alongside these organisations they are members of personal communities. If you want to understand people today, you need to understand both these parts of their lives.

---

1 John W. Meyer, Gili S. Drori & Hokyu Hwang, 'World Society and the Proliferation of Formal Organizations', in Gili S. Drori, John W. Meyer & Hokyu Hwang (eds.), *Globalization and Organization*, Oxford: OUP, 2006, pp. 25–49.

2 Some of this research is summarised in, for example, Stephen A. Stansfeld, 'Social Support and Social Cohesion', in Michael Marmot & Richard G. Wilkinson, *Social Determinants of Health*, Oxford: OUP, 1999, pp. 155–178; and Robert E. Lane, *The Loss of Happiness in Market Democracies*, New Haven: Yale, 2000, pp. 77–98.

3 *Social Trends*, 38, 2008, pp. 16–18.

4 Jim Bennett & Mike Dixon, *Single Person Households and Social Policy: Looking Forwards*, York: Joseph Rowntree Foundation, 2006, p. 8.

5 *Social Trends*, 38, 2008, p. 19.

6 *Regional Trends*, 38, 2004, Table 3 : 20.

7 This is a very rough estimate and assumes that half the 4.5 million single parents counted in the 2001 Census were aged 25 to 44, that this 2.25 million has remained reasonably constant since, and that most of them live alone with their children. In 2001 a third of lone mothers in the UK were under age 35. *Focus on Families*, Basingstoke: Palgrave/ONS, 2007, p. 6.

8 Adam Smith et al, 'Solo Living across the Adult Life Course', *CRFR Research Briefing*, 20, 2005.

9 *Social Trends*, 38, 2008, p. 19.

10 'Overwhelming majority of Britons want to marry', Civitas Press Release, 19 May 2008.

11 Anne Barlow et al, 'Cohabitation and the Law: Myths, Money and the Media' in Alison Park et al (eds.), *British Social Attitudes: The 24th Report*, London: Sage, 2008, p. 33.

12 In 2006 nearly 44% of all births were to unmarried mothers, 85% of which were registered by both mother and father and assumed to be cohabiting. *Health Statistics Quarterly*, 37, Spring 2008, Tables 2.1 & 3.2.

13 Anne Barlow et al, 'Cohabitation and the Law: Myths, Money and the Media' in Alison Park et al (eds.), *British Social Attitudes: The 24th Report*, London: Sage, 2008, p. 33; 'Social class of parents has a strong influence on children thirty years later', National Statistics News Release, 29 September 2005.

14 'Cohabitation, Separation and Fatherhood', *Findings*, Joseph Rowntree Foundation, 2002.

15 Simon Duncan & Miranda Phillips, 'New families? Tradition and Change in Modern Relationships', in Alison Park et al (eds.), *British Social Attitudes: The 24th Report*, London: Sage, 2008, p. 5.

16 56% of cohabiting parents lived in advantaged areas, against 68% of married parents. 'Overwhelming majority of Britons want to marry', Civitas Press Release, 19 May 2008.

17 Anne Barlow et al, 'Cohabitation and the Law: Myths, Money and the Media' in Alison Park et al (eds.), *British Social Attitudes: The 24th Report*, London: Sage, 2008, p. 30

18 Simon Duncan & Miranda Phillips, 'New families? Tradition and Change in Modern Relationships', in Alison Park et al (eds.), *British Social Attitudes: The 24th Report*, London: Sage, 2008, pp. 4–8.

19 Anne Barlow et al, 'Cohabitation and the Law: Myths, Money and the Media' in Alison Park et al (eds.), *British Social Attitudes: The 24th Report*, London: Sage, 2008, pp. 45–46.

20 Andrew J. Cherlin, 'The Deinstitutionalization of American Marriage', *Journal of Marriage and Family*, 2004, pp. 851–853.

21 Ibid. pp. 855–857.

22 Office of National Statistics, *Social Trends*, 38, Basingstoke: Palgrave, 2008, pp. 20–21.

23 'Divorces: England and Wales rate at 26-year low', 29 August 2008, **http://www.statistics.gov.uk**.

24 Carol Smart, 'Changing Landscapes of Family Life: Rethinking Divorce', in *Social Policy and Society*, 3(4), 2004, pp. 401–408.

25 Data for cohabiting unions was drawn from the British Household Panel Survey. See John Ermisch, 'Changing Patterns of Family Formation', **http://esrcsocietytoday.esrc.ac.uk** (accessed 1 May 2008).

26 The survey report claims that the number of couples continuing to cohabit rose slightly between 2000 and 2006, reflecting the longer duration of cohabiting unions. This (rather than an increase in cohabiting unions breaking up) would account for the fall from 59% to 56% in cohabitants who went on to marry. Anne Barlow et al, 'Cohabitation and the Law: Myths, Money and the Media' in Alison Park et al (eds.), *British Social Attitudes: The 24th Report*, London: Sage, 2008, p. 33.

27 The data in this section – though not always the interpretation – are drawn from Simon Duncan & Miranda Phillips, 'New families? Tradition and change in modern relationships', in Alison Park et al (eds.), *British Social Attitudes: The 24th Report*, London: Sage, 2008, pp. 15–22.

28 In the 2006 survey, 63% agreed that a same sex couple can be just as committed to each other as a man and a woman, while only 12% disagreed. Roughly a third agreed that a lesbian or gay couple could be as good parents as a man and woman, while around two-fifths disagreed. Simon Duncan & Miranda Phillips, 'New Families? Tradition and Change in Modern Relationships', in Alison Park et al (eds.), *British Social Attitudes: The 24th Report*, London: Sage, 2008, p. 21.

29 Ibid. p. 193.

30 Ibid. p. 192.

31 Ibid. pp. 196–97.

32 N. B. Ellison, C. Steinfield, & C. Lampe, 'The Benefits of Facebook "Friends": Social Capital and College Students' Use of Online Social Network Sites', in *Journal of Computer-Mediated Communication*, 12(4), 2007, **http://jcmc.indiana.edu.**

33 Liz Spencer & Ray Pahl, *Rethinking Friendship: Hidden Solidarities Today*, Princeton: Princeton University Press, 2006, pp. 109–110.

34 *Current Sociology*, 52(2), 2004, pp. 135–159.

35 Alison Park and Ceridwen Roberts, 'The Ties That Bind', in Alison Park et al (eds.), *British Social Attitudes: The 19th Report*, London: Sage, 2002, p. 203.

36 Sasha Roseneil & Shelley Budgeon, 'Cultures of Intimacy and Care Beyond "the Family": Personal Life and Social Change in the Early 21st Century', *Current Sociology*, 52(2), 2004, pp. 135–159.

37 Liz Spencer & Ray Pahl, *Rethinking Friendship: Hidden Solidarities Today*, Princeton: Princeton University Press, 2006, pp. 109–110.

HOW WILL ADULT RELATIONSHIPS CHANGE?
WHAT WILL SHAPE THE NEXT 20 YEARS?

- Individuals will have more time for family and friends
- Technology will change the nature of relationships
- Changing values will influence relationships
- Mobility will affect relationships
- The gap between rich and poor will remain a big influence

We have seen how relationships have changed for people between their late 20s and mid 40s, with:

- more individuals living on their own;
- hints that for some people cohabitation may be emerging as an alternative rather than a prelude to marriage;
- the role of the 'beanstalk' family in knitting generations together;
- a possible increase in the number of friends individuals have due to the Internet;
- some blurring of boundaries between family and friends.

What will influence the nature of relationships over the next 20 years?

Individuals will have more time for family and friends. Rising prosperity will be especially important. If per capita income grows at 2.5% a year overall – around its long-term rate – average incomes will be around 60% higher in 20 years' time, and after 28 years will have doubled.

Some of this greater wealth will be taken in shorter working time. There was a distinct, if intermittent trend in this direction during the twentieth century. More recently, the working hours of full-time employees in the UK have fallen from an average of 44 per week in 1997 to 42.5 10 years on.[1]

This decline is unlikely to accelerate, though, because many companies will face competition from parts of the world where working hours are longer, like the United States and some of the Asian economies. British firms won't want to increase their labour costs.

On the other hand, employees will continue to seek a better balance between work and the rest of life. This will encourage them to take some of their extra prosperity in fewer working hours, as well as longer holidays.

Mix up the interests of employers with the aspirations of their workers, and it is likely that individuals will have a modest increase in leisure time, which they will spend with friends and family. The statutory minimum entitlement to holidays, for example, is to be raised from 24 to 28 days in 2009.

Households will be able to afford more labour-saving devices, which will increase the time individuals can give to others. Between 1961 and 2001, the average time adults devoted to housework and preparing meals fell by an hour and 24 minutes a week. The drop would have been larger if retired and unemployed people were excluded from the figures.[2]

This long-term decline will persist as individuals become more prosperous, despite the recent economic downturn. They will eat out more often, eat more pre-cooked meals if they stay in, and use more labour-saving devices round the home, as robotics and technology come into their own. They will have more time for relatives and friends.

Cooking from scratch

British people claiming to 'always cook from scratch':
- 2003 – 24%
- 2008 – 41%

Might people spend more time cooking in the future?

Source: 'Scratch cooking makes a comeback', 2 May 2008, **http://www.talkingretail.com**

Delays in starting a family will increase leisure time. In Chapter 4, 'Will becoming an adult be more difficult?', we saw that graduates are highly likely to postpone having children as they take longer to establish themselves financially.

Without a baby to look after, couples who would have had children in their late 20s or early 30s will have more time to spend with friends and relatives.

The number of graduates will be swelled by more people going to university. We suggested that over the next two decades, a further fifth of school leavers might start a degree. As they reach their late 20s and delay having children for financial reasons, they too will have more time for friends.

Technology will change the nature of relationships, but by how much? Some commentators think that communication technologies will have little effect on relationships, while others expect the impact to be large. More probable is that technologies will at first be embedded in the existing pattern of relationships and then bring changes later, as they mature.

New technologies will tend to enhance offline relationships rather than damage them, as some fear. There have been concerns that individuals will be so absorbed by the Internet that face-to-face relationships will suffer. Online friends could displace offline ones.

However, a 2005 study of more than 4,000 British users of the Internet found no evidence that the Net was eroding social ties. Internet users, including people who had been online for more than five years, were just as willing as non-users to spend time face-to-face with other people.[3]

Communication technologies actually improves relationships by increasing contact between people who might otherwise be less in touch. This is especially true of those who are retired.[4] Perhaps surprisingly, the over 65s now spend longer online per active user than any other age group – an average of nearly 42 hours a month.[5] Like teenagers, they have the time.

> 'A 2005 study found no signs that the Internet was eroding social ties'

As children and older people devote more time to the Internet, will grandchildren and grandparents have greater contact with each other than ever before, strengthening the beanstalk family?

Relationships will be more fluid. Already mobile phones allow users to be continually present with friends and family. According to one source, 'What is new is the emerging feeling that one should be accessible everywhere and at all times'.[6]

This has made relationships more fluid. You can weave in and out of friends' lives throughout the day. Instead of making firm plans about when and where to meet, individuals are finalising details by mobile phone while they are out and about – 'approximeeting'.

Voice over Internet Protocol (VoIP), allied to wireless technology, will make relationships even more fluid. Users can now phone over the Internet via their computer at virtually no cost. In future, this will be standard for mobiles, too.

In time, close friends and family will be able to 'lifecast' their holiday experiences live on video throughout the day. This will add a new dimension to being constantly with friends while being apart.

As the functionality of mobiles and other technology improves, individuals will interact with each other in more varied ways – text, email, voice messages, video messages, phone conversations, video conferences and virtual reality. They will move rapidly from one type of communication to another, introducing a further element of fluidity.

How you display yourself to others through these different types of communication will be a growing concern. For a few hundred pounds you can now hire a 'digital biographer', who will take a detailed briefing from you over Skype and then enhance your presence on Facebook and other sites.[7] 'Looking good' is beginning to acquire a whole new meaning.

Will people have more friends, but fewer close ones? Some research has shown that the average individual has a network of 150 people, ranging from casual acquaintances to close friends.

As we saw in 'The story so far', communication technologies are enabling individuals to sustain a larger number of friends, and this may well push up the 150 figure. According to Dr Will Reader of Sheffield Hallam University, social networking sites are starting to have this effect, though close friends tend to number about five.[8]

A 2006 Microsoft survey of over 1,000 British people, presumably using a definition of 'friend' that excluded casual acquaintances, found that each person had an average of 54 friends – an astonishing increase of 64% since 2003. Nearly a third of the sample had made friends online.[9]

An American study, by contrast, found that the average circle of *close* friends had shrunk between 1985 and 2004. The mean number of people with whom adults could discuss matters important to them had dropped by nearly a third, from 2.95 people to 2.08. The number of respondents who said they had nobody with whom to discuss such matters more than doubled, to nearly 25%.

Within families, siblings, parents and children were less significant, but the number of people who mainly talked to their spouse about personal issues had increased – up from 30.2% of respondents to 38.1%. People seemed to be turning to close friends less and to their partner more.[10]

Could it be that the increase in friends and the smaller number of confidants are linked? As individuals lead busier lives, they have less time to make close friends, so that family becomes more important.

> 'Americans seem to be turning to their partner more and close friends less'

The Internet helps to compensate for this by allowing individuals to expand their overall circle of friends. But as they keep in touch with all their contacts online, they have less time to cultivate close friendships.

This reinforces the significance of their partners, which in turn encourages the collection of numerous scattered friends to help them feel connected – and so the pattern keeps reinforcing itself.

Might 'personal communities' polarise more sharply in future between one or two close ties and a growing number of weak ones? This could be especially true of the late 20s to late 40s age group, many of whom will be preoccupied with family responsibilities and have less time for friendships.

There will be new ways of meeting people. Even now, from chat rooms to dating websites, the Net has increased the potential for individuals to widen their circles of friends and contacts.

Making friends online

In 2007, a fifth of British Internet users over age 14 had met new people or made friends online. Of these, over half had met at least one of these new friends in person.

Source: Corinna Di Gennaro & William D. Hutton, 'Reconfiguring Friendships', *Information, Communication & Society, 10(5), 2007, p. 602.*

Opportunities to meet people will grow as the Net is used in increasingly varied ways. Parallel worlds like *Second Life* will feature more strongly in everyday life, especially as the technology becomes simpler to use. 'Second Lifers' report that it can be easier to make friends in virtual reality than in the real world.

If you are alongside a stranger in a virtual art gallery, for example, you can send them a short message. Doing so feels less of a risk because you are not physically with them. Unlike in real life, the other person can ignore you without appearing rude and you don't feel so rebuffed.

Technology may also be used to help people meet in real life: for example, there are 'love badges' now available in Japan, which individuals wear when going to a party. A single 32-year-old might set their badge to show they are available for a date.

When they start chatting to someone whose badge has been similarly programmed, each badge gives out a warm feeling, telling the wearer that the conversation is worth pursuing!

Changing values will influence relationships. The growing importance of choice, self-expression, happiness and self-improvement will be especially important.

More people will have more choice. Adults don't choose in a vacuum, of course. They are strongly influenced by their situation, including how they were brought up.

Before the Second World War, individuals were largely 'traditional'. They were shaped by their social and family backgrounds, and by the places where they grew up. Their upbringing determined the rest of their lives. This is still true of many people, especially those who can't afford to move far from home.

However, since the Second World War more and more adults have – to an extent – become 'unboxed' from their background. As mass consumption spread in the 1950s and '60s, consumer choice expanded phenomenally. Individuals came to feel that they were entitled to choose.

In addition, the trend towards more people going away to university gave larger numbers first-hand experience of different approaches to life, while greater affluence made it easier for them to choose their preferred lifestyle.

Upbringing began to compete with a wider range of influences. Individuals had to choose between alternatives rather than automatically follow in their parents' footsteps.

In future, ways of life that previously were reserved for better-educated and financially comfortable households will be experienced by other groups, too, as more people go to university and the country gets more prosperous.

Larger numbers will witness alternative lifestyles and be more conscious of their ability to choose. Unconventional relationships could grow in popularity.

Self-expression will acquire a new edge. For a growing number of people, being true to yourself and expressing who you really are is an important value. The plethora of books about spirituality and the multiplication of self-help groups reflect today's widespread interest in finding and nurturing your true self.

Jayne Middlemiss, the 34-year-old presenter of *Celebrity Love Island*, spoke for many people when she declared in 2006, 'In a nutshell, my philosophy is this: everyone has their own truth and if you stick to your truth then you'll be fine.'[11]

Authenticity ('I must express the real me') will be given a new twist by the accelerating pace of customisation. More and more goods and services will be tailored to the individual. Even now, for example:

- you can buy a car with so much choice of trim that the model is almost unique to you;
- teachers are encouraged to allow for pupils' different learning styles, so that learning can be 'personalised' for the individual;
- when outpatients need several hospital tests, the NHS provides someone to arrange the appointments so that the person can go straight from one to another without waiting.

As customisation forges ahead, individuals will increasingly expect the whole of life to match their expectations exactly. 'It must fit me exactly' will become a deeply entrenched value.

Consumers will expect organisations to provide an experience that satisfies their desires and preferences. Alongside 'I must express myself', consumers will demand '*You* must express me.' You must anticipate how I want to express myself.

> 'It must fit me exactly' will become a deeply entrenched value

This mindset will also make individuals more demanding of their relationships:

- they will expect relationships to fit them perfectly;
- they will withdraw faster from groups that don't work for them;
- they will become impatient more quickly with friendships that give them hassle;
- they may be less tolerant of people who are very different.

The desire to be with 'people like me', which has always been powerful, will be stronger still.

More people will pursue happiness as an end in itself. For the bulk of human history, individuals who were not part of an elite have been mainly concerned with the basic necessities and drives of life – food, shelter, security and starting a family.

Perhaps ours is the first era in which large numbers of ordinary people have had the luxury of searching for happiness. Certainly wellbeing (or happiness) is firmly on today's agenda – look at all the media attention it gets.

A 2006 study of 124 young people aged 15 to 25 in mainstream Britain found that happiness was the ideal they aimed for.

> ' "Happy" refers to the fact that central to our young people's world view is the belief that the universe and social world are essentially benign and life is OK. Of course, the young people recognised that difficult things happen (broken relationships, rape, divorce, violence); indeed, they had experienced some of these things themselves. But they also evidenced a belief that there are enough resources within the individual and his or her family and friends to enable happiness to prevail. There was no need to explain why happiness is the goal of life – this was self-evident to our young people.'[12]

These youngsters viewed life through the lens of happiness, which could be obtained mainly through relationships. They aimed to be happy by being themselves, and by connecting to family (who were an unquestioned source of security) and other people. Individuals should find happiness in whatever way they could, respondents said, provided they didn't harm others.

If this 'happy midi-narrative', as the authors described it, becomes a core value for future generations, relationships will be even more important than they are now. Family, which these young people strongly emphasised, will be central. Yet will an ethic of tolerance, which was a key part of the happy midi-narrative, be enough to sustain these relationships?

Self-improvement will be more highly valued. Of course, it is already important for many people who try to get fitter, improve their appearance or get higher qualifications. But might there be a step change? Instead of making a speech about wellbeing (as David Cameron did in the spring of 2006), might a future leader of the opposition talk about self-improvement?

- *Personal improvement could be a route to social status.* Buying the latest fashion item may have less social cachet than in the past. Increasingly, new items will be easily copied and sold more cheaply, so that something which is a status product one day will be in the hands of the masses the next. A more lasting way to impress others will be to show off your capabilities, such as your athletic prowess, your encyclopaedic knowledge of a subject or your ability to look good.
- *Improving performance at work will be vital* if companies are to avoid being left behind by global competitors. It won't be enough for workers to do well, they will be expected to do better. Appraisals, for example, may

increasingly require individuals to show not only that they have achieved particular targets, but that they have improved how they do their jobs. A culture of constant self-improvement will spread.

- *Technology will put self-improvement firmly on the map.* New 'smart' drugs will enhance the brain,[13] while other technologies will improve physical capacity. For instance, the US military has a programme called Exoskeletons for Human Performance Augmentation. It aims to develop battlesuits that contain sensors and machinery to read and amplify every muscle movement. The wearer would be able to carry heavier weapons over longer distances.[14] If successful, what might be the consumer applications?

Self-improvement will play a larger part in framing how people think about their lives. This will influence the type of things they do, including where they meet friends and how they spend time with them.

With the decision to marry increasingly becoming a statement, will a growing number of couples make getting married a declaration that they have achieved something or somehow improved themselves?

There is a tendency for couples to delay getting married until they feel they are financially set up. Will weddings increasingly make a statement that couples have arrived financially?

Mobility will affect relationships. It is often said that Britain is becoming a more mobile society, which is true in terms of people's willingness to travel and where they settle down, but is less true of moving house, as we shall see.

People will increasingly visit friends and relatives some distance away. This will be despite disincentives to travel, such as higher fuel prices, concerns about the contribution of transport to climate change, and – probably – the eventual introduction of national road pricing.

Offsetting these deterrants will be:

- *Higher incomes,* which will enable people to afford higher transport costs and travel greater distances. The increasing use of the car since 1995 has been associated with longer trips rather than more trips.[15]
- *Improvements in fuel efficiency.* Between 1971 and 2001 the running costs of motoring (tax, insurance, maintenance, fuel and oil) remained constant after allowing for inflation. Better fuel efficiency offset the oil price hikes of the 1970s, and the same is likely to happen in response to recent record prices.[16]

- *Advances in green technology,* which will reduce the carbon footprint of travel, especially by car. Cars will be lighter, for example, so that they use less fuel. Alternatives to petrol and diesel are being developed.
- *Tax cuts to offset national road pricing.* National road pricing will be designed to relieve traffic congestion, as London's congestion charge has done. Charges are likely to vary according to how much traffic is on the road. But this will meet resistance from motorists, who already think they are taxed enough. So there will almost certainly be tax cuts elsewhere as a sweetener – 'We'll introduce road pricing but halve council tax in return.' These tax cuts will help motorists afford the extra cost of road pricing (though the latter will still be effective: it will encourage road users to travel when there is least traffic). Rather than abandoning their cars, motorists will travel at different times and by less congested routes. People will continue to visit friends and family.

Adults will settle down further from home. There is already a slow trend in this direction. Census data show that Britain is gradually becoming more geographically polarised. The growth in car and home ownership since the 1970s has given individuals greater choice in where they live.

This is especially true of people with degrees. Graduates, who have tended to move to London and the South East, have been the most mobile.

In addition, old and young, native-born and migrant, black and white, and rich and poor people are pulling apart from each other. Individuals are choosing to live near other people like them, which is increasing geographical polarisation.[17]

Although there will be more opportunities to study for a degree near home, the large expansion of higher education over the next 20 years (see Chapter 4, 'Will becoming an adult be more difficult?') will encourage even more young people to move to a different part of the country to attend university or find a job. More graduates will live some distance from home, influencing how they relate to their parents.

Once established, households will tend to stay put. Those who move most often will be younger adults, especially if they are pursuing a professional or managerial career. But once children come along they will, like now, settle down and move less frequently. Older workers will remain the least willing to move.

The proportion of people who moved home because of jobs halved between 1984 and 1994, and there have been further falls since. Property owners stay an average of 16 years without moving. In an early-twenty-first-century RAC

Foundation survey, a quarter of respondents said they lived where they were because they had always been in the area or their family lived there.[18]

Staying put in 2000

People who had been living in their local area for:

- less than 5 years – **22%**
- 5 to 19 years – **35%**
- more than 20 years – **43%**

('local area' = 15–20 mins' walk from home)

Source: Melissa Coulthard, Alison Walker & Antony Walker, *People's perceptions of their neighbourhood and community involvement*, London: The Stationery Office, 2002, p. 90.

This trend to settle down and stay where you are is unlikely to be reversed – for several reasons:

- *The effect of both partners working.* If one changes job it can be a problem for the other to move. Couples will prefer to suffer the longer commute instead. This will be especially the case if they have children at school – uprooting the whole family is a formidable task.
- *The time workers spend in a job.* The time individuals spent with an employer increased from an average of six years and two months in 1992 to seven years and four months in 2000.[19] 'Jobs for life' have not come to an end, as many in the 1990s supposed. Individuals won't have frequent job changes prompting them to move home.
- *The greater mobility of work.* In 2002, approaching a fifth of all employees were working at home or, more often, 'on the road' – visiting clients, travelling to meetings and so on.[20] For a growing number of people, working from home will be as easy as working from the office. So if they do move job, there will be less need to move house.
- *The cost of moving home.* High rates of stamp duty and rising house prices in the long term (as growing demand meets supply shortages) will encourage owners to increase the size of their existing homes, as many are doing now, rather than move.
- *The value of local friends.* One piece of research found that each additional local friend reduces the probability of moving further than 20 miles away by more than 40%. The longer you stay in a place, the more local friends you acquire, and this makes it less attractive to move.[21]

Once they have settled down, individuals will stay in one place, put down roots and get to know other people in the area. Local friends – and often local family members – will continue to feature strongly in their lives.

The gap between rich and poor will remain a big factor. Poverty reduces the opportunity to socialise and develop friendships. It also puts huge stress on people, making it more difficult to maintain relationships, which tend to be more stable if you are better off.

At present, 55% of single parents live in disadvantaged areas, compared to 35% in areas that are classed as 'advantaged'.[22]

The 2001 Census revealed that cohabiting couples with children tended to live in poorer but more traditional parts of Northern England, where the decline of manufacturing had most disrupted working-class communities. The list of places where married couples with children lived was very different. With some exceptions, it read 'like a guide to the traditional "stable, well-to-do, family" districts of Southern England.'[23]

There are few signs that the gap between rich and poor will narrow significantly over the next 20 years, nor that large numbers will be taken out of poverty. As in so many other aspects of people's lives, relationships will be influenced by how much income they have.

---

1   Eurostat Labour Force Survey, Table EWHUNA.

2   Jonathan Gershuny, 'What Do We *Do* in Post-Industrial Society? The Nature of Work and Leisure Time in the 21st Century', *ISER Working Papers*, 2005(7), p. 15.

3   John Curtice & Pippa Norris, 'Isolates or Socialites? The Social Ties of Internet Users', in Alison Park et al (eds.), *British Social Attitudes: The 23rd Report*, London: Sage, 2007, pp. 239–259.

4   William H. Dutton & Helen J. Helsper, *The Internet in Britain 2007*, The Oxford Internet Institute, University of Oxford, 2007, p. 53, **http://www.oii.ox.ac.uk**.

5   Ofcom, *The Communications Market 2007*, section 4.1.12, **http://www.ofcom.org.uk**.

6   Knut H. Sorensen, 'Domestication: the Enactment of Technology', in Thomas Berker et al, *Domestication of Media and Technology*, Maidenhead: Open University Press, 2006, p. 55.

7   *The Times*, 31 July 2007.

8   James Randerson, 'Social network sites don't deepen friendships', 10 September 2007, **http://www.guardian.co.uk**.

9   'Britons Make More Time for Friendship than Ever Before', November 2006, **http://www.microsoft.com**.

10 Miller McPherson, Lynn Smith-Lovin & Matthew E. Brashears, 'Social Isolation in America: Changes in Core Discussion Networks over Two Decades', *American Sociological Review*, 71, 2006, pp. 353–375.

11 *Independent*, 4 July 2006.

12 Sara Savage, Sylvia Collins-Mayo & Bob Mayo with Graham Cray, *Making Sense of Generation Y: The World View of 15–25-year-olds*, London: Church House Publishing, 2006, p. 38.

13 Danielle Turner & Barbara Sahakian, 'The Cognition-Enhanced Classroom', in Paul Miller & James Wilsdon (eds.), *Better Humans? The Politics of Human Enhancement and Life Extension*, London: Demos, 2006, p. 80.

14 Eamonn Kelly, *Powerful Times*, New Jersey: Whatron School Publishing, 2006, pp. 92–93.

15 Nick Banks, David Bayliss & Stephen Glaister, *Motoring Towards 2050: Roads and Reality*, RAC Foundation, 2007, p. 19, **http://www.racfoundation.org**.

16 *Motoring Towards 2050*, London: RAC Foundation, 2002, p. 28.

17 Danny Dorling & Phil Rees, 'A Nation Still Dividing: The British Census and Social Polarisation 1971–2001', *Environment and Planning*, 35, 2003, pp. 1287–1313.

18 Edmund King & David Leibling, 'Commuting and Travel Choices', presentation to the RAC Foundation/Railway Forum Conference, 22 July 2003; Elizabeth Dainton, *The UK Commute: Healthy or Hazardous?*, RAC Foundation, 2007, p. 13. Both can be found on **http://www.racfoundation.org**.

19 Peter Nolan & Stephen Wood, 'Mapping the Future of Work', *British Journal of Industrial Relations*, 41(2), 2003, pp. 168–169.

20 Michael Moynagh & Richard Worsley, *Working in the Twenty-First Century*, Leeds: ESRC Future of Work Programme, 2005, p. 102.

21 Michele Belot & John Ermisch, 'Friendship Ties and Geographical Mobility: Evidence from the BHPS', ISER Working Paper 2006(33), 2006, p. 24.

22 'Overwhelming majority of Britons want to marry', Civitas Press Release, 19 May 2008.

23 Daniel Dorling & Bethen Thomas, *People and places: A 2001 Census atlas of the UK*, Bristol: Policy Press, 2004, pp. 142–143.

HOW WILL ADULT RELATIONSHIPS CHANGE? WHAT MIGHT BE THE IMPLICATIONS?

- How many people will live on their own?
- Will cohabitation become an alternative to marriage?
- How stable will couples be?
- The beanstalk family will flourish
- Friendships will consume even more time

Influences on relationships over the next 20 years will include, as we have seen:

- *more time* for family and friends;
- *technology,* which will enhance offline relationships, make them more fluid, expand the circle of acquaintances while narrowing that of close friends, and create new opportunities to meet people;
- *a growing focus on personal values* of choice, self-expression, happiness and self-improvement;
- *greater mobility* in terms of people's willingness to travel and where they settle down, alongside a continued reluctance to move house once they have settled;
- *the gap between rich and poor people.*

We look at how these drivers will affect the relationships of people aged between their late 20s and mid 40s, and consider some of the implications for business.

How many people will live on their own? In 'The story so far', we saw that the proportion of 25- to 44-year-olds living alone was projected to grow from 12% in 2003–04 to 17% in 2026. Solo living is currently growing faster among this age group than any other.

But might this change? Growing prosperity will make it more affordable to live on your own. On the other hand, young adults will be financially stretched as they pay off larger student loans and struggle to get on the housing ladder. Housing shortages could push up rents. Overall, it could well be financially harder to live alone.

More young people may share with a friend. Might there be a trend for thirtysomethings to live in larger households to keep down costs? And might boomerang children live at home for longer – into their late 20s and even their early 30s? This would have clear implications for the housing market.

So while some growth in solo living is likely (the trend is well entrenched), the rate of increase could easily slow down. This would affect retailing because single-person households consume differently. They use smaller quantities, for example, and are more inclined to buy from convenience stores than go to a supermarket.

If more thirtysomethings live in larger households, will housemates want to eat together (so that they start consuming like families) or live separate lives?

Will cohabitation become an alternative to marriage? Kathleen Kiernan has suggested that European countries are accepting cohabitation in stages:

Acceptance of cohabitation, stage by stage

Stage 1 – *Cohabitation is a fringe or avant-garde phenomenon*
Stage 2 – *Cohabitation is accepted as a testing-ground for marriage*
Stage 3 – *Cohabitation becomes an alternative to marriage*
Stage 4 – *Cohabitation becomes almost indistinguishable from marriage, as it acquires its own legal framework.*[1]

In 'The story so far', we saw that Britain has in general reached stage 2, with a small minority entering stage 3. In the years ahead, will there be a marked shift to stage 3 and the beginnings of stage 4?

The great majority of cohabiting couples want to marry,[2] and this is likely to remain the case. True, a low commitment culture pervades much of people's lives – but might there be a reaction against this in favour of stability, which marriage will symbolise? Marriage would be eroded more slowly.

The odds are on a slow move away from marriage rather than a dash to cohabitation as an alternative to marriage. Behind this gradual trend will be the expansion of young people's horizons as more of them go to university, where they will witness first-hand a wider range of lifestyles. For some of them, not having a conventional marriage will be a stronger option.

Equally important will be the persistence of poverty. For many poor people, a wedding will seem unaffordable. As now, couples may keep postponing marriage in the hope that one day they will have saved enough. Eventually, they will just accept their cohabiting status.

Frequently, those who are financially better off will also feel daunted by the costs of a wedding – 'Can we afford to meet everybody's expectations?' As is often the case today, many couples will want to feel that they have arrived financially before tying the knot. So the current trend for couples to marry when they are older will persist, reducing the number of marrieds in the thirtysomething age group.

As the drift away from marriage slowly continues, getting married may increasingly make a statement. 'This is not something we have to do, but we have chosen marriage for a reason.'

Often marriage will demonstrate commitment. But for a growing minority, especially in poor areas, will it be a sign that they have achieved something – that they have found a stable partner, or that they can afford to settle down?

These trends will influence how companies market their products. The desire for stability may favour solid, enduring brands such as Boots and Marks & Spencer. On the other hand, the minority who favour alternatives to marriage may be drawn to brands that talk about flexibility and living life your own way.

How stable will couples be? Recently the divorce rate has fallen, while cohabiting unions last for longer than before. Over the next 20 years, the pressures to separate will remain considerable, and will include:

- *The growing incidence of divorce,* which makes separation more acceptable. Divorce becomes more of an option when some of your friends have done it and survived.
- *The spread of 'it-must-fit-me' values,* which could make partners more demanding of their marriage and perhaps less willing to work at it. Longer life expectancy will also allow more time for partners to change, develop new expectations and grow apart from each other.
- *The emergence of happiness as the goal of life* for more and more people. Will happiness demote the ethic of self-sacrifice, which helps to glue marriages together?[3]
- *The effects of being poor* for the many couples who live in poverty or close to it. Couples will continue to be torn apart by the exhaustion of keeping their financial heads above water and the anxiety they'll sink.

Against these will be the natural desire of couples to stay together. Could there be a stand off between factors that encourage couples to separate and lovers' desire for a long-term relationship?

If so, the late-twentieth-century trend toward instability could flatten out. The recent fall in the divorce rate and the longer duration of cohabiting unions might suggest that we are reaching that point.

Stress within or the breakdown of intimate relationships can exact an enormous toll on individuals, distracting them from other activities, making them depressed and sometimes producing illness.[4] It almost certainly damages the performance of employees.

Will a growing number of employers provide 'family coaching' and other support for long-term relationships, especially marriage, to increase the wellbeing and performance of their staff?

> 'The late-twentieth-century trend toward instability could flatten out'

The beanstalk family will continue to flourish. This will be despite the trend for family members to live further apart, as more young people go away to university and then find jobs some distance from home.

Offsetting this scattering of the family will be:

- *Advances in technology,* which will allow family members to keep in touch with each other even though they live miles apart. Grandparents will receive online video clips of their grandchildren. Families will teleconference using large flatscreen monitors, or play a virtual game together in a parallel world.
- *A continued willingness to travel.* As many people are discovering, technological 'closeness' is no substitute for being physically with the other person. A virtual barbecue is not the same as a real one. So family members will still visit each other. For reasons we discussed in 'What will shape the next 20 years?', travel will almost certainly increase, which could be bad news for the environment.
- *The continued importance attached to families.* A striking feature of the 'happy midi-narrative' discussed in 'What will shape the next 20 years?' was the emphasis put on family by 15- to 25-year-olds, an age when you would expect them – certainly the younger ones – to be reacting against their parents. They saw their families as a source of happiness and of support when in trouble. Given their view of the world, this generation looks set to keep the beanstalk family very much alive when they have children themselves.

Thriving beanstalk families could be a joy for marketers. Just as advertisers use children to reach parents, will grandchildren increasingly be used to reach grandparents? And will grandparents, an expanding market for children's products, fuel a resurgence of traditional toys as they nostalgically share their childhoods with their grandchildren?

Friendships will consume even more time than they do today.

> ■ *People will have more time for friendships* (as well as family), as leisure time continues to increase slowly, more everyday chores are automated and graduates delay starting a family.
>
> ■ *Individuals will be able to keep in touch with more friends* as communication technologies advance. Already the Internet has made it quicker and easier to maintain contact. In future, relationships will be sustained through new and cheaper forms of communication. Even more than today, when you leave an area you won't have to leave your friends behind. You will remain in touch online.
>
> Individuals may acquire 'convoys' of friends who travel with them through their lives. To one or two school friends you might add some friends from university, and then a few friends from each subsequent phase of your life. Gradually you will build up a sizable convoy of people whom you contact regularly and who offer varying forms of support. To some extent this happens now, but will these convoys be larger and more significant in future?
>
> ■ *Immediate friends will be constantly present* in more varied ways, as electronic forms of communication multiply. Texting and voice conversations will be supplemented by video messaging, personal websites that display your evolving biography – and many other ways of keeping in touch.
>
> Everyday existence will continue to grow more fluid as different parts of your life flow in and out of each other – from texting one set of friends while you are at work, to keeping in touch with another group by video message, while always meeting face-to-face with a third group.

Though relationships have always mattered, we have entered an age when they are becoming more central to people's lives than perhaps at any time since the Industrial Revolution.

> ' " Convoys" of friends may travel with individuals throughout their lives'

Parents and children are spending more intentional time together, as we saw in chapter 3, 'How will we bring up our children?' Relationships – or 'social capital' – are playing a bigger role at work than ever before.[5] People are more constantly in touch with each other – look at the time they spend on their mobile phones!

In the 'network society', business will be judged by its contribution to relationships. Are its products damaging relationships or helping to make them more healthy? Are company employment policies making relationships at home more difficult? Are relationships at work a source of wellbeing? Coming soon, perhaps, will be relationship audits to asses companies' performance in these areas.

> 'Relationships are more important than at any time since the Industrial Revolution'

1 Kathleen Kiernan, 'Cohabitation in Western Europe: Trends, Issues, and Implications', in A. Booth & A. C. Crouter (eds.), *Just Living Together: Implications of Cohabitation on Families, Children, and Social Policy*, Mahwah, NJ: Erlbaum, 2002, pp. 3–31.

2 'Overwhelming majority of Britons want to marry', Civitas Press Release, 19 May 2008.

3 One study found that spouses who believe that 'marriage is for life, even if the couple are unhappy' are significantly happier in their marriages and report fewer marital problems. Paul R. Amato et al, *Alone Together: How Marriage in America is Changing*, Cambridge, MA: Harvard, 2007, p. 198.

4 See, for example, M. Willitts, M. Benzeval & S. Stansfeld, 'Partnership history and mental health over time', *Journal of Epidemiology and Community Health*, 58, 2004, pp. 53–58.

5 For 65% of jobs, emotional skills were 'very important' in 2006. In 52% of jobs 'aesthetic skills' – looking and sounding the part – were also 'very important'. Alan Felsted et al, *Skills at Work, 1996–2006*, Cardiff/Oxford: ESRC, 2007, p. 47.

CHAPTER 6

WILL ETERNAL YOUTH REPLACE THE MIDLIFE CRISIS? THE STORY SO FAR

- Middle age is occurring later in life
- The trend to stop working at an earlier age has been reversed
- Family circumstances have diversified
- Today's middle-aged people are the 'lucky generation'
- Middle-aged people on low incomes are not so fortunate

It is easier to talk about middle age than to define it. The government thinks you have passed middle age (and become 'old') if you are 60; employers, if you're 50; while individuals themselves may not feel old till after 65 (or even 75).

There is as much uncertainty about when the middle years begin. A mother who starts a family when she is 20 may feel she is middle-aged by 40. Someone else may not feel middle-aged till their 50s. Indeed, individual experiences are so varied that some sociologists resist talking about middle age at all.

Nevertheless, there is a clear stage of life, often described as middle age or midlife, when many people see their children leave home, witness their own parents grow old and perhaps die, experience the menopause if they are female and become grandparents. People begin to see the future less in terms of their potential and more in terms of their limitations.

'People start to see the future less in terms of their potential and more in terms of their limitations'

This phase of life is one that follows having young children (or the capacity to have children) and precedes retirement. Retirement marks a convenient end. The mid 40s are a very rough starting point. The table below shows how this segment of the population has grown both in numbers and as a proportion of the total since 1986.

Size of the middle-aged population (000s)

Year	Numbers aged 45–59	Numbers aged 60–64	Total	% of total pop.
1986	9,212	3,069	12,281	21.7
1996	10,553	2,785	13,338	22.9
2006	11,744	3,240	14,984	24.7

Source: *Population Trends*, 131, 2008, table 1.4.

The middle years are of increasing interest to business. Currently forming a quarter of the population and still growing in size, people in their midlife are and will remain highly significant as consumers. As their children grow up, many have more to spend on themselves.

In future, employers will have an ageing workforce. With fewer young people available for full-time employment (see chapter 4, 'Will becoming an adult be more difficult?'), older workers will become a prized resource. Employers will want these workers to be as productive as possible. Encouraging more older workers to stay in employment has also become a government priority, not least to boost the tax take.[1]

Middle age is occurring later in life. This is partly due to the general ageing of the population, which has created space for middle age to start later in the journey through life.

Between 1860 and 1960, life expectancy for men aged 65 in the UK rose by slightly more than a year across the whole period. Since 1960, it has increased by almost one year *per decade*. For women, life expectancy has been rising at an ever-faster rate since 1920.[2] As people live longer, life expectancy is creeping up to an older age.

At the other end of the life course, individuals have been entering adulthood at a later age. As we saw in chapter 4, the time when most people left school at age 15 or 16 is long gone.

Currently, 60% of 16- to 18-year-olds remain in full-time education. Over 40% of the 18-plus age group go to university. Longer education has delayed adulthood, and the effect has rippled through the life journey. The start of middle age has been delayed.

In addition, people are healthier for longer than in the past. In 2002, for example, men could expect to live disability-free lives till the age of almost 61 on average, compared to just over 58 in 1981.[3] Middle age not only happens at an older age, but it also lasts longer as people grow 'old' later than before.

> 'Middle age happens at an older age and lasts longer'

The trend to stop working at an earlier age has begun to reverse. Employment among workers over age 50 fell sharply during the late 1970s and 1980s, before climbing slowly from the mid 1990s. But it has still not recovered to the level of 30 years ago.

Only around three-fifths of 55- to 59-year-old men are currently working, compared to four-fifths in the late 1970s, while among men aged 60 to 64 two-fifths are employed – against 70% 30 years before.

The figures for women currently in work are around three-fifths of those aged 55 to 59 and one-third of 60- to 64-year-olds. A much higher proportion of women than men work part-time (around a quarter of 55- to 59-year-olds, for example).[4]

The employment rate of 55- to 64-year-old men and women overall has risen gradually since the mid 1990s, with the increase in the number of sixtysomething women at work being especially marked.

Despite this steady rise, there are two peaks formed by early leavers from the workforce. People on higher incomes are one. As members of comparatively generous final salary pension schemes, they are in a better position to cease working than most employees, who stay on till around the retirement age.

People on lower incomes form a second peak. Few would describe themselves as 'retired': many draw disability benefits. There is a clear connection between low income and poor health. If your earnings are modest, you are more likely to stop working for health reasons.[5]

Family circumstances have diversified. As society has become more ethnically mixed, family patterns in midlife have become more varied. Rising divorce rates also mean that more people are either living on their own, cohabiting or in a second marriage. 'Blended' families, involving stepchildren, are more common.

Variations in caring responsibilities illustrate this growing diversity.

Fewer couples in their midlife have children at home. For example, if we use the General Household Survey quoted opposite to look at women aged 50 to 54, a total of 51% of those who were born in the early 1930s had at least one child living with them when they reached this age. Among those who were born five years later, the figure was 44% and for those born 10 years later it was 39%.

This reflects:

- **the long-term decline in adult children living at home**, partly due to more students at university (though the growing number of graduates returning home has to some extent reversed the trend);
- **greater prosperity over the past 40 years**, which has also allowed young adults going from school to work to move out of their family home earlier. Higher incomes have enabled them to set up on their own.

Figures for women born after 1941–45 are not available in this particular study. But the decline in those with children at home is likely to have slowed and perhaps levelled off, for the reasons described in 'What will shape the next 20 years?'.

Percentage of women aged 45 to 64 with children in the household (by age group and birth cohort)

Age	1926–30	1931–35	1936–40	1941–5
45–49				
Parent with dependent child in household	N/A	N/A	34	33
Parent with non-dependent child in household	N/A	N/A	32	29
50–54				
Parent with dependent child in household	N/A	17	10	13
Parent with non-dependent child in household	N/A	34	34	26
55–59				
Parent with dependent child in household	5	3	3	4
Parent with non-dependent child in household	26	27	21	17
60–64				
Parent with dependent child in household	1	1	1	N/A
Parent with non-dependent child in household	14	15	8	N/A

Source: Maria Evandrou & Karen Glaser, 'Changing Economic and Social Roles: The Experience of Four Cohorts of Mid-Life Individuals in Britain, 1985–2000', *Population Trends,* 110, 2002, p. 23.

Note: Data drawn from General Household Survey.

More middle-aged people are caring for an older person. Longer life expectancy means that a growing number of men and women are living into their 80s and 90s, and becoming dependent on their children at a later age.

At the turn of the millennium, for example, 28% of 55- to 59-year-old women born in the early 1940s helped to look after a 'sick, handicapped or elderly person', mostly older relatives. Just 19% of women who were 15 years older had done so at that age (see table below.)

To an extent, caring also seems to be consuming more time. Among 60- to 64-year-old women, 8% from the 1936–40 cohort provided care for over 20 hours a week in the late 1990s, against 5% of women this age born 10 years earlier.

Percentage of women aged 45 to 64 who care for older relatives (by age group and birth cohort)

Age	1926–30	1931–35	1936–40	1941–45
45–49				
Carer	N/A	N/A	21	23
Carer for over 20 hours a week	N/A	N/A	3	5
50–54				
Carer	N/A	21	25	24
Carer for over 20 hours a week	N/A	3	5	5
55–59				
Carer	19	23	21	28
Carer for over 20 hours per week	5	5	7	7
60–64				
Carer	19	22	26	N/A
Carer for over 20 hours per week	5	9	8	N/A

Source: Maria Evandrou & Karen Glaser, 'Changing Economic and Social Roles: The Experience of Four Cohorts of Mid-Life Individuals in Britain, 1985–2000', *Population Trends*, 110, 2002, p. 23.

Note: *Data drawn from General Household Survey.*

Few couples work, have children at home and care for an elderly relative in their middle years. Among those born in 1941–45, only one in nine women between ages 45 to 49 in the late 1980s and early '90s combined all three of these roles. When they reached 55 to 59 10 years later, the proportion was a mere 3%.

Many more 45- to 49-year-old women had two of the three roles. Nearly two-fifths of women born in 1941–45 were in this category in the late 80s and early 90s. But by the time these same women reached 55 to 59, the figure had dropped to just over a fifth. At both stages, the proportion who were carers and parents of dependent children, but were not employed, was less than 4%.[6]

Being 'caught in the middle' – caring both for dependent children and frail parents while in paid work – seems to be an atypical experience, though it is likely to be more common for those born after 1945:

- who will have had their children at a later age;
- who will be more likely to have inherited children from a previous union;
- whose parents have a better chance of being alive because of longer life expectancy.

Becoming a grandparent is very much part of being middle-aged nowadays. About three-quarters of adults will become grandparents, and the average age of doing so is about 54, a little younger than in previous years.[7]

Grandmothers are more likely to be alive and active than in the past, and smaller families mean that they have fewer grandchildren to compete for their attention. Grandparents with lower education and income tend to be younger, to have more grandchildren and to live closer to them.[8]

Close involvement with grandchildren peaks among grandparents aged under 60 and then falls among older groups. Two-fifths of grandparents live within 15 minutes' travelling time of a grandchild.[9]

Although they have considerable contact with young grandchildren in particular, grandparents provide less support for working parents than is sometimes assumed. In 1998, only a quarter of grandparents with grandchildren under the age of six looked after them during the day. Just 14% took a grandchild under 13 to or from school

Grandparents play a particularly important support role when the parents of their grandchildren split up. More than two-fifths of grandparents in that position say they put themselves out to look after their grandchildren, compared to under three in 10 when parents stay together. Grandmothers are especially important.

Most grandparents enjoy their frequent contact plus limited responsibilities. They seem to provide support without interfering too much, and are happy with their role.

The main exceptions are those who provide extra support to grandchildren of separating parents. They are substantially more likely to be dissatisfied – their involvement is more than they bargained for. With higher rates of divorce, will this dissatisfaction spread?

Today's middle-aged people are the 'lucky generation' in terms of lifestyle. They have higher incomes and greater wealth than previous generations, for all sorts of reasons – for example:

- *Society is more prosperous* and, as we have noted, since the mid 1990s more fiftysomethings have had jobs.
- *More women are employed*, boosting the incomes of couples. Partly offsetting this, however, has been the increase in divorce, which reduces the standard of living of both partners. In such cases there are two homes to look after instead of one.

■ *They are more likely to own their home. They can look forward to higher pensions.* People now retiring are among the first to get the full benefits of the State Earnings Related Pension Scheme if they don't have a private pension. Most of those who have contributed to an occupational scheme can look forward to a relatively generous pension based on their final salary, whereas future generations will have to settle for less generous private pensions based on contributions.

Proportion of households owning their own property, by age and year (in %)

Age	1995	2000	2005
40–49	79	79	81
45–54	80	81	82
55–64	76	77	85
60–69	72	74	78

Source: British Household Panel Survey, reported by Richard Boreham & James Lloyd, *Asset Accumulation across the Life Course,* London: ILC-UK, 2007, p. 24.

For many people, earnings peak in their late 30s – as shown in the table below. Mean averages peak at an older age than median ones because of the small number of very high salaries which keep climbing till later in life. The table shows that workers in their middle years tend to have less to spend than younger age groups.

On the other hand, as children leave home, parents in their middle years have more money for themselves, so they may feel better off.

Gross annual pay for all employees in the UK, 2007

Age	Median (£)	Mean (£)
18–21	9,817	10,097
22–29	18,093	19,833
30–39	22,774	27,321
40–49	22,307	28,717
50–59	20,486	25,670
All employees	19,943	24,908

Source: *Annual Survey of Hours and Earnings,* London: ONS, 2007, Table 6.7a.
Note: *The table refers to employees on adult rates who have been in the same job for more than a year.*

How are the middle-aged spending their income? The table below compares the spending of 50- to 64-year-olds with people who are younger and older than they are. The proportion of income spent on many categories seems remarkably stable across the age groups.

There is a steady increase in the percentage spent on food, however, despite smaller households as individuals get older. This probably reflects the lower average incomes of the fifty- and sixtysomethings, with more of them unemployed or retired. The fall in 'other expenditure items' partly reflects smaller mortgage payments.

Middle-aged people are spending a larger portion of their income on recreation and culture, and to a certain degree on household goods and services, than younger people. Presumably midlife couples in employment are more able to splash out now that, in most cases, their children have left home.

In 2004, 95% of 52- to 54-year-olds owned a CD player, dropping to 90% for those aged 60 to 64. Of the 52 to 54s, 79% had a computer, 60% had a digital TV and 74% had a DVD player. The figures for 60- to 64-year-olds were 64%, 46% and 56% respectively.[10]

Household expenditure as a percentage of total expenditure by age of household reference person, 2006

Item	Age 30–49	Age 50–64	Age 65–74
Food & non-alcoholic drinks	9	11	13
Alcohol, tobacco & narcotics	2	3	3
Clothing & footwear	5	5	4
Housing, fuel & power	9	9	11
Household goods & services	6	7	7
Health	1	2	2
Transport	14	14	14
Communication	3	2	2
Recreation & culture	12	16	16
Education	2	1	1
Restaurants & hotels	8	7	7
Miscellaneous items	8	8	8
Other expenditure items	19	17	13

Source: *Family Spending, 2007*, London: ONS, 2008, p. 109.
Notes:
The household reference person is the head of the household, roughly speaking.
Housing costs exclude mortgage interest payments, council tax and Northern Ireland rates.

A small (but growing) proportion of the middle-aged are buying properties overseas, while others move within the UK, often to the countryside or seaside.

As discussed in chapter 5, 'How will adult relationships change?', most people don't move home, or if they do, they remain in the same area. This is especially true of older age groups, for whom a sense of belonging to the place where they live is of particular importance.

Middle-agers have become firm members of the consumer society. With more money for themselves, many couples are well positioned to enjoy a consumer lifestyle. Staying young – by keeping fit, buying beauty products and having cosmetic surgery – is an important part of this.

Influenced by consumer values, people in their middle years seem to be more individualistic than the age group above them, but less so than generations coming behind.

For example, 35- to 54-year-olds are more supportive of increased government spending on poor people than those who are under 35, but they are less supportive than the 55s and over.[11] Consumer values are tempered by a lingering sense of solidarity with those less fortunate.

Middle-aged people on low incomes are not so fortunate, of course. About a third of this age group are either in poverty or close to poverty. They depend heavily on state support, which will probably be their main source of income, rather than earnings.[12]

As we have seen, compared to higher-income groups, they are more likely to be out of work involuntarily and to experience poor health. Though it is possible to escape poverty, the odds are that if you have been poor for most of your earlier life, you will remain so in middle age.

1 *Opportunity Age: Meeting the Challenges of Ageing in the 21st Century*, Vol. 1, London: HM Government, 2005, pp. 16–40.
2 James Banks & Richard Blundell, 'Private Pension Arrangements and Retirement in Britain', *Fiscal Studies*, 26(1), 2005, p. 37.
3 *Social Trends*, 37, 2007, p. 81.
4 James Banks, 'Economic Capabilities, Choices and Outcomes at Older Ages', *Fiscal Studies*, 27(3), 2006, p. 288; James Banks & Maria Casanova, 'Work and Retirement' in Michael Marmot et al (eds.), *Health, Wealth and Lifestyles of the Older Population in England*, London: IFS, 2003, p. 129.
5 James Banks, 'Economic Capabilities, Choices and Outcomes at Older Ages', *Fiscal Studies*, 27(3), 2006, pp. 290–294.
6 Maria Evandrou & Karen Glaser, 'Changing economic and Social Roles: The Experience of Four Cohorts of Mid-Life Individuals in Britain, 1985–2000', *Population Trends*, 110, 2002, p. 25.
7 Peter K. Smith, 'Grandparents and Grandchildren', *The Psychologist*, 18(11), 2005, p. 684.
8 Anne Gray, 'The Changing Availability of Grandparents as Carers and its Implications for

Childcare Policy in the UK', *Journal of Society & Politics,* 34(4), p. 573.

9   This and the next four paragraphs are based on Geoff Dench, Jim Ogg & Katarina Thomson, 'The Role of Grandparents', in Roger Jowell et al (eds.), *British Social Attitudes: The 16th Report,* Aldershot: Ashgate, 1999, pp. 135–57.

10 Banks et al, *Retirement, Health and Relationships of the Older Population in England: The 2004 English Longitudinal Study of Ageing,* London: IFS, 2006, p. 276.

11 Peter Taylor-Gooby & Rose Martin, 'Trends in Sympathy for the Poor' in Alison Park et al (eds.), *British Social Attitudes: The 24th Report,* London: Sage, 2008, p. 249.

12 *Households Before Average Income: An Analysis of the Income Distribution 1994/95–2006/07,* London: Department of Work & Pensions, 2008, p. 17.

WILL ETERNAL YOUTH REPLACE THE MIDLIFE CRISIS? WHAT WILL SHAPE THE NEXT 20 YEARS?

- The number of middle-aged people will grow
- They will be more healthy
- More of them will be employed
- Their family responsibilities will change
- People with middling incomes may feel less well off

The number of people in their middle years will continue to grow. Numbers of 45- to 64-year-olds are projected to increase from a total of nearly 15 million in 2006 to over 16.5 million in 2026 and 17 million in 2036 (see table below). Among key issues for this group will be:

- health;
- employment;
- caring responsibilities;
- how they spend their money;
- the persistence of poverty.

Projected middle-aged population in five-year age groups (000s)

Age	2006	2016	2026	2036
45–49	4,151	4,557	4,013	4,848
50–54	3,683	4,549	3,992	4,496
55–59	3,910	3,988	4,393	3,879
60–64	3,240	3,450	4,293	3,778
Total	**14,984**	**16,544**	**16,691**	**17,001**
Percentage of total population	24.7	25.5	24.1	23.4

Source: *National Population Projections: 2006-based*, London: ONS, 2008, pp. 64–65.

Will they be more healthy? In 'The story so far', we noted that people in their middle years have better health than in the past. Will these health improvements continue?

A big factor will be people's lifestyles. In each of the last four decades of the twentieth century, mortality improvements (a key health indicator) were significantly greater for adults born between 1925 and 1945 – now mostly past their middle age – than for people born before them.

This was largely due to people smoking less. It may also have been the result of healthier diets in the early 1940s, despite – or even because of – wartime rationing. Were youngsters eating more vegetables and less starch?[1]

These lifestyle improvements have persisted in the generations coming up behind, who are now middle-aged or due to become middle-aged over the next 20 years. Notably, the decline in smoking has continued. Obesity – currently much in the news – will be more of a problem for people becoming middle-aged *after* the next 20 years.[2]

There have been a number of environmental improvements that should also enhance the health of those who will enter middle age. These include better quality air. The 1956 Clean Air Act blew away much of the smog in London and other cities, bringing long-term health benefits to children brought up since then.

People in their fifties experience multiple transitions that encourage them to take stock of their lives. An awareness of growing old means that this group is receptive to messages about exercise, diet and other measures which will help them to keep healthy. This, too, should continue the improvement in health experienced by previous generations.

Medical advances will have a significant impact. Already, people in their middle years are benefiting from the improved detection and treatment of many cancers, for example, while new anti-TNF drugs are bringing positive results for patients with some rheumatic diseases.

A different medical paradigm is slowly beginning to emerge. Traditional medicine has been largely reactive. Symptoms occur and the doctor treats them. The emerging predict-and-prevent paradigm, however, puts much greater emphasis on detecting an individual's proneness to a disease, and then intervening at an earlier stage to prevent or manage it. Screening for breast cancer is a classic example.

As our knowledge of the genetic component of many diseases improves, there will be more tests to see if you are predisposed to a particular disease, and action will be taken earlier to treat it. The gradual shift to predict-and-prevent should bring significant health improvements to people in their midlife.

A key issue will be how far this new paradigm is available to everyone on the National Health Service. Will a tax-funded NHS have enough money?

With the government reportedly ready to allow patients to top up their treatment by paying for more expensive and allegedly more effective drugs, will wealthier people eventually gain most from predict-and-prevent medicine?

Poverty is strongly associated with poor health. Data from 2002 and 2004 for those between 50 and the state pension age confirm what numerous other studies have revealed: there is a strong correlation between health and wealth, including pension wealth and owner-occupied housing. At each point of the wealth distribution the wealthier you are, the better health you have.[3]

Being poor causes all sorts of stress. Life often feels out of control, for instance. You may be anxious about debt, paying the next bill or making sure your children can keep up with their friends in the latest fashion. Stress seems to be one of the pathways from poverty to poor health.[4]

Among middle-aged people, it is hard to see the gap between rich and poor narrowing significantly over the next 20 years. The gap appears to be firmly entrenched for those currently in younger age groups, who will carry this inequality into their middle years.[5]

> **'The health gap will continue to track the wealth gap'**

By middle age poor people will have experienced more stress and damaging life events, such as unemployment, than rich people.[6] This will take an increasing toll on their health.

So while the midlife group as a whole can expect better health, improvements will be smaller for those on lower incomes. The health gap will continue to track the wealth gap.

How many midlifers will be in employment? To help achieve an 80% employment rate overall, the government aims to have a million more 50- to

64-year-olds in work 'in the longer term' – an increase of about 15%.[7] Will this target be achieved?

Potentially, there could be a large demand for older workers.

- **The economy will keep growing**, despite the current downturn, and this will create jobs.
- **There will be a labour-intensive bias to many jobs**, despite automation. One of the effects of technology is to make possible more advanced products and processes – which require human collaboration. This increases the time spent interacting with other workers, making many tasks more labour-intensive. Rather than technology reducing the amount of jobs created, the volume of new jobs for each percentage point of economic growth may actually increase.[8]
- **Fewer younger workers will enter the labour market**, mainly because larger numbers are staying on in education. At the same time, more and more baby boomers will reach retirement, leaving plenty of vacancies to be filled. An estimated 13.5 million job openings will be created between 2002 and 2012, of which almost 12.2 million will be replacements for existing workers.[9] Will older workers be asked to stay on in employment to ease the labour crunch?

But will employers want older people? It is often claimed that older workers bring experience and maturity to the job. In an ageing society, an older employee may also relate better to customers of a similar age than a younger person.

- **There is no reason, it is said, why older workers should not be as productive as younger ones.** In future, middle-aged people will have spent much of their lives adapting to changes in the workplace. Facing change when they are older won't faze them as much as previous generations.

  Yet comparing productivity is difficult. A larger proportion of midlife people leave the workforce than is the case for younger workers. It is not unreasonable to assume that these leavers include the least productive employees.

  If that's true, any sample of older workers will tend to be skewed toward those more productive ones who remain in employment. So looking at the productivity of middle-aged workers in relation to younger ones may not be a fair comparison.

- **Might it be that older workers are less productive than younger ones?** For example, there is clear evidence that certain cognitive functions decline with age.[10] This is particularly true of the speed of information processing. For those over 50, the older you get, the greater the degree of decline.[11]

It may be that experience and other benefits brought by middle-aged employees outweigh such disadvantages. Employers may shift their middle-aged workers into jobs where the decline in cognitive (and other) functions matters less.

But say the evidence grew that older workers really were less productive than younger people. Might employers turn to youthful immigrants to fill their vacancies instead? Getting an extra million middle-aged British people into work would become a tall order.

■ *If employers relied more heavily on immigration, would enough foreign workers be available?* Unless Turkey joins the EU, migrant labour from within the Union could well be insufficient in the long run. As wages in Eastern Europe rise closer to the European average, people from those countries will have less incentive to work abroad. Immigration controls may curb new arrivals from outside the EU.

■ *Employers could find themselves caught between a rock and hard place* – between less productive older workers (assuming that is the case) and the lack of possible replacements.

Will middle-aged workers want to continue in employment? The employment rate among fiftysomethings has picked up since the mid 1990s, partly reflecting a greater willingness to work (see chart opposite).

This trend is likely to persist as workers save more for a pension, and as the state pension age for women is raised from 60 to 65 between 2010 and 2020 (to bring it into line with men). The latter will bring more older women into the workforce.

But slowing the trend down will be older employees whose declining health makes it difficult for them to work. Will they stop working, or will employers make it easier for them to continue – either by finding them a more suitable job or by allowing them to work part-time? (We discuss this more fully in chapter 7, 'Will "retirement" disappear?'.)

Overall, the rising employment rate for the over-50s looks set to continue, at least for a while. But whether this will be enough to bring an extra million older people into the workforce, as the government hopes, is more uncertain.

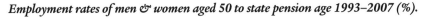

Employment rates of men & women aged 50 to state pension age 1993–2007 (%).

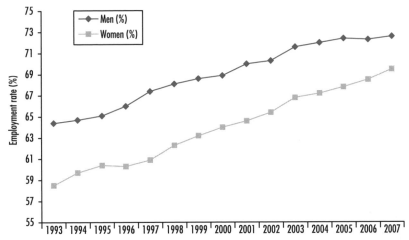

Source: ONS Labour Market Statistics – Integrated FR LFS TIME PERIODS, tables YBUN, YBUO.

How will family responsibilities change for people in midlife? Families will certainly be very different as divorce, cohabitation, ethnic diversity and income variations produce an ever-widening range of domestic arrangements. As in 'The story so far', we focus on individuals' caring responsibilities when considering the next 20 years.

The long-term decline in middle-aged parents whose children live with them is likely to slow, and may even go into reverse. Till recently, rising prosperity meant that young adults could afford to leave home earlier, while growing numbers of young people have been moving away to university.

Offsetting these trends in future will be:

- *The tendency for couples to start a family at an older age.* This tendency kicked in around 1970 – among a cohort that will be age 60 in 2030 – and has become stronger since. In 2000, for example, 10% of births were at ages above 36.7.[12] These children will still be at home when their parents reach their middle years.
- *The increase in separation and divorce,* which is leading to more second partnerships. As more people remarry and start a new family (or acquire stepchildren), children will be living at home when parents are in their midlife.
- *The growing number of boomerang children,* for the reasons discussed in chapter 4, 'Will becoming an adult be more difficult?'. Larger student debt and the higher cost of housing will encourage more twentysomethings to live at home till they find their feet financially.

More middle-aged people will have an older parent to care for – a continuation of the current trend.

A 2003 study projected that for people around age 60, the proportion with a living mother would rise from 22% for those born in 1911 to just over 50% for the 1971–74 cohorts, who will enter their middle years between 2016 and 2020. This will be due largely to the improved mortality of older people. The figures were expected to be similar for fathers.

For the generations coming up behind, however, the proportion of 60-year-olds with an older mother is projected to tail off gradually to 40% for those born in 2000 (who will reach 60 after the middle of the century).

The main reason for this slowdown is the older age at which women are having children. Giving birth when you are 35 rather than 25, for instance, means that when your child reaches 50, you will be 85 instead of 75.

Each extra year of life carries a greater risk that you will die. So there is less chance of an 85-year-old living to 90, when their child would be 55, than of a 75-year-old living to 80.

Being older when you have children means that you are less likely to be alive when your children are middle-aged.[13]

> 'More middle-aged people will have parents still alive by 2020, but fewer will do so thereafter'

Up to 2020, then, a growing proportion of people in their middle years will have their mothers still alive – perhaps around 50%. The percentage will then begin to fall away slightly as the post-1974 cohorts come through. The trend will be similar for fathers.

Not all these parents will need looking after, of course. But a good proportion will need care from children who are in the later years of middle life.

As we noted in chapter 5, 'How will adult relationships change?', in 2001 over half of adult children who had their own families lived near enough to their mothers to see them weekly. They will be sufficiently close to offer practical support to their parents as they age.

Will adults in midlife be 'caught in the middle'? In 'The story so far', we saw that caring for both dependent children and frail parents while in paid work is a very uncommon experience, especially for those in their late 50s or older.

Over the next 20 years, however, being caught in the middle is likely to become more widespread because of the trends we have just described:

- ■ ***More couples will have dependent children*** as they enter middle age, either as a result of having children when they are older or starting a second family.

■ *Improved mortality* means that more older parents will still be alive.
■ *The rising employment rate* for the over-50s is set to continue.

Caring for dependent children and older relatives while holding down a job will still be a minority experience. But for some in their middle years, it will be an increasingly complicated task involving stepchildren and the parents of former partners.

In particular, compared to less-educated people, individuals with higher qualifications will be more likely to care for an older parent in their middle age and/or to have at least one child under 18 living at home.[14]

This is because spending longer in education and then taking time to get established in a job tends to result in later childbearing. In turn, having children at a later age means that your children will be relatively young when you enter middle age.

At the same time, your parents are likely to be comparatively old. Better-educated children tend to have better-educated parents, who will have followed the same pattern. If you are a doctor and start a family when you are 30, for example, your mother might well have given birth to you at a similar age. So when you are 50, your mother could be 80.

Well-educated people also tend to live longer. As a result, when a better-educated person reaches midlife, their comparatively well-educated parents are more likely to be still alive and possibly in need of care.

Better-educated people are most likely to have dependent children and dependent parents in their middle years.

Will grandparents be less available to their grandchildren? A large majority of people in their middle years will continue to be grandparents. Though they don't provide as much support for working parents as is sometimes thought, they are an important source of care, especially for lower income families who can least afford to pay for childminders and nurseries.

On the eve of the millennium, 29% of grandchildren whose parents had separated received some daytime care from their grandparents, while 20% of grandchildren whose parents had not separated had some care from this source. Grandmothers provided the bulk of this support.[15]

However, the employment of older women is increasing. They will also retire later, when their state pension age is raised to 65 by 2020. There is clear evidence that the amount of care given by grandmothers declines if they have a job. Will the childcare given by grandmothers fall during the next decade?

> **'Will the amount of childcare given by grandmothers fall in the next decade?'**

If so, there could be a serious conflict between two of the government's policy goals – increasing the number of young mothers in work and increasing the employment of older people. Achieving the latter will make it harder for low-income mothers to find the free childcare they need if they are to return to work quickly. Single parents will suffer most.[16]

How financially well off will people in their middle years be? In 'The story so far', we saw that many of today's middle-aged people (the 'lucky generation') are fortunate compared to their predecessors.

Their household incomes are higher because of rising prosperity and the greater number of women at work; a larger proportion own their own homes; and they can look forward to more generous pensions.

How rosy are the prospects for future generations? Tomorrow's midlifers will certainly benefit from a general increase in prosperity. If the economy was to grow by 2.5% a year (roughly its long-term trend), average incomes would rise by 60% in 20 years and double after 28 years.

But this doesn't mean that middle-aged people will feel 60% richer in 20 years' time.

- **They will have larger mortgages to repay** than people currently in their middle years, having bought when prices were higher. Some may have made only modest repayments, to allow them to spend more on bringing up their children. Will there be a growing trend to pay only the interest? 'My children can pay off the mortgage when I die!'
- **They will need to save more for retirement.** This will be especially true of workers with private pensions. A growing number of these pensions will be based on contributions rather than on final salary, as most are now. With the latter, if contributions are insufficient to pay the expected pension, the employer makes up the difference. (This is not uncommon because people frequently live longer than pension companies foresee.) Defined contribution schemes contain no such safety net, and so tend to be less generous.
- **They will face larger financial demands from their children.** Parents who started a family when they were older will have dependent children at home when they are in their early (and even late) 50s. As we have seen, more parents will be in this position than in the past. In addition, young people will be spending more time in education, which will make them financially dependent on their parents for longer.
- **They may inherit less from their baby-boom parents than they expected.** Conventional advice is that it is wise to have a retirement income of at least two-thirds of your previous salary. But will this be enough for baby boomers who have lived their entire lives in a consumer culture? As they spend out on holidays, new kitchens and other consumer products, and live for longer, growing numbers may release extra income by re-mortgaging their homes. Equity release schemes have been getting more popular. Individuals will have less to pass on to the next generation when they die.

How far will these developments offset the benefits of greater prosperity? The answer will vary according to income.

Those in roughly the top fifth of earnings, who accounted for 45% of the nation's income in 2006–07,[17] will probably feel substantially more prosperous. They will be able to pay off their mortgages, put aside enough for retirement and support their children, even if they inherit less than they anticipated.

Middle-aged people with incomes around the median, which was £377 a week in 2006–7,[18] may feel relatively less well-off than their immediate predecessors.

Many will still have a mortgage hanging round their neck; they will be saving frantically for retirement; a significant number will be supporting their children – and their parents may have re-mortgaged the family home. Will they see themselves as the *un*lucky generation?

A large number of middle-aged people will be poor. Poverty is normally defined as being on 60% of median incomes or less. In Britain there is a large bunching of people around this 60%, with individuals often moving in and out of poverty. Around a fifth of the country is poor.[19]

Though it is not inevitable, obviously if you have been poor for much of your early life you are likely to be poor in your middle age. In addition, two particular groups are at risk of poverty:

■ **Couples on modest incomes who split up** and move into separate homes. Living costs jump considerably if you are on your own. There is no one to share the heating bills and so on. Women, normally on the lower income within a couple, lose the benefit of their former partner's higher earnings (despite any divorce settlement). With higher rates of separation, in future more middle-aged people will be in this position.

■ ***Those who leave work*** for health reasons or because they have been made redundant. It is notoriously difficult to get back into work if you are middle-aged. Though the number of unemployed 50- to 64-year-old men has declined in recent years, the total still stands at a little below 25%. For women aged 50 to 59, the figure is slightly higher.[20] Many are drawing incapacity benefit, and finding that unemployment is a fast track to poverty.

The government is trying to help workers with health problems to remain in employment, but it is too early to know how successful it will be. The workforce may also benefit from general improvements in health. On the other hand, if work continues to be more demanding, will greater numbers suffer from stress and eventually leave their jobs?

1 R.C. Willetts et al., 'Longevity in the 21st Century', paper presented to the Faculty of Actuaries, 15 March 2004, and to the Institute of Actuaries, 26 April 2004, pp. 21–38.

2 Adult obesity rates, largely reflecting childhood diets, only began to climb sharply in the 1980s and didn't exceed 10% of the adult population till just before 1990. Foresight, *Tackling Obesities: Future Choices – Project Report*, London: Government Office for Science, 2007, p. 24.

3 James Banks, 'Economic Capabilities, Choices and Outcomes at Older Ages', *Fiscal Studies*, 27(3), 2006, p. 288.

4 See, for example, Richard Wilkinson, *Mind the Gap: Hierarchies, Health and Human Evolution*, London: Weidenfeld, 2000.

5 Between 1994–95 and 2006–07, inequality within the whole UK population increased slightly. See *Households Before Average Income: An Analysis of the Income Distribution 1994/95–2006/07*, London: Department for Work & Pensions, 2008, p. 22.

6 Paula M. Lantz et al, 'Stress, Life Events, and Socioeconomic Disparities in Health: Results from the Americans' Changing Lives Study', *Journal of Health and Social Behaviour*, 46, 2005, pp. 274–288.

7 *Opportunity Age: Meeting the Challenges of Ageing in the 21st Century*, Vol. 1, London: HM Government, 2005, p. 19.

8 Michael Moynagh & Richard Worsley, *Working in the Twenty-First Century*, Leeds: ESRC Future of Work Programme, 2005, pp. 10–11.

9 Institute for Employment Research, *Bulletin*, No. 73, 2004.

10 James Banks, 'Economic Capabilities, Choices and Outcomes at Older Ages', *Fiscal Studies,* 27(3), 2006, pp. 294–95. However, this is contested. Some studies suggest that the decline in cognitive and other functions has been exaggerated. See Kirsten Benjamin & Sally Wilson, *Facts and Misunderstandings about Age, Health Status and Employability*, London: DWP, 2005, pp. 14–26.

11 Felicia A. Huppert, Elizabeth Gardener & Brenda McWilliams, 'Cognitive function', in James Banks et al (eds.), *Retirement, Health and Relationships of the Older Population in England: The 2004 English Longitudinal Study of Ageing*, London: IFS, 2006, p. 217.

12 Michael Murphy & Emily Grundy, 'Mothers with Living Children and Children with Living Mothers: The Role of Fertility and Mortality in the Period 1911–2050', *Population Trends*, 112, 2003, p. 43.

13 *Ibid.* p. 37–39.

14 Emily Agree, Beverley Bissett & Michael S. Rendall, 'Simultaneous Care for Parents and Care for Children among Mid-Life British Women and Men', *Population Trends*, 112, 2003, pp. 29–36.

15 Anne Gray, 'The Changing Availability of Grandparents as Carers and its Implications for Childcare Policy in the UK', *Journal of Society & Politics,* 34(4), 2005, p. 563.

16 *Ibid.* p. 575

17 *Households Before Average Income: An Analysis of the Income Distribution 1994/95–2006/07*, London: DWP, 2008, p. 23.

18 This is before housing costs. *Households Before Average Income: An Analysis of the Income Distribution 1994/95–2006/07*, London: DWP, 2008, p. 24.

19 They were below 60% of median incomes in 2006/07 – 18% before housing costs and 22% after housing costs. *Households Before Average Income: An Analysis of the Income Distribution 1994/95–2006/07*, London: DWP, 2008, p. 40.

20 ONS Labour Market Statistics, Integrated FR LFS TIME PERIODS, tables LWFK, LWFL, **www.statistics.gov.uk**.

WILL ETERNAL YOUTH REPLACE THE MIDLIFE CRISIS? WHAT MIGHT BE THE IMPLICATIONS?

- Middle age can be a time of considerable happiness
- Healthy living will be a stronger theme
- Employers will need to adapt to an older workforce
- Brands will speak to more varied family circumstances
- The middle-aged will have more diverse lifestyles

Your experience of happiness changes as you get older. Research from across 80 countries shows a remarkably similar pattern. Happiness is a U-shaped curve: people are happiest towards the beginning and end of their lives.

> 'People are happiest towards the beginning and end of their lives'

Most people reach rock bottom at age 44. They will be stuck in this trough till their 50s when, so long as their physical health holds up, their happiness levels rise and the risk of depression declines. The pattern is much the same whether you are rich or poor.

In an interview, researcher Professor Andrew Oswald suggested that the most plausible reason for the U-curve is that people are especially aware of their limitations in their mid 40s.

Many people may start adult life expecting too much of themselves. When they don't achieve their hopes, they become disappointed. Coming to terms with this disappointment later in their middle years leaves people more content as they head towards retirement.[1]

Though experiences vary greatly, once you accept your limitations, middle age (and the early years of retirement) can be a time of considerable satisfaction.

You have less responsibility: children leave home, and dependent parents will perhaps have passed away. You may have more opportunity to live for yourself and seek fulfilment. You can experience a 'second youth', doing things you have always wanted to do but never had time for.

But much depends on your health, your work situation, family responsibilities and how well off you are. Developments in each of these areas will have implications for business.

Most people will be more healthy in their middle years, due partly to advances in healthcare.

The gradual shift to predict-and-prevent medicine will trigger increased usage of products that help individuals to monitor and manage their health. For example:

- genetic screening will tumble in price;
- new diagnostic devices will enable you to take and analyse a blood sample at home rather than using a doctor and a laboratory;
- gastric pacemakers to take away your appetite are theoretically possible;
- exercise games played via computer will become even more sophisticated.

The bulk of the National Health Service budget is spent on people near the end of their lives. But as predict-and-prevent medicine advances, a greater amount will be devoted to other age groups, especially those in their middle years. How to fund these extra treatments will be hotly debated.

To ease the funding pressures, governments will continue to seek greater efficiency within the health service. Already private companies are being invited to run some NHS activities – hip operations, for example – in the hope that they will be more cost-effective.

This trend is likely to accelerate. Will the NHS eventually become a commissioning body – commissioning, branding and paying for services which it currently provides directly, but which in future would be supplied by private and charitable enterprises?

Healthy living will become an even more popular theme. Middle-aged people, aware of their limitations but also wanting to make the most of the rest of their lives, will be especially receptive to health messages.

They will increasingly demand:

- healthy foods;
- housing and planning policies that make it easy to walk and cycle;
- more health-based standards to ensure that individuals are protected from pollutants released into the environment;
- technologies that are designed with older people in mind – such as a mobile phone screen that you can see without your reading glasses.

The government will continue to want more fifty- and sixtysomethings to have jobs. Boosting the employment of this age group will increase tax revenue, cut the amount government spends on incapacity benefit and enable people to save more for retirement.

Employers will also want more older workers as the supply of younger adults shrinks. As we noted in 'What will shape the next 20 years?', migrant labour from the EU is unlikely to make up the shortfall in the long term, while immigration curbs may limit new arrivals from outside the EU.

Employers will need a very different mindset as they come to terms with an ageing workforce. For example:

- *They will have to spend more on training and retraining older workers.* At present, companies spend most of their training budgets on people in their 20s and 30s. Increasingly, they will have to spend more on older workers, and gear their training to the needs of this age group. Material may have to be taught more slowly, for example, than with younger people.
- *Working practices may need to be adapted to older employees.* With some cognitive functions declining in middle age, what employment arrangements will best suit changes in the human brain? For instance, some jobs may have to be slimmed down to help older workers manage rapid change – they won't have so much to cope with. But will older workers fear they will become less marketable if they have a narrower set of skills?
- *Employment may have to be more flexible.* To retain workers whose health has deteriorated, employers may need to introduce more part-time options, including phased retirement schemes so that individuals can scale down their employment gradually. Will more workers who can afford them request sabbaticals, perhaps to use their skills in Africa for a few months? This could be part of a 'second youth' – trying things you couldn't do when you had dependent children.
- *New reward packages may be required for this age group.* They might include training, health check-ups, phased retirement possibilities, sabbaticals and retirement planning, perhaps as part of a menu. Each item would be worth so much, with workers choosing what they wanted from the menu within a particular limit.

Family responsibilities among the middle-aged will vary greatly. Brands will want to avoid stereotypes that don't fit and which often mask the considerable diversity of people's lives.

> 'Brands will want to avoid stereotypes that don't fit'

One stereotype is being 'caught in the middle' – trapped between caring for children, supporting an ageing parent and holding down a job. As we saw in 'The story so far', very few people are in this situation nowadays – just 3% of 55- to 59-year-old women at the turn of the millennium.

Improved mortality, more couples with dependent children and higher employment levels among the fiftysomethings will increase the proportion over the next 20 years. But they will still be very much a minority.

More common will be middle-aged workers with just one of the family responsibilities – a dependent child or an older relative needing their care. This group will tend to have a higher level of education and be among the most affluent. Brands may want to take these family circumstances into account when talking to the wealthier section of the population.

Another stereotype is the joy of being a grandparent. As we have seen, while this is true in many cases, it is least true when grandparents help care for grandchildren whose parents have split up.

The pleasure of being a grandparent lies in having frequent contact, knowing that your responsibilities are limited and being in control of your involvement. When the parents of your grandchildren separate, you may have to provide more care than you bargained for. With divorce rates continuing to rise, more grandparents may find themselves in this position.

The joys of grandparenting can also be less when the children of grandparents are better educated and so more likely to live further away. Grandparents may be frustrated that they can't see their grandchildren more often, despite emailed photos and other forms of modern communication.

Companies marketing products to grandparents would be wise to take these different contexts into account.

Variations in wealth will affect the lifestyles of middle-aged groups – and again, this will be extremely important for brands.

People at the richer end will benefit from rising prosperity and be better off than their counterparts today. For them especially, midlife will offer a chance to recreate something of what it was like to be young. As now, for example, this group will want active – but safe – leisure pursuits.

Middle-aged people in 20 years' time will be today's 30- to 40-year-olds. They will have used the Internet for most of their working lives, and will be comfortable with further new technologies as they develop. Will they use these technologies to express themselves in new ways?

They could provide a large market for virtual reality, which is set to follow the Internet as the next big thing. By 2020 v-commerce could replace e-commerce, with 3D virtual equivalents of shopping malls.[2] Tesco, for example, is looking to rework its whole online environment to make it more three-dimensional and game-like.[3]

> **'Aspects of an individual that were dormant in real life may flourish in a virtual one'**

There will be new opportunities for individuals to make and display things. The online world *Second Life* allows participants to build houses and infrastructure, display works of art and provide various kinds of entertainment – all in virtual reality.

As these opportunities multiply over the next 20 years, middle-aged people will be able to try alternative careers and develop a host of new hobbies. Aspects of themselves that were dormant in real life may flourish in a virtual one.

A large middle group will share the country's rising prosperity, but they may not feel a lot better-off. They will find their finances are being squeezed by:

- mortgage repayments;
- saving for a pension;
- the financial needs of their children;
- potentially smaller inheritances than they expected, as their baby boomer parents re-mortgage their homes to sustain their lifestyles and pay for their long-term care in old age.

A substantial group of poor people will remain. More people could reach the fringes of poverty as a result of divorce, while the increasing demands of work may force more employees to leave their jobs due to stress.

On the other hand, the government may succeed in helping those who would otherwise be off sick to stay in employment. This would reduce the number of poor people in middle age, since even low-paid jobs pay more than incapacity benefit.

Both the main political parties want to contract out elements of the welfare state to the private and voluntary sectors – such as helping people back into work. Might assisting this group by, say, reducing the numbers on incapacity benefit, become a significant business opportunity?

---

1 'Forty-Four Most Unhappy Year of Life: Study', **http://www.abc.net.au** (accessed 24 July 2008).

2 Report of a study by Oxford University's Social Issues Research Centre, *Retail Week*, 28 September 2007.

3 **http://www.intelligent-commerce.com** (accessed 26 June 2008).

CHAPTER 7
WILL 'RETIREMENT' DISAPPEAR?
THE STORY SO FAR

- Retirement has become an increasingly significant phase of life
- Our idea of retirement has evolved from a rest, to a reward, to a right
- Pathways to retirement are fairly rigid
- Government has taken steps to meet a long-term pensions crisis

People have mixed feelings about retirement. Some look forward to a well-earned rest after years of hard work. Others fear that retirement will mean the loss of an active life – not earning an income, no longer raising children, and being eased out of civic responsibilities.

As they approach retirement age, many people would like the best of both worlds – a bit more rest along with some continuing purposeful activity. But there are few opportunities in the workplace for older people to take an easier job or work part-time. It is often said that company employment practices are to blame.

There are other reasons why retirement is a big issue for business, ranging from pension provision (and its implications) to the consumer behaviour of the retired.

Men and women in the UK of pensionable age, 1951–2001 (in 000s)

Year	Men (aged 65 and over)	Women (aged 60 and over)	Total
1951	2,247	4,580	6,827
1961	2,385	5,362	7,747
1971	2,841	6,282	9,123
1981	3,327	6,708	10,035
1991	3,630	6,927	10,557
2001	3,928	6,917	10,845

Source: *Annual Abstract of Statistics*, 2007, table 5.3.

Retirement has become an increasingly significant phase of life over the last half-century. The table above shows how the number of people of retirement age grew rapidly between 1951 and 1981, and has continued to grow (though more slowly) since.

People have been retiring at an earlier age. The proportion of older men in employment or looking for work fell dramatically during the twentieth century as life expectancy increased (see table below). Retirement by 65 became widespread.[1] An average man spent 17% of his life in retirement in 1950. By 2005 the figure had risen to 31%.[2]

In addition, retirement has become a distinct phase of life for the growing number of working women in the UK. The proportion of women of working age in jobs or looking for jobs rose from 59.4% in 1971 to 73.8% in 2006.[3] Retirement, in the sense of retiring from employment, is no longer an experience mainly for men.

Labour force participation of men age 65+ in the UK and life expectancy at birth, 1891–2001

Year	Labour force participation rate (%)	Life expectancy (years)
1891	65	41.9
1901	61	49.4
1931	48	58.4
1951	31	66.2
1991	8	73.2
2001	8	75.7

Source: *Sarah Harper, Ageing Societies: Myths, Challenges and Opportunities,* London: Hodder, 2006, p. 95.

Our idea of retirement has evolved from a rest, to a reward, to a right.[4] Will it eventually be considered a relic?

> 'In 1961 as many as 40% of 65- to 69-year-olds went to work'

Retirement was seen as rest before the 1960s, when many older employees continued to work till their late 60s or beyond. In 1961 as many as 40% of 65- to 69-year-olds went to work.[5] Retirement was seen as a short period of rest once you were too frail to work.

Retirement as a reward emerged in the 1960s and 1970s with the spread of occupational pension schemes. Schemes required pensions to be paid at a fixed age, typically 60 or 65, and didn't allow recipients of a pension to keep working for the same employer. So a growing number of people stopped work when their pension was due.

The number of companies with fixed retirement ages rose from a quarter in the 1940s to two-thirds in the early 1960s.[6] By the end of that decade, membership of occupational schemes had reached a peak of some nine million men.[7]

Retirement became something you could look forward to at a certain age – a reward for all your hard work. Workplace 'pre-retirement' courses, which helped employees prepare for retirement and which spread rapidly in the 1970s, included the idea of retirement as a recompense for contributing to society.

It was not a long step to the notion that retirement is a right. Retirement as a reward did not fit comfortably with the reality that many workers were contributing to a pension, which would be paid as an entitlement.

So retirement came to be seen as a period of funded leisure, to which you had a right at the end of your working life. 'I've paid my National Insurance. I've paid into my pension. I'm entitled to this reward.'

The emergence of retirement as a right is one reason why raising the pension age, to keep up with longer life expectancy, is so politically charged. Starting pensions at an older age can be seen as eroding your right to retirement. Retirement has become a right to be defended.

Retirement as a relic? In 2000, a Cabinet Office report on 'active ageing' argued:

'The very concept of retirement needs to be challenged. Retirement fits well with a situation where leaving one's lifelong job is associated with the end of one's working life. This is an increasingly inaccurate description of what happens. It would be useful in the short term to blur, and in the long term to abolish, the concept of retirement.'[8]

'Abolishing' retirement was a dramatic way of saying that the present cliff edge between work and retirement should give way to a more fluid transition.

> 'In 2000 a Cabinet Office report called for the abolition of retirement'

Instead of moving straight from work to not working, individuals should have greater freedom to wind down their employment gradually and expand their leisure, community and family activities.

Routes from employment to retirement would be more flexible, with individuals having much greater freedom to work part-time for a while, do a less demanding job, and go on working at a reduced level beyond their theoretical retirement age, if they wanted.

Retirement as we now understand it would give way to a phase of life in which employment, leisure and unpaid forms of work existed side by side, in proportions tailored to fit each individual.

This is a far cry from how things are today, but it is a goal shared across the political spectrum. Might we inch towards it over the next 20 years? One day, could the current version of retirement be seen as a relic of the past?

This hope for change and fluidity contrasts with the rigid nature of retirement past and present. In a culture where choice is highly prized, older workers now want to feel free rather than being tied down.[9]

But retirement as it has evolved since the war has had several rigidities – not least:

- *Fixed retirement ages,* as we have seen, with few opportunities to work beyond.
- *Inflexible hours.* Surveys repeatedly find that before retiring, older workers want opportunities to scale down their employment gradually. Yet the chance to phase yourself into retirement remains rare. You still work full-time, then stop completely.
- *Age discrimination,* which adds to the difficulty of staying on in employment. Among many studies pointing in this direction, a 2003 survey found that 35% of working and retired people claimed to have been discriminated against at work on grounds of age. This was far higher than for any other category such as race, gender or disability.[10]

The government has recently taken steps to make retirement more flexible and reduce these rigidities.

- *It has made it easier and more attractive to keep working.* In 2005 it pushed up the extra amount you get if you delay drawing your state pension.[11] Since 2006, individuals have also had the option of receiving an occupational pension and continuing to work for the same employer, where schemes allow it. (The government hopes that occupational schemes will amend their rules to make this possible.) In defined circumstances, public servants – a fifth of the national workforce – are now allowed to work beyond their retirement age, either full- or part-time, while simultaneously drawing their pension.
- *It has reduced age discrimination at work* in response to an EU directive. Employees have had the right to challenge age discrimination at work since 2006. In particular, employers are not allowed to force workers under 65 to retire on grounds of age unless they can show 'objectively' that only a younger worker can do the job. Employees wishing to work beyond 65 can make a formal request, to which employers are required to respond (though they are not required to grant it). When it reviews these arrangements in 2011, the government has promised to scrap this default retirement age if it is no longer appropriate.

■ *It has introduced a new right to request flexible work.* The right for parents with young children to request flexible working was extended to carers of adults in 2007. Since the peak of caring responsibility falls between ages 45 and 65, this new right could significantly extend flexible work for older employees. 90% of companies receiving requests from parents for flexible work have responded positively.[12] Could a similar pattern hold for older workers? If so, might caring responsibilities encourage a significant number to work fewer hours, creating phased pathways to retirement?

A long-term crisis in paying for retirement became apparent in the early 2000s, as several problems came to the fore – an ageing population, inadequate savings amongst younger people, the unsustainable nature of the new Pension Credit and the incredible complexity of pension arrangements.

Complicated in detail, Britain's pension system comprises three tiers:

■ *Tier one* consists of the basic state pension, paid for by current taxpayers through National Insurance. Originally, the state pension was intended to provide a safety net against poverty for most people, but this role has now been assumed by the Pension Credit, which is an additional means-tested supplement to the basic pension.
■ *Tier two* provides a further layer of income for those who, broadly speaking, don't have some form of private pension. The tier comprises the State Earnings-Related Pensions Scheme (SERPS) and the State Second Pension (S2P), which replaced SERPS in 2002.[13] Employees must make contributions unless they belong to a private scheme that has contracted out.
■ *Tier three* consists of private pensions for people who are not relying on the second tier – either occupational schemes provided by employers or personal schemes, such as 'stakeholder' pensions, taken out by individuals.

Our ageing society poses a fundamental threat to today's pension system. People are living for longer.

'In 1950, a man aged 65 could expect on average to live to the age of 76. Today, he can expect to live to 85, and by 2050 to 89. Women will live for even longer – on average, perhaps, into their early 90s. This is a huge change, ranking among the greatest social achievements of the last century.'[14]

The UK pension system at a glance

TIER 1 Funded by current National workforce through Insurance & taxes	TIER 2 Funded by current workforce (unless contracted out) through National Insurance	TIER 3 Voluntary, funded by employer & employee contributions or individuals alone, with tax incentives
Basic State Pension	SERPS (till 2002) – earnings-related	Occupational pensions – final salary or defined contribution
Pension Credit (for those in poverty)	State Second Pension (from 2002) – to become flat rate from 2012	Personal pensions such as stakeholder pensions

Source: Adapted from Alison O'Connell, *A Guide to State Pension Reform*, London: Pensions Policy Institute, 2003, p. 11.

How to fund these extra years of retirement has become a pressing question.

The proportion of the population at work is shrinking. This is due to longer life expectancy, lower birth rates since 1970, which mean there are not as many young workers to replace those who are retiring,[15] and young people spending longer in education, which reduces their availability for full-time jobs.

In 1950 pensioners numbered 19% of the working-age population. In 2006, the figure was around 27%. On current trends (with no later retirement), it would be 47% in 2050![16] Can we expect the working-age population to support a retired population half its size?

Younger age groups are not saving enough to be sure of an adequate income in retirement. Active membership of occupational pension schemes has declined in the private sector – from 6.3 million in 1995 to 3.6 million in 2007.[17] Fewer people under ages 45 to 50 are paying into a scheme.

In particular, companies have been closing final salary schemes to new members. Often they have replaced them with defined contribution (DC) schemes, in which the level of pension is based not on final salary but the amount of contributions. Unlike final salary schemes, DC schemes don't guarantee a certain level of pension when you retire.

If a poor return on investment or longer life expectancy reduces the expected annual value of the pension, the individual has to bear the risk. The employer won't fund the difference.

Largely because individuals tend not to make up the shortfall (they are scarcely aware of the risks involved), DC pensions are generally lower than final salary ones. On one estimate, final salary schemes promise pensions twice as generous as DC ones.[18]

Employers have been switching to defined contribution schemes for a number reasons:

- *Longer life expectancy* has increased the cost of pensions, which in final salary schemes is a cost to the employer.
- *Falling interest rates in the 1990s* cut returns on investment and pushed up the price of annuities (which are used to fund pensions when individuals retire). The higher price was an extra burden for the employer rather than resulting in higher contributions by the employee, or a lower pension, as in DC schemes.
- *Gordon Brown's 1997 tax on dividends paid to pension funds* cost the final salary schemes some £5 billion a year. Final salary schemes had to meet this cost in full rather than being able, as in DC schemes, to pass it on to scheme members in the form of lower pensions or higher contributions.
- *The crash in share prices in the early 2000s* wiped out any surpluses left in final salary schemes, creating thumping deficits that employers had to fund.[19] Unlike DC schemes, they couldn't expect scheme members to make up the deficits.
- *Financial Reporting Standard 17* (FRS17) has required since 2002 that companies be more transparent in reporting the balance of assets and liabilities in their pension schemes. A deficit is now more visible, threatening the company's share price. Switching to DC pensions means that if a scheme doesn't perform as well as expected, the risk is borne by the individual (who gets a smaller pension) rather than the company (who has to make up the deficit).

As well as encouraging employers to prefer DC schemes, these developments forced companies to shore up their final salary schemes to protect existing pensioners and those approaching retirement.

To afford the extra payments, employers cut back their contributions to DC schemes. In 2006, average employer and employee contributions to DC pensions were 9% of earnings (with employers making the largest contribution), against 19% for final salary schemes.[20]

Younger workers have steadfastly failed to increase their payments, both to offset the smaller employer contributions and to compensate for the greater risks of being in a DC scheme.

In the mid noughties, an estimated nine million people were not saving enough for retirement, a number that seemed likely to grow as the shift to DC schemes continued.[21] Demands that the pension system be reformed intensified.

The Pension Credit has also been storing up problems for the future. This means-tested payment was introduced in 2003 to tackle pensioner poverty, which had become extensive by the turn of the millennium; the state pension was not high enough to stop many retired people being poor.

Though the Credit has raised the incomes of many poor pensioners substantially, what you receive is not predictable. Payments depend on savings, the size of any private pension built up over the years and the level of income you need to qualify – which changes annually.

So individuals cannot know before they retire what they will get, which makes it almost impossible for people on modest incomes to judge whether it will be worth their while to save for an additional private pension, if they can afford it; they might be better off on the Credit but they cannot be sure. For some, the Credit reduces the incentive to save because savings cut the amount of Credit you can claim.

If the government continues – as it does now – to raise the basic state pension in line with prices and the Pension Credit in line with earnings, over 60% of pensioners will be drawing the Credit (with all its limitations) in 2050.[22] Government spending would have to rise considerably. The system appears unsustainable.

Pensions have become far too complicated, prompting calls for a much simpler system. Piecemeal reforms over many years made Britain's pension arrangements increasingly complex. The Pension Credit added yet another layer of complexity. Even experts found the system almost impossible to fathom. 'Make it simpler!' became an urgent cry.

The government now plans to reform the pension system, having appointed a Pensions Commission chaired by Lord Turner, which produced recommendations in 2005.[23] Though departing from these recommendations in some of the detail, the government's plans are based on the Turner Report.[24] They include:

- *New savings arrangements from 2012,* comprising 'personal accounts' in a new national savings scheme. Employees will pay into these accounts at least 4% of earnings (within a lower and upper band), employers 3% and the government – through tax relief – 1%. Workers will be automatically enrolled in these accounts unless they opt out (either by joining another pension scheme or choosing not to save at all).

- *Reform of the state pension.* At least from the end of the next Parliament, and possibly from 2012, the basic pension will be increased in line with earnings rather than prices; the State Second Pension will evolve into a flat-rate top-up to the basic pension, and changes in contribution requirements in 2010 will allow more women to qualify for a full state pension. These measures will cut the number of people who rely on the Pension Credit and will lift retirement incomes for those on modest earnings.

- *A gradual raising of the pension age,* to take account of longer life expectancy. The pension age will be increased from 65 to 66 over a two-year period from 2024, to 67 over two years from 2034 and to 68 over two years from 2044.[25] This will help to pay for the reform of the state pension.

- *Making pensions more simple.* On 'A-Day' – 6 April 2006 – a new tax regime for private pensions greatly simplified taxation arrangements. Abolishing 'contracting out' for defined contribution schemes from 2012 will further reduce some of the administrative complexities. Also from 2012, the government will make available to individuals a single pension forecast, rolling into one cash figure entitlements to the basic pension, the State Second Pension (and its predecessors) and the Pension Credit. This will make it much easier for people to know how much state pension they are due to get if they remain employed.

In 'What will shape the next 20 years?', we ask whether these reforms will go far enough.

---

1 Comparable figures for women are problematic because it is difficult to distinguish between working women who retired and women who stopped working once they were married.

2 *Security in Retirement: Towards a New Pensions System,* cm 6841, London: DWP, 2006, p. 140.

3 Derived from ONS LFS Time Series, table YBTN.

4 This is based on Sarah Harper, *Ageing Societies: Myths, Challenges and Opportunities,* London: Hodder, 2006, pp. 94–124.

5 Sarah Harper, *Ageing Societies: Myths, Challenges and Opportunities,* London: Hodder, 2006, p. 94. This 40% is higher than the 31% of men aged 65+ who were in employed in 1951 shown in the earlier table, 'Labour force participation of men . . .'. This is because the table refers to all men aged 65+ rather than the group 65- to 69-year-olds referred to by the 40% figure here.

 6 Sarah Harper, *Ageing Societies: Myths, Challenges and Opportunities*, London: Hodder, 2006, p. 95.

 7 *Pensions: Challenges and Choices: The First Report of the Pensions Commission*, London: The Stationery Office, 2004, p. 115.

 8 *Winning the Generation Game: Improving Opportunities for People Aged 50–65 in Work and Community Activities*, London: HMSO Performance and Innovation Unit, 2000, p. 47.

 9 Michael Moynagh & Richard Worsley, *The Opportunity of a Lifetime: Reshaping Retirement*, London: CIPD, 2004, p. 49.

10 *Age, Pensions and Retirement: Attitudes and Expectations*, London: CIPD, 2003, tables 5 & 14.

11 The extra weekly sum if you defer was increased, and an option of receiving a lump sum payment instead was introduced.

12 *Security in Retirement: Towards a New Pensions System*, Cm 6841, London: DWP, 2006, p. 150.

13 S2P was introduced as a more generous alternative for those on modest incomes. Instead of being paid on an earnings-related basis, individuals accrue a flat-rate additional payment on top of their basic state pension.

14 *Security in Retirement: Towards a New Pensions System*, Cm 6841, London: DWP, 2006, p. 7.

15 Using ONS population estimates, in 1976 the 60–64 age group was 68% of the size of the 15–19 group. In 2006, it was 81% of the size of the younger group.

16 *Security in Retirement: Towards a New Pensions System*, Cm 6841, London: DWP, 2006, p. 8.

17 *Occupational Pension Schemes 2005: The Thirteenth Survey by the Government Actuary*, London: Government Actuary's Department, 2006, p. 33; 'Occupational Pension Schemes Annual Report 2007', ONS, 2008, p. xv.

18 *Security in Retirement: Towards a New Pensions System,* Cm 6841, London: DWP, 2006, p. 60.

19 The pension deficit of Britain's top 100 companies doubled between 2002 and 2003, to more than £55 billion, according to an annual survey by Lane, Clark and Peacock (reported on **www.yourmoney.com**).

20 *Security in Retirement: Towards a New Pensions System*, Cm 6841, London: DWP, 2006, p. 34.

21 *Pensions: Challenges and Choices: The First Report of the Pensions Commission*, London: The Stationery Office, 2004, p. 165. 'Enough for retirement' is conventionally understood as two-thirds of your pre-retirement income.

22 *Pensions: Challenges and Choices: The First Report of the Pensions Commission*, London: The Stationery Office, 2004, p. 225.

23 *A New Pension Settlement for the Twenty-First Century: The Second Report of the Pensions Commission*, London: The Stationery Office, 2005.

24 *Security in Retirement: Towards a New Pensions System*, Cm 6841, London: DWP, 2006.

25 The pension age for women is being raised to 65 between 2010 and 2020, to bring it into line with that of men.

WILL 'RETIREMENT' DISAPPEAR?
WHAT WILL SHAPE THE NEXT 20 YEARS?

- Retired people may need higher incomes than now
- Life expectancy will rise further
- It will not be easy to save enough for a pension
- More people will retire at an older age
- Work will be more flexible for *some* groups of older workers

Retirement will stay near the top of the policy agenda over the next 20 years. This will be partly because of the number of people involved. As the table below shows, numbers aged 60 and over are projected to increase from 12.3 million in 2006 to 18.5 million in 2026 – from over a fifth of the population to more than a quarter.

A growing proportion of this group will be baby boomers, who will mostly be better off than their predecessors (for reasons described in chapter 6, 'Will eternal youth replace the midlife crisis?').

People coming after them will be less fortunate. As a result, concerns will mount about the financial security of future generations when they retire.

Projected number of people aged 60 and over and their proportion of the population, 2006–2036

Year	Number aged 60 and over (000s)	Proportion of population (%)
2006	12,297	21.3
2016	15,303	23.6
2026	18,512	26,7
2036	20,810	28.6

Source: *National Population Projections: 2006-based,* London: ONS, 2008, pp. 64–65.
Note: *The 'principal projection' is used.*

How much income will retired people need? The conventional view is that two-thirds of pre-retirement income should be enough. But as more and more baby boomers retire, we are entering uncharted waters. What will be an adequate income in retirement for somebody who has lived their whole life in our modern consumer society?

By 2011 the oldest of the boomers will have reached the 'traditional' retirement age of 65. People born halfway through the 1960s will be reaching age 65 in 2030.

Baby boomers will be the first generation to have lived almost their entire lives in a society dominated by mass consumption. Post-war babies became the teenagers of the 1960s, spending 20% of their money on clothes by the end of the decade and almost half on various forms of entertainment.[1] Boomers' identities have been significantly bound up with consumption.

With consumer-shaped values very different to those of their parents, boomers' expectations of retirement will differ, too. Will two-thirds of their final salary be sufficient for them to enjoy retirement in the ways they expect?

- *A new 'experience economy'* of travel, food, entertainment and lifestyle is growing rapidly for those who can afford it. The newly retired, with more time on their hands, will want to enjoy it to the full.
- *Baby boomers won't want to grow old in the same way their parents did.* Many will be active and fit when they retire, and will want to take advantage of medical advances to stay that way. In particular, when they grow very old they will expect residential homes to be of a higher standard than they often are today.
- *Costs of healthcare will escalate.* Around 1,500 drugs, including about 200 cancer drugs, were thought to be in late-stage development at the start of the new century.[2] The molecular revolution, fuelled by research into DNA, will produce many more. The NHS will not be able to afford them all. As some are doing now, older people with the financial wherewithal will demand the right to pay for additional treatments on top of what's available on the National Health Service, but without losing their NHS entitlement.

All this need not negate the conventional wisdom about how much income retired people will need. Just as television is cheap in terms of cost per hour viewed, so the electronic media may provide retired people with abundant new forms of entertainment at a price they can afford. We 'ain't seen nothing yet' in terms of virtual reality, online games and other Internet activities.[3]

On the other hand, baby boomers could find that two-thirds of pre-retirement income is not enough for the lifestyle they aspire to. Growing numbers could well re-mortgage their homes to fund the deficit. Watching them, younger generations might raise their estimates of the income they will need in retirement. To build up their savings, might they retire later?

Will life expectancy keep rising? The answer will be another influence on the timing of retirement.

Prediction is difficult. On the one hand, life has been lengthening at a faster pace. In the two decades between 1961 and 1981, the projected life expectancy at birth for men increased by nearly three years, whereas over the following two decades it jumped by almost five. Projected life expectancy at birth for women has also accelerated, but more slowly.[4]

In each of the last four decades of the twentieth century, mortality improvements were significantly greater for those born between 1925 and 1945 than for people born earlier. Reasons may include:[5]

- *better lifestyles,* especially the decrease in smoking habits;
- *improved diet,* not least the consumption of more fresh vegetables, milk and fish after the Second World War;
- *the introduction of the NHS,* and medical advances such as the greater use of antibiotics.

Mortality improvements seem set to continue as the 1925–1945 age group passes through retirement into very old age. But will the gains be maintained for younger ages?

On the other hand, there is some evidence that improvements for the 1925 to 1945 cohorts have been greater than for later generations.[6] This would suggest that the increase in life expectancy is slowing down. Professor Jay Olshansky of the University of Chicago believes that obesity and infectious diseases could bring a levelling off and even a decline in life expectancy.[7]

Medical advances and better lifestyles may extend lives more quickly.[8] In particular, techniques to delay cell damage – which is what causes body organs to fail – could have a big impact. Future life expectancy is surrounded by uncertainty.

Changes in life expectancy will have a threefold impact:

- *They will affect the funding of final salary pensions.* The Pensions Regulator has warned that every two years of increased life expectancy will add 5% to 10% to companies' liabilities for their final salary schemes.[9] If longevity continues to increase, companies will have to prop up these schemes, leaving them with less money to pay into defined contribution (DC) pensions. Age groups below roughly 50 at the turn of the millennium will lose out.
- *Life expectancy will affect annuity rates for defined contribution schemes.* When someone in a DC scheme comes to draw a pension, the amount of pension

their savings will buy depends on the annuity rate, which in turn depends partly on life expectancy.[10] Were lives to lengthen at a faster rate, the pot of savings for people nearing retirement would have to spread over more years, which would lessen the amount paid annually. Would individuals respond by working till they are older, giving them more time to save for a larger pension?

- *Life expectancy also affects the state pension.* If people live for longer and the amount of pension stays the same, the overall cost of state pensions will rise. Since the state pension is funded by current taxpayers, people in work would have to shell out more to support those who are retired. The government has announced plans to raise the state pension age from 65 to 68 in stages between 2024 and 2044. This will produce savings that will help to fund a higher pension from 2012, when increases in the state pension will be linked to earnings rather than prices. But if people live longer than expected, will government dare to raise the pension age by even more?

Might the state pension age be adjusted automatically? This would be one way of dealing with the uncertainties surrounding life expectancy.

Sweden, for example, has an automatic process for reducing the state pension – for a given number of years worked – as life expectancy lengthens. The lower pension is announced well in advance, so that people have time to adjust their expectations. They can plan to work till they are older if they want to maintain their previous level of pension.[11]

A similar approach in Britain, but perhaps with automatic changes to the pension *age* rather than the level of pension, would take some of the politics out of raising the retirement age. It would be consistent with attempts to de-politicise other contentious issues, such as interest rates and, more recently, the treatment of planning applications.

> '**Individuals' expectations about the length of their retirement may clash with the smaller pensions available**'

The state pension age would go up (or down) in incremental stages as life expectancy changed. Private pensions would almost certainly follow suit.

An independent body might collect information about life expectancy and make the announcement. Older workers would know in plenty of time when they could expect to retire, while younger workers would be able to adjust their expectations as longevity changed.

People's expectations about when they will retire currently lag behind reality.[12] If this gap persists, a painful crunch may occur: individuals' expected timing of retirement would clash with the smaller pensions available as people live for longer.

Will individuals save enough to retire at the age they expect? The answer will depend on three things.

First will be the shift to defined contribution schemes. Among people with a private pension, those aged roughly 50 and over at the turn of the millennium are most likely to belong to a final salary scheme, in which employers take most of the risks.

As we saw in 'The story so far', the shift to defined contribution schemes (where risks fall on the individual) has often been accompanied by smaller employer contributions.[13] So on current trends, final salary pensions will usually be more generous to employees, as well as less risky for them, than DC ones.

As growing numbers of people in DC schemes approach retirement and start to think seriously about their retirement incomes, the realisation will sink in that the previous generation had a much better deal. How will these younger workers respond?

- *Will they work till they are older* to make up the shortfall?[14]
- *Or will they demand that employers make larger pension contributions* to help them out?
- *Alternatively, will they press employers to share more of the risks* in the form of hybrid schemes that combine elements of both DC and final salary? These schemes already exist. You are guaranteed a minimum pension (perhaps a proportion of your final salary), but the final amount could be larger depending on life expectancy, how the scheme performs, and so on. Risks are shared between the individual and the employer. Might hybrids become the way forward?

The coverage of private sector pensions will be a second factor. The proportion of private sector workers in an occupational scheme fell from around 37% in 1991 to about 26% in 2004.[15] This doesn't mean that three-quarters of the private sector workforce won't get a pension. Some will have a personal scheme, such as a stakeholder pension.

Those with neither an occupational nor a personal pension will usually get SERPS – the State Earnings-Related Pension Scheme – or its replacement, the State Second Pension (which will become most generous for people on modest incomes). Everyone who has paid National Insurance, of course, will also get the basic State Pension.

Unless they opt out, from 2012 workers who are not in a private pension scheme will be automatically enrolled into the new 'Personal Account' – a national private pension scheme for people who are not saving for a private pension.

Based on research in other countries, the government expects that automatic enrolment will boost the take-up of private pensions (either through the Personal Account or some other scheme). Inertia will stop people opting out.

But how many workers will remain enrolled, especially those on modest incomes? Though contributions will be phased in between 2012 and 2015, employees will have to contribute 4% of their 'banded earnings', not far off the size of an annual pay increase in many cases.

- *Younger workers* may prefer to repay their student loan or save to buy their first home.
- *Will some parents opt out?* The costs of childcare may seem more pressing, for instance. In addition, the growing number of couples who start a

family in their mid to late 30s will be at a particular disadvantage when it comes to saving for retirement. In their 50s they will still be supporting their children. They could find it harder to make up any shortfall in their private pension contributions.

■ *People on low incomes* may prefer to take their chances with the Pension Credit, the means-tested top-up to the state pension. Rather than pay into a private pension, it may be more sensible to wind down their existing debts and rely on the Credit when they retire. Quite a few people could be in this position. The Pensions Policy Institute believes that, despite the government's planned reforms, individuals eligible for the Credit will fall by only a small amount – broadly speaking, from 45% of pensioners in 2005 to 40% in 2050.[16]

If many on low incomes opt out of private pensions, more people could end up relying on the Pension Credit than the government currently expects. Taxpayers would face higher costs.

On the other hand, if large numbers opt in, might they later complain that they had been ill-advised – that they would have done better to opt out, use their contributions to repay any debts, and rely on the Pension Credit if necessary?

For example, in 2008 the difference for a single person between the basic state pension of £90.70 a week and the Credit's means-tested, guaranteed income of £124.05 was £1,734 a year.

To generate an income of that size would require a pension pot of about £30,000. Many low earners will struggle to save this much. Why should they make the sacrifice if they end up with the same income as someone who hasn't saved?

Accusations will mount that the government is using automatic enrolment to steer low-earning workers into a pension scheme when they would have been wiser to stay out. Equivalent action in the private sector would amount to a huge mis-selling scandal. Will public concern about this shove pensions policy to the top of the government's in-tray?

How much people pay into private pensions will have obvious implications for retirement incomes. Under automatic enrolment, workers will have to contribute a minimum of 4% of their earnings between an upper and lower income band; employers at least 3%; and the government, instead of providing tax relief, 1%.

But for many people, 8% in all could be on the low side to secure an adequate retirement income. If you start in your 20s and contributions stay at 8% throughout your working life, then – along with the basic state pension – you *might* end up with nearly two-thirds of your pre-retirement income.[17]

But this would leave little room for things to go wrong – for your pension to be smaller than expected because of longer life expectancy, or for breaks in contribution for one reason or another.

What would happen if individuals temporarily opted out of an occupational scheme while they were saving to buy a house, or when they stopped work to start a family, or what if they took a 'pension holiday' to help their children repay their student loans? 'It's only a short break', the person might think, without realising that it could cut the value of their pension significantly.

What about employers? Might they increase their contributions? At present their payments to DC schemes are depressed, possibly because they have spent so much money propping up their final salary schemes. If the latter need becomes less urgent, they may be able to contribute more to DC pensions.

Or will the 3% minimum lower their expectations? 'Why should we pay in 6%, which is twice the legal minimum?'

And what if pensions continue not to be particularly valued by younger workers, as is often the case today? Might employers prefer to put the money into salaries or other benefits that employees value more highly?

In 2006 the government estimated that seven million people were not saving enough for their retirement.[18] If large numbers continue to under-save after 2012,

Employment rates for men and women of state pension age and above in the UK (men 65+, women 60+).

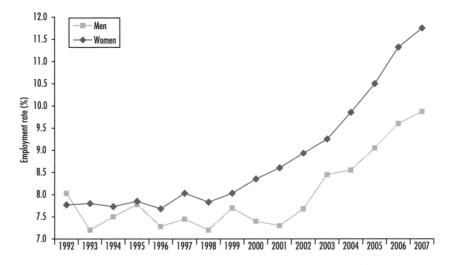

Source: ONS Labour Market Statistics – Integrated FR LFS TIME PERIODS, tables YBUQ, YBUR.
Note: Percentage is the average of quarterly figures.

government will have to look again at pensions policy. Would a further elevation of the retirement age, to give people more time to save, be an option?

Will individuals work beyond the retirement age? The normal retirement age is generally understood to be the age at which people can draw their occupational pension or the full basic State Pension.

The retirement age is set to go up:

- *The state pension age for women* will be gradually made equal to that of men (age 65) between 2010 and 2020.
- *The state pension age for both sexes* is then due to rise in stages to 68 by 2044, as we have seen. It may even have to rise to 69 or 70 to give people time to save enough for retirement.
- *The retirement age for many public servants* will almost certainly have to rise, too. Pension arrangements for the public sector are generous compared to private schemes. Most pensions are still based on final salary and are often paid at a younger age, encouraging earlier retirement. They are under-funded, which means that future taxpayers (most of whom are in the private sector) will have to pick up the tab for pensions due to today's public servants. The amounts are huge.[19] Taxpayers will ask, 'Why should we pay for their pensions, which are so much more generous than ours?' The government has taken some steps to limit the burden on future generations, but it is widely recognised that these steps are not enough.[20] To reduce its liabilities, sooner rather than later the government may have to push up the age at which public sector pensions are paid to existing workers – from 60 to 65 for civil servants, teachers and NHS employees.[21]

Growing numbers have already been working beyond their retirement age, though the trend has yet to take off. As the chart above shows, the employment rate for women aged 60 and above has risen from 7.8% in 1998 to 11.8% in 2007. For men aged 65 and over, the rate has increased from 7.3% in 2001 to 9.9% in 2007.

Despite the retirement age going up, will more people work beyond the age at which they are entitled to a full pension?

> 'Government will have to push up the age at which public sector pensions are paid'

Several factors will encourage later retirement.

- *Workers may need longer to save for a pension.* As we have seen, their expectations of retirement may require a larger income than in the past. Life expectancy may lengthen by more than anticipated. Individuals with private pensions may not have contributed enough.

- *The financial incentives are at last in place.* The basic state pension has been made more generous if you delay taking it. You can also draw an occupational pension while continuing to work (for the same employer). In addition, as has always been the case, you don't have to pay National Insurance after the state pension age (lifting your take-home pay by, say, almost 10%). It now pays to work beyond the retirement age. Other incentives include the option of working half-time while drawing your private pension, or postponing your state pension so that you get more per week when you finally take it. Your income after tax might not be far off what you earned full-time previously.

- *The default retirement age will be changed.* Under the current age discrimination laws, employers cannot require workers to retire before 65 unless a younger worker is 'objectively' needed to do the job. The government is to review these arrangements in 2011. Age Concern and others hope that the default age will be scrapped. But this would meet resistance from employers, who argue that it would be difficult to dismiss under-performing workers if there was no default age. However, it might be that if the default age were abolished, a nudge into retirement (or even dismissal) would be practical and legal if employers regularly conducted thorough employee appraisals. Might a future government abolish the retirement age partly to encourage such appraisals, leading to the better management of people? A compromise might be to raise the default age steadily over a number of years till it is too high to make much difference.

- *Skill shortages may intensify* as large numbers of baby boomers retire. Education employers, for example, are alarmed at the number of senior teachers who will leave the workforce in the next few years. Will there be enough replacements? Other professional and associate professional groups face similar problems. Recently, employers have recruited immigrants to fill some of their skill gaps. But this may be more difficult in future as public concerns – about over-crowding, for example – mount.

Will older workers be increasingly valued for their experience and maturity, and will employers give them incentives to stay on after their normal retirement age?

On the other hand, poor health could make later retirement difficult. Many workers will feel too tired and stressed to continue beyond their retirement age. Indeed, as global competition makes work ever more demanding, will a growing number of 'worn and torn' workers want to leave *before* their full pension is due?

Or will health and safety regulations tighten further, so that work becomes less stressful? Employers' legal responsibility for work-related stress has increased in recent years and this trend seems set to persist.

As now, decisions about retirement will be complicated. The table below shows how men in a higher social class live for longer than those in a lower one. The pattern for women is similar.

High-status workers tend to remain physically fitter towards the end of their working lives than people in lower-status jobs. So they are able to keep working for longer. But they usually also have larger earnings and bigger pensions, which can reduce their need to do so.

By contrast, workers on modest earnings may have a stronger financial need to stay in employment, yet be prevented by health reasons.

How these health and wealth considerations play out will do much to determine the number of people who work beyond their retirement age, and will of course vary from person to person.

Life expectancy (in years) at age 65 by social class – males

Social class	1972–76	1982–86	1992–96	2002–05	Gain, 1972 – 2005
I	14.0	15.5	17.0	18.3	4.3
II	13.3	14.5	15.7	18.0	4.7
IIIN	12.6	13.6	15.4	17.4	4.8
IIIM	12.2	13.1	14.3	16.3	4.1
IV	12.2	12.7	13.9	15.7	3.5
V	11.6	11.6	12.6	14.1	2.5

Source: 'Variations persist in life expectancy by social class', ONS Press Release, 24 October 2007.

Will work be more flexible for those approaching retirement? Flexible work would include the option of working part-time, perhaps four days a week initially and then half-time before you eventually retire. It might also include the opportunity to do a less-demanding job.

Either possibility would allow you to ease yourself into retirement gradually. Research repeatedly shows that older workers would welcome this degree of flexibility.

Phased retirement would create new opportunities for individuals to combine work, a greater degree of leisure, and family and community activities – in proportions that fit their circumstances. Making the transition to retirement gradually would be a lot less daunting for the many who view it as an approaching cliff edge.

Yet phased retirement schemes are not widespread – for several reasons:

- *They require management time to set up.* Jobs may have to be redesigned, for example. But management time is generally in short supply.
- *They could make skill shortages worse.* If a job is split in two to cater for an existing employee, another person may have to be recruited to fill the other half. In a tight labour market, someone with the appropriate skills may not be available.
- *Employers have not needed them.* In most cases, retiring workers have had relatively few skills, reflecting the low-skills tradition of Britain's economy. So retirement has not greatly increased skill shortages. Where a retirement would have created difficulties (normally at higher skill levels), employers have sometimes persuaded the individual to return, for instance as a consultant – in effect a form of phased retirement.

Will phased retirement become common in future? Much will depend on what balance is struck between employers' need for older workers and the willingness of these workers to stay in their jobs.

As far as the *employer* is concerned, on the plus side, older workers often have years behind them (the 'company memory') and tend to have high levels of tacit knowledge ('the way we do things round here'). Losing such employees can be a real blow.

On the other hand, as we have just noted, older workers usually have fewer qualifications than younger ones. Some cognitive functions also decline as you age. It can take longer to process visual information, for instance, and to learn new things. Employers may have an incentive to replace workers who are under-qualified or slowing down with younger ones.

From the *employees'* standpoint:

- *People on the highest incomes* will still be able to afford to retire on their due date, and will generally find some other form of part-time activity.
- *Workers on high, but not top, incomes* tend to be healthier than those on lower earnings and so better able to continue in employment. Growing numbers may want to keep working because they haven't saved enough for retirement.
- *Lower-paid workers* may also want to stay on to enhance their retirement incomes, but ill-health is more likely to prevent them from working – full-time, at least.

Put these different considerations together and you could have a situation where people with specialist skills – workers whom employers want to keep on – are both better-paid and (therefore) more healthy than most.

But their incomes may not be sufficiently high that they can afford to retire. Consequently, a number may want to remain in employment and will be healthy enough to do so. Their desire and ability to keep working would lessen the need for employers to bring in phased retirement as an inducement to stay on.

Where phased retirement might be developed first is among workers with key skills who are highly paid, who have made adequate savings for retirement and who don't have a strong desire to continue working. Employers may have to offer them phased retirement as an encouragement to stay on, at least part-time.

Might phased retirement evolve in three stages?

1. *The occasional part-time consultancy post* for a former employee, which already happens today.
2. *A handful of phased retirement schemes* designed for limited groups of older workers with specific skills.
3. *A growing demand for phased retirement* among other workers who like the look of these schemes. Might public demand eventually force government to make phased retirement a legal entitlement, and might this be introduced initially for older employees with caring responsibilities, as an extension of their current right to request flexible work?

---

1 Dominic Sandbrook, *Never Had It So Good: A History of Britain from Suez to the Beatles*, London: Little, Brown, 2005, p. 409.
2 Derek Wanless, *Securing our Future Health: Taking a Long-Term View: Interim Report*, London: HM Treasury, 2001, pp. 173–175.

3 For example, Nintendo has successfully appealed to the 65+ generation with games that track mental acuity and provide gentle, interactive brain and body exercise.

4 *Population Trends*, 90, 1997, table 13; *Population Trends*, 118, 2004, table 5.1. Life expectancy for women increased by three years from 1961 to 1981, and then by just over three-and-a-half years between 1981 and 2001.

5 'Mortality', *Analysis,* Issue 160, Hewitt Consulting, July 2007.

6 R. C. Willetts et al., 'Longevity in the 21st Century', paper presented to the Faculty of Actuaries, 15 March 2004, and to the Institute of Actuaries, 26 April 2004, pp. 21–38.

7 Quoted in 'Mortality', *Analysis*, Issue 160, Hewitt Consulting, July 2007.

8 Rising levels of childhood obesity may not be translated into higher levels of adult obesity, and even if they are they will not impact retired age groups within our next-20-years time frame.

9 TAEN (The Age and Employment Network) Newsletter, Spring 2008, p. 4.

10 This is also true of final salary schemes, except that the risk falls on the employer rather than the employee.

11 L. Horngren, 'Pension Reform: The Swedish Case', *Journal of Pension Management*, 7(2), 2001, p. 134.

12 In a 2005 survey of managers, just 35% thought that the average person would retire as early as age 65, but 80% thought that they personally would do so. *Tackling Age Discrimination in the Workplace: Creating a New Age for All*, London: CIPD, 2005, p. 18.

13 Total contributions to final salary schemes in 2006 were around 19% compared to 9% for DC schemes. *Security in Retirement: Towards a New Pensions System*, Cm 6841, London: DWP, 2006, p. 34. According to *The Economist* (14 June 2008), employers' payments into final salary schemes in October 2007 was 14.2% of payrolls, compared to 5.8% for DC schemes.

14 This seems highly likely. James Banks & Richard Blundell, 'Private Pension Arrangements and Retirement in Britain', *Fiscal Studies*, 26(1), 2005, pp. 48–49.

15 *Security in Retirement: Towards a New Pensions System,* Cm 6841, London: DWP, 2006, p. 33.

16 'PPI Projections of Future Eligibility for Means-Tested Benefits', December 2007, **http://www.pensionspolicyinstitute.org.uk**.

17 For example, *Financing Retirement*, an online source of advice, recommends that people in their 20s put aside 10% of their monthly income to get a pension two-thirds of their final salary. **http://www.financingretirement.co.uk** (accessed 2 July 2008).

18 *Security in Retirement: Towards a New Pensions System,* Cm 6841, London: DWP, 2006, p. 36.

19 In 2006, estimates of how big this liability was varied from the Treasury's £530 billion to an Institute of Economic Affairs figure of over £1,000 billion, equivalent to 80% of GDP. *The Times*, 22 September 2006.

20 Robert Chote et al (eds.), *The IFS Green Budget 2008*, London: IFS, 2008, p. 176.

21 The government has already done this for new entrants to public sector pension schemes.

WILL 'RETIREMENT' DISAPPEAR?
WHAT MIGHT BE THE IMPLICATIONS?

- People will keep working till they are older
- State pensions will be changed – again
- A new Lifelong Savings Account is needed
- Widespread pensioner poverty is a real risk
- Might retirement be abolished one day?

What is likely to happen over the next few decades? While experiences will vary, three developments are almost certain:

- people will continue to work till they are older;
- the state pension will come back onto the agenda;
- encouraging people to save will become a political issue once more.

Workers will stay in employment till they are older. This will apply less to people who were over 50 at the turn of the millennium and who are more likely to belong to final salary schemes.

Younger generations, however, are more likely to keep working.

- *Many will not have saved enough for retirement.* The income they need (in real terms) may well be higher than for age groups before them; life expectancy could lengthen faster than projected; and a significant minority may opt out of private pensions (or take lengthy breaks) when automatic enrolment is introduced in 2012.
- *Good incentives now exist to remain at work.* There are generous payments if you postpone your state pension, and it is now legally possible to draw an occupational pension and continue in work for the same employer.
- *The default retirement age is likely to be raised or abolished.* The law governing the dismissal of employees would then apply to workers aged 65 plus. Many workers will find it easier to stay on.
- *Labour market pressures will exist for certain skills.* Employers will want to retain older workers whose skills are in short supply.

Based on current trends, the number of people working beyond their retirement age is likely to be quite modest over the next decade or so, but could grow significantly thereafter.

In the immediate future, employers will be able to do quite a bit to encourage workers who would have retired in their late 50s or early 60s to stay on. For employers, keeping older workers will be more than just a matter of good HR practice. Tight labour markets for some skills will make it a commercial priority. Senior managers who have ignored the issue could end up in trouble with their Board – 'Why didn't you warn us about these shortages?'

Key issues for employers will include:

- *Recognising which skills will be least available,* and developing policies to retain older workers who have them.
- *Recognising what incentives will be needed* to retain employees with the required skills. Phased retirement may be attractive to people whose skills are in high demand but whose desire to stay on is limited.
- *Responding to the needs of workers they wish to keep.* This may include looking for ways to assist older workers whose sight is impaired, for example, and developing training packages to fit the learning requirements of older people.
- *Developing a friendly culture for older workers.* How many employers have developed a culture that honours experience, for instance?

Further changes to the state pension regime are likely. Planned reforms of state pensions and the Pension Credit will increase public spending by an estimated 1.5% of the country's national income between now and 2050-51. The increase will only begin after 2020, so when it comes the actual rise will be more than 1.5% (to make up for the smaller increase between now and 2020).[1]

> 'If government spends so much more on older people, will it be able to spend enough on younger age groups?'

Economic growth – which has been averaging between 2.5% and 2.75% a year – could make this extra spending possible without taxes having to be pushed up.

But government spending on the NHS is also expected to rise a lot faster than national income, certainly up to 2017-18 and probably beyond.[2] Healthcare costs tend to grow more rapidly than the economy.

If government were to spend so much more on pensions and health, which will benefit mainly retired people, there will be no room to increase spending in real terms on education, transport and other concerns of younger age groups – unless, of course, taxes go up. Will taxpayers stand for this? Easing the burden of state pensions on the taxpayer could become a priority.

In addition, as we discussed in 'What will shape the next 20 years?', the automatic enrolment of individuals into 'personal accounts' could run into difficulty. In particular, low earners might be better advised to pay off their existing debts and have their retirement incomes made up by the means-tested Pension Credit. Protests on behalf of low-paid workers are likely.

Might government respond by removing the requirement to be automatically enrolled for those workers who earn less than a certain amount? The trouble with that is more people would then be eligible for the Pension Credit, which would push up taxes. Would taxpayers meet these extra costs?

These are some really knotty questions that a future government will have to address.

The proposed 'personal accounts' pension scheme may not work as well as the government hopes. More people than expected could well opt out, while contributions may not be sufficient to provide the size of pension individuals will need.

The underlying approach is at odds with the fluid nature of modern society. Today's workers switch rapidly from task to task. Individuals use their mobile phones to change meeting arrangements at the last minute. People 'go with the flow'. They don't want to be boxed in.

Yet workers who have enrolled into personal accounts will be locked into a savings scheme for one purpose only – a pension. This will not suit their flexible lives. Younger people may feel that retirement is eons away, and that repaying their student loan and buying a home are more immediate priorities. They won't want to be tied down by a pension scheme.

A more flexible approach is likely to chime with the public mood. The Tomorrow Project has proposed a Lifelong Savings Account that would offer a different way of thinking about savings.[3]

A Lifelong Savings Account would bundle together various savings schemes that the government currently supports, such as pensions, Independent Savings Accounts (ISAs) and the Savings Gateway (designed to encourage lower earners to save). The Lifelong Account might also include the Child Trust Fund. Payments into the Account would start from birth.

It would be built around the entire life course rather than retirement alone. Individuals could save up to buy 'assets' that they required now and that would also boost incomes in old age. These assets might consist of:

> ■ *Learning* – students would buy a university course by paying the fees upfront. Acquiring skills would boost the person's earnings, enabling them to save more for retirement.
> ■ *Housing* – saving up for a deposit or paying off a mortgage. If people got on the housing ladder earlier and paid off their mortgage more quickly, they would be able to save more for a pension.
> ■ *A pension,* as now.

As people travelled through life, they could both put money into their savings 'rucksack' and draw money out. Individuals might carry this rucksack for the whole of their lives.

The Government intends that the Child Trust Fund will be converted into an ISA automatically when children reach 18 (though children will be free to withdraw the money). It would be only a small step to restrict withdrawals to funding education or paying for a deposit on a home – assets that would benefit the person later in life. Individuals could be given a 'rucksack' with some savings in it when they were born.

Employers and government would make contributions, as well as workers. The government's contribution would replace today's tax relief for pensions.

Contributions might be set at the levels proposed for personal accounts – 4% of a specified income band for employees, 3% for employers and 1% for the government. (A government contribution would be more visible to savers than tax relief, strengthening the incentive to save.)

Savers could choose from a wide range of private schemes, including an adapted version of the new personal accounts, but their savings would be channelled through a single designated bank account. The bank would inform the authorities how much has been saved, so that employers and government could calculate their contributions.

Individuals would receive an annual savings forecast, helping them to see what their current savings would be worth if they retired at a variety of ages. This would be a regular reminder to individuals to plan for retirement.

Together with the planned simplified forecasts for state pensions, these forecasts would be sent to everyone in the same week (though they might have been prepared earlier) to attract media attention and provoke public discussion.

This would bring savings to the forefront of people's minds at least once a year and help individuals become better informed.

Our proposal for a Lifelong Savings Account has a strong affinity with the KiwiSaver in New Zealand and is more ambitious than the Conservative Party's proposed Lifetime Savings Account.

> **'Pension forecasts would be sent to everyone in the same week to attract media attention and provoke public discussion'**

The KiwiSaver has influenced government thinking on personal accounts, but the government has rejected the New Zealand idea of letting people make withdrawals not only for pensions, but to help buy their first home or pay off their mortgage. This is a missed opportunity both to encourage savings among young adults and hasten the process of becoming mortgage-free.

If people had smaller mortgage payments in midlife, when they are more receptive to messages about saving for retirement, they would be able to pile up more for their old age. Entering retirement without a mortgage would also reduce their costs (allowing them to afford a smaller pension), while providing them with an asset – a fully-owned home – that they could convert into a source of income.

Might something akin to our proposed Lifelong Savings Account be introduced in the years ahead, not least to make saving more relevant to younger age groups who are frequently reluctant to put money aside?

Widespread pensioner poverty will be a real risk if no measures are taken to prevent it. Several developments could increase substantially the proportion of pensioners who are poor, particularly in the 2030s and beyond.

- Ideas about what is a reasonable standard of living in old age may change radically, as consumerist generations leave work with higher and higher expectations of their retirement. More people may be poor when measured against these rising expectations.
- Longer life expectancy may reduce the amount of pension paid to people in defined contributions schemes, and put pressure on government to limit increases in the state pension. More people would be receiving the pension – because they are living longer – than is currently anticipated.
- Despite the government's personal accounts scheme, individuals may still not save enough for their retirement (for the reasons we have discussed).
- Opportunities to work till you are older to boost your pension *could* be more limited than people expect. 'Worn and torn' workers could be forced

out of employment for health reasons. Since these workers are most likely to be on low earnings (because of the close relationship between health and wealth), their chances of escaping poverty in old age would be bleak.

There are of course ways that this scenario could be avoided – and we have discussed a number of them: by the second quarter of the century, a considerable number of people on middling incomes and above may well be working till their late 60s and early 70s; the pension age could be raised more quickly as life expectancy lengthens; a stronger savings culture might emerge if saving was made more attractive; retired people may use their homes to boost their retirement incomes.

This more optimistic future is far from certain, however. A number of new policies may have to be introduced to bring it about. Policy-makers need to face the very real risk that pensioner poverty could reach near-crisis proportions.

Might retirement itself be abolished one day? As noted in 'The story so far', 'abolishing' retirement is a strong way of saying that the present clean break between work and retirement needs to give way to a much more fluid transition.

Instead of people moving straight from work to retirement (which is equated with not working), they would have greater freedom to wind down their employment gradually and expand their leisure, community and family activities.

Retirement as we understand it today would give way to a phase of life in which individuals mixed employment, leisure and unpaid forms of work in a combination geared to their particular circumstances. People would continue in jobs till they were much older, but for shorter periods of the week.

Some older people on high incomes are able to do this today, but it is far from the norm. It could start to become more common, however, as phased retirement is introduced for specific groups of skilled workers.

The 'abolition of retirement' is unlikely in the next 20 years, but might foundations be laid for people to have a fundamentally different experience of retirement in the decades that follow?

---

1   Carl Emmerson, Matthew Wakefield & Gemma Tetlow, 'The Pensions White Paper: Who Wins and Who Loses?', *PMI News*, August 2006, The Pensions Management Institute.

2   Robert Chote et al (eds.), *The IFS Green Budget 2008*, London: IFS, 2008, pp. 137–140.

3   The proposal is discussed in more detail in Michael Moynagh & Richard Worsley, *The Opportunity of a Lifetime: Reshaping Retirement*, London: CIPD, 2004, pp. 112–121 and 132–135.

CHAPTER 8
WILL THE OLDEST OLD HAVE A BETTER LIFE?
THE STORY SO FAR

- Life has been lengthening at a faster pace
- Very old age is perhaps the most demanding phase of life
- Care for very old people has changed immensely
- The quality of life for the oldest old has improved considerably overall

Being very old is about a state of mind as much as age. Perceptions of ageing depend on where you stand. To a child, someone in their 50s can seem very old. Many people in their 80s, on the other hand, do not see themselves as old and resist the label.

There is a subjective and objective element to being very old (as with some of the other stages of life). It is partly a matter of how you feel. It is often associated with increasing dependence on others – due to growing frailty and disability.

At the same time, it is not unrelated to age. When you reach your late 80s and 90s, people tend to think you are among the 'oldest old', another term for this phase of life. For statistical purposes, we define the very old as people aged 85 and over.

Number (000s) and proportion of 85-year-olds and above in the UK population, 1951–2001

	1951	1961	1971	1981	1991	2001
85 & over	224	346	485	603	895	1,128
% of total population	0.4	0.7	0.9	1.1	1.6	1.9

Source: *The Annual Abstract of Statistics,* London: The Stationery Office, 2003, table 5.3.

The number of oldest old increased fivefold between 1951 and 2001. Over the same period, the age group climbed from 0.4% of the population to 1.9%. The most rapid growth was in the 1980s (see table above). In 2006, the total reached an estimated 1.24 million people, representing 2.1% of the population.[1]

Wales has the highest proportion of people aged 85 and over – 2.25% in 2006, which was significantly higher than the UK average. Northern Ireland has the lowest (see table below).

The increase in 85s-plus creates opportunities for business. Growing very old can be an unpleasant experience: friends die, you lose some of your physical and mental capacities, care services are not always up to scratch and you may dread ending up in a nursing home.

Business can do much to improve the quality of this stage of life. The pharmaceutical industry is developing treatments to delay mental and physical decline. Products are being developed to enhance independent living. New housing can be sensitive to the needs of the very old and providers of care can improve the quality of their services.

Companies can allow flexible working to help their older staff support an elderly relative. Might employers come to see this as part of their corporate responsibility?

Number (000s) and proportion of 85s and over in the four countries of the UK, 2006

Age	England	Wales	Scotland	N. Ireland	UK total
85–89	695	45	63	18	820
90 and over	360	22	32	8	423
Total, 85 and over	**1,055**	**67**	**95**	**26**	**1,243**
% of population	2,080	2,260	1,860	1,490	2,050

Source: *Population Trends*, 132, 2008, table 1.4.
Note: Figures have been rounded to the nearest thousand as per the source.

Life has been lengthening at a faster pace, which goes a long way to explaining the rise in the number of oldest old.[2] Over the two decades between 1961 and 1981, life expectancy at birth for men went up by nearly three years, whereas over the following two decades it jumped by almost five (see chart below).

Life expectancy at birth for women has accelerated more slowly – by three years between 1961 and 1981, and then by just over three-and-a-half years from 1981 to 2001.

However, life expectancy *at older ages* has increased more sharply. Whereas between 1961 and 2001 men's life expectancy at birth rose by 11.5%, life expectancy at age 60 leapt by 32% and at age 80 by 36.6%.

Across the same period, life expectancy for women at birth increased by 8.9%, at age 60 by 22.1%, but at age 80 by 38.1%. Life expectancy itself is lengthening with age.

Life expectancy at birth and at ages 60 and 80 (UK)

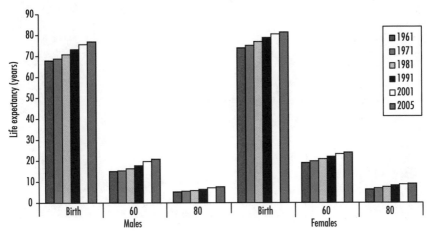

Source: *Population Trends*, 90, 1997, table 13; *Population Trends*, 132, 2008, table 5.1.

Longer life spans among the very old may reflect social improvements such as:

- *better housing* – fewer old people now die of hypothermia caused by poor heating or insulation in winter;
- *advances in medicine,* such as better treatments for cancer;
- *improvements in lifestyle,* such as the decline in smoking.

But these explanations are contentious; it is difficult to say how much weight should be attached to each one.

What is more certain is that greater increases in life expectancy for men in comparison to women are set to change the gender balance of the oldest old.

An enduring feature of this age group has been that many more women than men are contained in it, reflecting women's longer lives. But whilst men are living till they are older, the proportion of the 85-and-over age group who are female is projected to fall from nearly 70% in 2006 to just under 60% in 2026.[3] The stereotype that old age means old women will have to be revised.

Very old age is perhaps the most demanding phase of life. Individuals often experience declining health and greater loneliness, sometimes age discrimination and, not infrequently, poverty.

> **'Dementia more than doubles every five years – from 1% at age 65 to 21% at 85'**

Many of the oldest old suffer from chronic ill health. At age 85, on average 70% of the rest of an individual's life will be spent with difficulties in moving around and over 50% with hearing problems. The prevalence of dementia is thought to increase by more than double every five years from around 1% at age 65 to 21% at 85.

Women tend to report more chronic conditions and more disability than men. They also live a greater proportion of their life with multiple conditions. At 85, women will spend over 10% of their remaining life with a combination of cognitive impairment, physical illness and disability. The figure for men is 4%. The extra years for an 85-year-old women are not predominantly healthy years.[4]

Even so, Shakespeare's gloomy view of 'the last scene of all' – 'sans teeth, sans eyes, sans taste, sans everything' – is far from true of everyone. And where health does decline, many of the oldest old are able to put a positive gloss on it. A condition may not be seen as limiting once the person has adapted and become used to it.

Age discrimination in healthcare still exists. A large 1999 study found that people over 75 who were suspected of having cancer were less extensively investigated than younger patients. When diagnosed, they were offered fewer treatment options.

These discrepancies were not explained by the frailty of the older patients, nor by the presence of other complicating illnesses.[5]

Stereotypical attitudes are deeply entrenched. A report in 2000 by the King's Fund, a healthcare thinktank, stated that:

'Older people tend to be stereotyped as a homogeneous group characterised by passivity, failing physical and mental health and dependency. Such views are observable in society generally but also among healthcare and social care professionals, who may have more frequent contact with older users with complex health needs.'[6]

However, things may be getting better. In 2006, an official report found that explicit age discrimination had declined, except in mental health services. Other forms of ageism did remain, though, ranging from patronising attitudes to not taking the needs and aspirations of older people seriously.[7] Overt forms of ageism are in retreat, but more subtle forms persist.

> **'Overt forms of ageism are in retreat, but more subtle forms persist'**

The oldest old are at risk of loneliness, though the risk should not be exaggerated. Interviews with older people suggest that the essence of 'ageing well' is the ability to sustain relationships that meet the needs of intimacy, comfort, support, companionship and fun.

Interdependence among the very old is vital. This includes a determination 'not to be a burden' on others, an emphasis on helping one another and the importance of being part of a community, one where people look out for each other.[8]

The Economic and Social Research Council's 'Growing Older Programme' found little evidence that people aged 65 and older were lonelier than in the past, though the number declaring that they were never lonely had probably decreased.[9]

The experience of the very old tends to differ from that of younger retired people. Loss accelerates as close friends and relatives die or move away.

Unlike the over- 65s as a whole (for whom figures were stable), between the early 1980s and the early 2000s the number of 85s plus who were living on their own increased substantially – by over a third for men and one quarter for women.[10] But this was less than the growth of the oldest old population overall, which nearly doubled.

In one survey, 17% of the 75s and over classed themselves as very lonely and over 50% as moderately so. Sadly, nearly a fifth sometimes felt that life was not worth living. The figures would almost certainly have been higher for the 85-plus age group.[11]

For many, poverty is another feature of 'grand old age'. Though the proportion of pensioners living in poverty has fallen (see box below), almost two million pensioners are still living below the official breadline – a figure that suddenly rose by 300,000 in 2006-07.[12]

The very old tend to be in a worse position than younger pensioners. The over 85s, especially women, generally have lower incomes and are more likely to be poor.[13]

Pensioners in poverty

> *27% in 1997*
>
> *17% in 2004–05*

Source: 'Monitoring Poverty and Social Exclusion in the UK 2006', *Findings,* York: JRF, 2006.

Even if they escape 'official' poverty and have a little more to spend, the oldest old often struggle to make ends meet. Holidays, trips to the hairdresser or going out for a meal can be out of the question.

Survival strategies include heating one room rather than the whole house, buying food on the sell-by date and searching out second-hand clothes.

As people become frailer, their lives are increasingly confined to their immediate physical and social environments. The wealthier you are, the easier it is to jump these limitations. You can afford a taxi to visit a friend. You don't need to worry so much about the phone or the heating bills. You can pay to have your home cleaned or even redecorated.

But for poor people the opposite is the case: you're trapped within your surroundings. If your home is cold, there is no escape.

Very old people with health needs are increasingly cared for in the community. This reflects a long-term change in the philosophy and practice of looking after the very old, which has moved through four phases:

- *Doing to people* in the 1940s. This was as much about containment in large geriatric hospitals and mental health asylums as about care.
- *Doing for people,* not least with the advent of smaller residential care and nursing homes from the 1960s. The paternalistic aim was to look after people in a more cosy environment.
- *Doing with people,* a growing ambition from the 1970s. The 1988 Griffiths Report, whose recommendations were picked up in the 1990 NHS and

Community Care Act, stressed partnership with older people in decisions affecting their care.
- *Doing by people* – the current emphasis. The intention now is that individuals should have more choice and control. They should be in charge, receiving 'assistance' in making their decisions rather than simply 'care'. Instead of deciding in partnership with older people what form of care should be provided by the state, local authorities are starting to give individuals a personal budget – a sum of money they are entitled to – which they can spend on whatever care *they* think is most appropriate, from whatever source they like.[14]

Institutional care has declined. The NHS and Community Care Act transferred the public funding of residential and nursing home care to local authorities, and led to a shift in the balance of care. Fewer people are now cared for in homes and care is increasingly based within the community – the recipient's home or a local centre.

Between 1991 and 2001, at a time when the oldest old population was going up, the number of residential and nursing care homes in Great Britain shrank by 11%, though Scotland bucked the trend with an 11% increase.[15] Places in Britain's care homes have continued to drop since.[16]

The greatest fall has tended to be in deprived areas with poor levels of health – so much so that in 2001 many inner London boroughs were sending more residents to care homes outside their boundaries than inside. In such cases, friends and family (who often don't have transport) have to travel longer distances to visit.[17]

Community care has increased. During a survey week in September 2006, local authorities in England provided or purchased 3.7 million hours of home care services, mostly for people aged 65 and over. This was more than double the amount in 1992. The proportion of these hours provided by the private and voluntary sectors soared from 2% in 1992 to 75% in 2006.[18]

More hours of help are being provided – but to fewer households. Of households getting some kind of care, the proportion receiving intensive care (more than five hours of help and six or more visits a week) increased from 21% in 1995 to 50% in 2006. Councils have been focusing more heavily on people with the greatest needs, and providing less support to households where the need is least.[19]

> 'The proportion of care provided by the private and voluntary sectors soared from 2% in 1992 to 75% in 2006'

Informal care is extensive. In the 2001 Census, 5.9 million people (3.4 million women) reported that they cared for relatives, friends and neighbours. Many would have been caring for older people. 348,000 of these carers were aged 75 and over, nearly 8% of the age group.

Two-thirds of all carers were caring for fewer than 20 hours a week, while a fifth were involved for 50 hours or more. Among those caring for people aged 85 and older, about half devoted at least 50 hours a week. Caring tasks ranged from keeping an eye on the person to providing physical help.[20]

Overall, the quality of life for the oldest old has improved. Compared with previous generations, those aged 85 and older live in much warmer homes (90% had central heating in 2006 compared to 50% in the 1980s[21]), they are less likely to need residential care (which many would rather avoid), the care available is better and their standard of living is higher.[22]

> 'Some of the stereotypes of old age are being chipped away'

This has helped to bring about the beginnings of a more positive view of the final stage of life. Being very old in modern society has tended to be seen negatively: as 'God's waiting room', a period of dependence and a time when many 'lose their marbles'.

But as growing numbers in their late 80s and 90s live active and in many respects healthy lives, some of these stereotypes are being chipped away. Terms like 'OAP' (old-age pensioner), which conjure up a picture of old people with walking sticks, are used less frequently.

Increasingly, care professionals no longer treat the very old as passive recipients of help who must be told what they need. The emphasis now is on respecting the autonomy of the oldest old and helping them make informed decisions.

The experience of being very old is improving. Many elderly people live fulfilled lives. Where they become dependent on others, they have more choice, experience less overt discrimination in healthcare and are treated with greater respect.

Is it too much to hope that as society begins to see the oldest old with new eyes, we may be at the start of a complete transformation in people's views? In future, will we no longer perceive old age as an 'ante-chamber to death', but rather as something akin to the crown of life?

---

1 *Population Trends*, 132, 2008, table 1.4.

2 The other important reason was the relatively high number of births seen between the end of the nineteenth and the beginning of the twentieth centuries. Ercilia Dini & Shayla Goldring, 'Estimating the Changing Population of the "Oldest Old" ', *Population Trends*, 132, 2008, p. 10.

3 *The Annual Abstract of Statistics*, London: The Stationery Office, 2008, table 5.3.

4 Carol Jagger, 'Sans Everything? Quality of Life for the Oldest Old', in Ian Stewart & Romesh Vaitilingam (eds.), *Seven Ages of Man and Woman: A Look at Life in Britain in the Second Elizabethan Era*, Swindon: ESRC, 2004, pp. 33–34.

5 David G. Green & Benedict Irvine, 'Introduction', in John Grimley Evans et al., *They've Had a Good Innings*, London: Civitas, 2003, p. 5.

6 Cited by Sarah Harper, *Ageing Societies*, London: Hodder, 2006, p. 252.

7 *Living Well in Later Life: Summary Report*, London: Commission for Healthcare Audit, 2008, pp. 8–9.

8 Mary Godfrey, Jean Townsend & Tracy Denby, 'Building a Good Life for Older People in Local Communities', *Findings*, York: JRF, October 2004.

9 'Loneliness, Social Isolation and Living Alone in Later Life: Full Report', **http://www.regard.ac.uk**.

10 Cecilia Tomassini, 'The Oldest Old in Great Britain: Change over the Last 20 Years', *Population Trends*, 123, 2006, p. 34.

11 Carol Jagger, 'Sans Everything? Quality of Life for the Oldest Old', in Ian Stewart & Romesh Vaitilingam (eds.), *Seven Ages of Man and Woman: A Look at Life in Britain in the Second Elizabethan Era*, Swindon: ESRC, 2004, p. 35.

12 'Monitoring Poverty and Social Exclusion in the UK 2006', *Findings*, York: Joseph Rowntree Foundation, December 2006; *Households Below Average Income 1994/96 – 2006/07,* London: Department of Work & Pensions, 2008, table 6:6tr: Individuals below 60% median income before housing costs.

13 The median gross weekly income of women over 80 was £109 in 2001–02, compared with an average weekly income of £189 for pensioners aged 75 and over, and £203 for pensioners under 75. 'Why are older pensioners poorer?', *PPI Briefing Note Number 6*, London: Pensions Policy Institute, 2003.

14 Ray Jones, 'A Journey through the Years: Ageing and Social Care', *Ageing Horizons*, 6, 2007, p. 42.

15 Laura Banks et al., 'Changes in Communal Provision for Adult Social Care: 1991–2001', *Findings*, York: Joseph Rowntree Foundation, July 2006.

16 For example, an estimated 13,400 care home places were lost across Britain between January 2002 and April 2003, and 745 independent care homes were closed. *The Responsibility Gap*, London: Henley Centre/Salvation Army, 2004, p. 52.

17 Laura Banks et al., 'Changes in Communal Provision for Adult Social Care: 1991–2001', *Findings*, York: Joseph Rowntree Foundation, July 2006.

18 *Social Trends*, 33, 2003, p. 150; *Social Trends*, 38, 2008, p. 111.

19 *Social Trends*, 38, 2008, p. 111.

20 *Social Trends*, 34, 2004, p. 121.

21 Cecilia Tomassini, 'The Oldest Old in Great Britain: Change Over the Last 20 Years', *Population Trends*, 123, 2006, p. 35.

22 In 2006, registered residential services for older people were meeting 79% of National Minimum Standards, compared to 59% four years earlier. *The State of Social Care in England 2005–06*, London:CSCI, 2006, p. 41.

WILL THE OLDEST OLD HAVE A BETTER LIFE? WHAT WILL SHAPE THE NEXT 20 YEARS?

- The number of very old people will grow sharply
- Longer life spans will drive this growth
- These extra years of life could be reasonably healthy
- Qualify of life will improve in other ways
- How very old people are cared for will gradually change
- A crisis of long-term care is unlikely
- The story will be less rosy for those who are poor

The number of very old people will grow sharply, as shown in the table opposite. Among them will be a lot more 100-year-olds – up from 10,000 in 2006 to a projected 53,000 in 2030.[1] If the monarch was to send everyone a birthday card on their 100th birthday, as happens now, in 2030 Buckingham Palace would be sending out 145 cards a day.

Trends worth highlighting include:

- *The overall increase in the number of oldest old,* projected to grow from 2.1% of the population in 2006 to 3.4% in 2026 and 4.8% 10 years later.
- *The accelerating rate of growth.* From 2006 to 2016, the proportion of very old people in the population is expected to grow by 0.4%, over the following decade by 0.9% and then from 2026 to 2036 by 1.4%. It is projected to slow somewhat thereafter.
- *The faster growth in very old men* compared to women. In 2006, men comprised an estimated 30.5% of the 85s and over; this is projected to grow to 36.8% in 2016, 41.2% in 2026 and 42.4% in 2036. Men are expected to make ground rapidly on women between 2006 and 2016, but their sprint will tail off over the following two decades.

We cannot emphasise enough, however, that these projections are subject to an increasing margin for error the further into the future they go.

Projected size of the 85+ population in the UK, 2006–56

Year	Male (000s)	Male (% of all males)	Female (000s)	Female (% of all females)	Total (000s)	Total (% of all)
2006	379	1.3	864	2.8	**1,243**	**2.1**
2016	608	1.9	1,045	3.2	**1,653**	**2.5**
2026	965	2.8	1,378	3.9	**2,342**	**3.4**
2036	1,495	4.1	2,029	5.5	**3,524**	**4.8**
2056	2,305	5.9	3,035	7.7	**5,340**	**6.8**

Source: *National Population Projections: 2006-based,* London: ONS, 2008, pp. 64–65.

Longer life spans will propel the increase in the oldest old. In particular, more and more people born between 1925 and 1945 will join the ranks of the extreme elderly. Someone born in 1925 will be 85 in 2010; those born in 1945 will reach 85 in 2030. Over the next quarter-century, more and more of the very old will be people born between 1925 and 1945.

This is a group that has experienced bigger improvements in life expectancy over the past 40 years than previous generations and also, it seems, age groups coming up behind. The lengthening of life appears to have been due to:

- *changes in lifestyle:* notably, less smoking;
- *the availability of free healthcare,* following the launch of the NHS in 1948;
- *advances in medicine,* for example the use of antibiotics;
- *environmental improvements,* such as less air pollution following the 1956 Clean Air Act;
- *healthier diets* – did wartime rationing encourage youngsters to eat more vegetables and less starch?

Advances in life expectancy over such a long period should continue into the final years of life for those born from 1925 to 1945.

'It is likely that mortality improvements in the first decade of the twenty-first century will be greatest for people in their 60s and 70s. In the second decade, they will be greatest for people in their 70s and 80s, and so on.'[2]

Especially important will be rapid developments in medicine. For example, drugs will increasingly take into account genetic make-up, so that they can treat variations in the underlying pathology of a disease. Your version of prostate cancer may be different to someone else's.

A growing number of cancer specialists, though by no means all, believe that within the next couple of decades most cancers will become controllable diseases. You will still have cancer, but you will live with it for much longer.[3]

These and other advances could prolong life spans by more than expected. Professor David Blake, director of the Pensions Institute at Cass Business School, London, has noted that official figures have 'continually underestimated the longevity of elderly people.'[4] Will there be larger numbers of the extremely old than we expect?

These extra years of life could be reasonably healthy. Some think the oldest old are likely both to live longer and suffer fewer serious medical complaints than before. But experts are divided on the latter.

Some believe in what is called the 'compression of morbidity'. As lives get longer, ill-health (morbidity), including minor complaints, will be compressed into a shorter proportion of the life span. Ill-health will be experienced later and, relatively speaking, for less of an individual's life than before. The same medical and other advances that extend life will reduce the amount of disease an individual experiences during those extra years of life.

Some UK research supports this. While life expectancy was lengthening, the proportion of 85s and older who were unable to walk outdoors on their own fell from 48% in 1980 to 41% in 2001. The proportion unable to walk up and down steps on their own also dipped: from 31% to 24%.[5]

A number of US studies have found that an increasing percentage of the over-65s are free from any disability and a decreasing proportion suffer from immobility. According to one source:

'The present data indicate that senior mortality rates are declining by about 1% per year and disability is declining by about 2%.'[6]

At the other extreme are the pessimists. They fear an 'expansion of morbidity'. Lives will be longer, but the extra years will contain more frailty, ill-health and disability. The factors driving longer life expectancy will not deliver greater health. Your cancer may be controlled, but that won't stop you losing your sight. The rising incidence of dementia as people age is a particular concern.

This idea has been dubbed the 'survival of the unfittest'.[7] It seems to be supported by surveys of how individuals rate their own health. Publishing their findings in 2004, government statisticians declared: 'Living longer; more years in poor health'. Poor health included minor ailments.

Between 1981 and 2001, years of poor health as a proportion of men's total average life span rose from 9.2% to 11.5%. For women, the figures moved from 13.2% to 14.4%. Though people were living for longer, a larger portion of their lives was being spent in ill-health – the so-called 'failure of success'.

But as the table below shows, the trend has now gone into reverse. By 2004 there had been a very slight reduction in the proportion of men's lives that were unhealthy. The trend for women was more marked, rectifying completely the decline between 1981 and 2001. Might this be further support for the 'compression of morbidity' argument?[8]

Years of poor health as a proportion (%) of life expectancy at birth

	1981	2001	2004
Men	9.2	11.5	11.4
Women	13.2	14.4	13.2

Source: 'Health Expectancy: Living Longer, More Years in Poor Health'; 'Life Expectancy (LE), Healthy Life Expectancy (HLE) and Disability-Free Life Expectancy (DFLE) at Birth and Age 65: By Country and Sex, 2004', ONS, http://www.statistics.gov.uk.

Note: 'Poor health' is derived from figures for 'healthy life expectancy', which are based on answers to the General Household Survey question: 'Over the last 12 months would you say your health has on the whole been good, fairly good or not so good?'

A compromise view says the story is 'both-and'. Morbidity will both be compressed and expand! Severe disorders will decline, but less serious ailments will become more common.

Medical advances, for example, will both prolong life and lessen the worst forms of ill-health. Resources will be concentrated on tackling the severest conditions. There will be new treatments for diseases like Alzheimer's.

But less troubling complaints will become more widespread. To-be-expected wear and tear, such as back pain, will increase as the body ages.

The 2001 Wanless Review of Britain's long-term health needs found evidence of this. Levels of very serious ill-health were falling, but minor problems were on the up.[9] If these trends continue, the oldest old will be healthier overall, but will have more minor complaints.

We should be cautious, however. The evidence is not firm and more research is needed to form a definite view.[10] The balance of evidence supports a relatively optimistic stance, but we can't be sure.

Quality of life will improve in other ways. The oldest old will not only live longer and a little more healthily; they will also have higher incomes than previous generations, be less lonely and be treated with greater respect.

The very old will be financially more fortunate. The over-85s will still have higher rates of poverty compared to others who are retired, and they won't be as well off as their children, but they will be in a better position than their parents. In particular:

- *They will share the country's rising prosperity.* From 2012, the government plans to increase the basic State Pension each year in line with earnings rather than prices (which have determined state pension levels since 1981). Because earnings go up faster than prices, elderly people who rely heavily on the state pension will benefit significantly. For the first time in 30 years, this part of their income will keep pace with the growing prosperity of the working population.

- *More of them will have a private pension.* This will be especially true of people who turn 85 in the 2020s. An 85-year-old man in 2020, for example, will probably have retired at age 65 in 2000. He could well have had 20 years in the State Earnings-Related Pension Scheme, and many of those years would have been when the scheme was most generous. Or he might have spent much of his life in a final salary, and so relatively ample, occupational scheme.

- *More of them will own their own homes.* Among those who are now in their mid 80s and older, 61% are owner-occupiers. This will leap to 73% for those who will be 85 to 89 in the early 2020s.[11] More of the very old will be able to boost their incomes, if they want to, by borrowing against the value of their homes. They will be able to use the extra income to fund a higher standard of care if they need it.

- *They will benefit from the rising prosperity of their children.* A 2006 study found that nearly half the pensioners interviewed received some help, mainly financial, from family and friends. Most often this took the form of gifts of electrical items, and also involved practical help such as with decorating.[12] As the economy grows and the children of the 85-plus group become better off, the financial value of such gifts will increase.

Very old people will also be less lonely. This may come as a surprise to those who expect more and more of the extreme elderly to live alone, with family scattered far and wide, and with an increasing sense of loss as relatives and friends pass away.

This has indeed been true for a good many in their final years, at least till recently. More 'oldest old' people have been living on their own. Take women aged 85 and over living in a household with other generations. The proportion fell from 42% in 1971 to 13% in 2001.[13']

Proportion (%) of people aged 75+ in England and Wales who are projected to be married, 2003–2031

Year	Men	Women
2003	62.4	26.2
2011	63.0	30.4
2021	63.0	36.1
2031	59.9	37.0

Source: 'Marital Projections for England and Wales: 2003-Based Principal Projections', Government Actuary's Department, http://www.gad.gov.uk.

Over the next 20 years, however, some important trends will reduce loneliness.

■ *A higher proportion of very old women will be married* (see table above). This is partly because more men will live beyond 85, as we have seen. But it will also be because marriages peaked in the early 1960s.[14] During this nuptial boom, women who'll become 85 in the 2020s were in their prime marrying years. A 'typical' woman reaching 85 in 2024, for example, could well have tied the knot at age 23 in 1962.

■ *More of them will have children.* Heavy losses of men in the First World War left many women childless. The proportion of such women later declined. This means that compared to any previous generation in Britain (and perhaps future ones), over the next 25 years there will be more women aged 80 plus with at least one living child. The proportion will increase from two-thirds to three-quarters. Among generations born since 1945, however, the percentage of childless women has gone up once again. So the proportion of very old women with children will then tail away in the following decades, as generations born since 1945 reach their 80s.[15]

■ *Technology will improve communications.* In particular, wall-mounted flatscreen TVs will continue to fall in price. Screens will get larger, and teleconferencing will allow tiny video cameras to shoot live pictures from one sitting room to another via the Internet. In time, a scattered family might agree to have breakfast 'together' each Saturday and catch up on one another's news. Elderly friends may leave their screens and cameras on, so that they are present with each other throughout the day, even though their sitting rooms are far apart. Experience of communication technologies to date suggests that these virtual meetings won't reduce face-to-face contact – quite the reverse. Being in touch electronically may encourage *more* visits. Instead of elderly relatives being 'out of sight, out of mind', online visual encounters may focus the mind: 'we really ought to visit my mum, you know.'

Might loneliness, a scourge of old age, become a thing of the past? *Stereotypical views of the very old will decline.* Age discrimination, whether overt or implicit, will continue to be challenged. Representatives of older people, such as Age Concern, will keep up the pressure. They will be supported by those working with the very old, whose professional values will include a stronger stand against all types of age discrimination.

Might baby boomers begin to challenge old-fashioned views about the final years of life? Many will have parents who are over 85 and they will often play a part in the decisions their parents make. Their expectations, which will often differ from those of the very old, will influence how their parents are treated.

Baby boomers have spent their lives championing the rights of women, ethnic minorities and gay people. As they care for their elderly parents, they will resist age discrimination when they come across it.

Their lives have also been shaped by the consumer society, and more recently by the 'experience economy' in which experiences are sold – an entertainment experience, the experience of eating out or the customer experience. 'Will the experience be good enough?' boomers will wonder, as they help their elderly relatives sort out professional care.

> 'Baby boomers will influence the quality of what is on offer to the oldest old'

At the back of their minds, of course, will be an awareness that they too will one day grow old. When they go with their parents to look at the possibility of sheltered accommodation, they will perhaps be asking themselves, 'Could *I* put up with that?'

In these different ways, baby boomers will influence the quality of what is on offer to the oldest old. Standards will go up – from how a very old person is treated in a hotel to what is available in a nursing care home.

How very old people are cared for will gradually change. As we saw in 'The story so far', developments over the past 25 years have included more care in the community, a big shift from public to private residential homes and, more recently, the introduction of personal budgets for recipients of state-funded 'personal' care. What will change in future?

The oldest old will spend longer in their own homes, which will cut the demand for residential care. Reasons for this will include:

- *Healthier ageing* – if people live for longer with more minor ailments but fewer severe conditions, independent living at home will be easier.
- *More married couples* – the increase in married couples among the elderly will mean that more frail old people will be cared for by a partner. Women will benefit most. As the table on p. 203 suggests, the proportion whose husbands are still alive will rise significantly.
- *More oldest old people with children*, as we have seen. Contrary to what some think, many of these children will be within easy travelling distance of their parents. In 2001, just over half the adult population living separately from their parents saw their mothers weekly. The figure had remained stable since 1995.[16]

Of course, quite a few adult children have jobs which may affect their availability to care for an older person. In 2004–05, nearly a third of people providing informal care, mostly (but not exclusively) to the elderly, were in full-time employment.[17] As the state pension age for women rises between 2010 and 2020, the number of carers at work will grow. In 2020, for example, a woman whose mother was aged 89 and gave birth to her at age 25 would be 64 years old. She would have to work another year before getting the state pension.

Does this mean that fewer children will be free to care for their elderly parents? This seems unlikely. Workers with dependent relatives are already entitled to request flexible work to care for them. Employers are not obliged to respond positively. But as they have done with parents wanting to care for young children, most will probably grant these requests. More of our oldest old than in the past will be cared for by their children.

- *Advances in technology*. Textiles with embedded sensors to monitor heart rate are currently being trialled. So, too, are nurse-robots that rely on sensors scattered around your home to learn your habits, walk you round the room, remind you to take your medicines and compensate for the abilities lost in very old age.[18] Many other developments are in the pipeline.[19] Though robotics has promised more than it has delivered so far, real advances are being made. As devices are adapted to caring roles and production costs fall (in China, for example), robots will provide more and more help to people with limited mobility. Pointers to the future are today's robotic lawnmowers and vacuum cleaners that train themselves and operate without human assistance.

New forms of care will spread. Firstly, care will be more personalised. State-funded personal budgets, allowing those elderly people with disabilities to buy nursing and 'personal' care from any source, are being introduced. The government plans to also pilot the use of personal budgets for other forms of health care.[20]

In time, a growing number of the oldest old may be given a pot of money to cover *all* aspects of treatment for their condition. They will take their custom wherever they choose. As they do so, they (and the relatives who help them) will increasingly behave as consumers. Professionals will have to respond.

> 'Services for older residents could be bundled together and sold as a package'

But choice is not always pleasant. You can be confused by the options and anxious you'll make the wrong choice. Those who assess whether you are entitled to a personal budget may increasingly be called upon to advise how the money should be spent. Will they have the time and the knowledge to do this? Or will a new breed of care adviser emerge?

Secondly, services for older residents could be bundled together and sold as a package. In the US, real estate brokers have begun not only to sell houses, but also to assemble a network of pre-screened, dependable local suppliers of a wide range of homeowners' needs. These are offered at preferred prices. Homeowners pay the agency to join the network, and then buy the services direct from the supplier.[21]

Will packages of gardening, cleaning, pre-cooked meals, various forms of personal care and other services become increasingly available to the oldest old? Their ballooning numbers may establish a viable market in some areas. Private care agencies could create these bundles according to their clients' needs.

Thirdly, new forms of community for the oldest old may be developed. For instance, the Joseph Rowntree Foundation is pioneering a continuing-care retirement community outside York.[22] Within the garden village of New Earswick are 152 bungalows for elderly people.

The concentration of older people there makes it economic to pool risk and provide care that is both affordable and tailored to individuals' needs. Residents have the option of paying a service charge that covers all the nursing care they will need. It can be met from a loan against the bungalow which is repaid from the individual's estate.[23].

In future, will continuing-care retirement communities be scattered throughout a neighbourhood rather than being on a dedicated site? Where a growing number of older people creates a critical mass, these communities might form without individuals having to move home.

> **'New forms of community may be developed for the oldest old'**

Care agencies could develop bundles of services, including personal and nursing care, for elderly people who were scattered across the area. A fixed charge, also covering any nursing care required, might be covered by a loan as in the Joseph Rowntree scheme, to be repaid from the individual's estate when their home is sold.

This would help the oldest old to stay longer in their homes and remain part of their local communities. It would have some of the advantages of sheltered accommodation, but without the disadvantage of having to move. Retired people might start settling in areas where these schemes exist.

Will there be a crisis of long-term care? Alarm bells have sounded. Many experts fear there will be a growing 'care gap' between the care individuals need and what the state is willing to pay for. In 2008, the government launched an enquiry to examine this issue in England.

At present, in most of the UK the government pays the costs of nursing care if you enter a residential home but not the costs of personal care, unless you are poor. In Scotland, the government foots the whole bill, but doubts have been raised about whether this will be affordable in the long run.

Outside Scotland individuals resent contributing to their care costs, which can be very high. Some people are taken by surprise – the NHS is free, so they expect long-term care to be free, too. Paying for care reduces the nest egg they may have built up to leave to their children when they die. It can feel as if they are being penalised for having saved.

The costs of long-term care should be manageable for a while – perhaps over the next 20 years – even though the number of oldest old is going up.

- *Serious ill-health may not rise as fast as longevity.* We have seen that as life expectancy lengthens, years spent with severe conditions could well decline as a proportion of individuals' lives, while minor ailments increase. Demand for primary care would grow faster than for residential care.
- *People will be able to live longer in their own homes.* A higher proportion of very old people than in the past will have a spouse or a child to look after them, while advances in technology will provide further support.
- *Costs of care can be reasonably contained.* Staff account for 85% of the costs of residential care.[24] So long as adequate labour is available, these staff costs can be expected to climb at roughly the same rate as average earnings in the wider economy. If shortages emerge, immigration may well come to the rescue. Will robotics also play a significant role as time goes by?
- *The amount paid by the individual can be made more acceptable.*[25] For example, using 2005 figures, government could double the threshold to £42,000 before individuals pay for 'personal' care themselves. The cost to taxpayers would be a manageable £250–300 million a year. This would allow someone to stay in a residential home for approaching two years in some parts of the country before having to pay for (non-nursing) costs. If they sold their house to meet costs thereafter, they would still be left with a sizeable sum to pass on to their children. Might the sting be taken out of existing arrangements?

Will the problem be more acute by the mid twenty-first century? The oldest old population will be growing at a faster rate from the mid 2020s. Less support will be available from spouses because of the increase in divorce among baby boomers, while the decline in the birth rate will mean that fewer children will be able to provide care.

On the other hand, science and technology will have advanced phenomenally. Medical developments may reduce the amount of serious disease experienced by the very old, while robotics and other technologies could make independent living much easier.

The future is highly uncertain. So how will government respond? Funding long-term care by raising taxes or introducing compulsory insurance, as some have suggested, would almost certainly be a vote-loser.

Younger people would be paying for a benefit they would not see for years, and might not even need at all. 'I'd rather have the money now', most taxpayers are likely to think.[26] Will the government make some small adjustments but leave the basic system unchanged?

The story for poor people will be different from the experience of those who are better off, as in other stages of life.

Fewer poor people will reach age 85. In 2002–05, a 65-year-old in the lowest social class could expect to live till 79, whereas someone in the highest class could look forward to being alive until 83.[27] The elderly in poor areas will, as now, have worse health than richer people, since poor health is closely associated with poverty.

Their incomes will also be lower, of course, which will prevent them topping up state-funded care if it is inadequate. They will be less able to afford technologies that will support independent living. Their marriage partner will be more likely to have died, which will add to the difficulty of staying in their own home in old age. Life will be tougher all round.

---

1 *National Population Projections: 2006-based*, London: ONS, 2008, pp. 64–65.

2 R.C. Willetts et al., 'Longevity in the Twenty-First Century', paper presented to the Faculty of Actuaries, 15 March 2004, and to the Institute of Actuaries, 26 April 2004, p. 72.

3 For example, at a National Cancer Prevention Conference in London on 17 November 2005, Prof. Karol Sikora, Professor of Cancer Medicine and Honorary Consultant Oncologist at Imperial College School of Medicine, Hammersmith Hospital, claimed that by 2025 cancer could be 'under control', rather like diabetes. Over 40 drugs for highly specific cases of cancer are likely to be licensed in the US over the next five to 10 years. See **http://www.canceractive.com**.

4 *The Times*, 26 November 2007.

5 *Pensions: Challenges and Choices: The First Report of the Pensions Commission*, London: The Stationery Office, 2004, p. 31.

6 James F. Fries, 'Reducing Disability in Older Age', *Journal of the American Medical Association*, 288(24), 2002, p. 3164.

7 Christina Victor, 'Will Our Old Age Be Healthier?', in John A. Vincent, Chris R. Phillipson & Murna Downs, *The Futures of Old Age*, London: Sage, 2006, pp. 139–140.

8 There is a 'high overall correlation' between 'healthy life expectancy' based on respondents' perceptions of their health, and other measurements of morbidity. So changing expectations of health are unlikely to explain the new trend between 2001 and 2004. See Madhavi Bajekal et al., 'Healthy Life Expectancy at Health Authority Level: Comparing Estimates from the General Household Survey and the Health Survey for England', *Health Statistics Quarterly*, 16, 2002, pp. 25–35.

9 Derek Wanless, *Securing our Future Health: Taking a Long-Term View: Interim Report*, London: HM Treasury, 2001, p. 142.

10 Derek Wanless, *Securing our Future Health: Taking a Long-Term View: Interim Report*, London: HM Treasury, 2001, pp. 139–142; *Pensions: Challenges and Choices: The First Report of the Pensions Commission*, London: The Stationery Office, 2004, pp. 28–32.

11 NOP, 'Financial Research Survey 2000' in *Impact of an Ageing Population for the FSA*, London: FSA, 2002, p. 14.

12 Nicola Dominy & Elaine Kempson, *Understanding Older People's Experiences of Poverty and Material Deprivation*, London: DWP, 2006, p. 5.

13 'Demographic Aspects of Population Ageing', in 'ESRC Seminar Series: Mapping the Policy Landscape', ESRC, 2007, p. 12.

14 Mike Murphy & Pekka Martikainen, 'Demand for Long-Term Residential Care and Acute Health Care By Older People in the Context of Ageing Populations: A General Overview of Drivers for Care and a Case-Study of Finland with Particular Emphasis on Age and Proximity to Death', paper prepared for workshop: Ageing, Care Need and Quality of Life, Rostock, 30 January-1 February 2008, 21 May 2008 version, p. 5.

15 Emily Grundy, 'Ageing and Longevity: Too Much of a Good Thing?', PowerPoint presentation kindly made available to the authors in June 2008.

16 Alison Park and Ceridwen Roberts, 'The Ties That Bind', in Alison Park et al (eds.), *British Social Attitudes: The 19th Report*, London: Sage, 2002, p. 192.

17 *Social Trends*, 37, 2007, p. 105.

18 *The Times*, 15 June 2004.

19 See, for example, *Media Laboratory: Projects*, Massachusetts Institute of Technology, April 2008, pp. 5-8, 31-2, 40, **http://www.media.mit.edu**.

20 The government's commitment to preventive care was reaffirmed in *High Quality Care for All: NHS Next Stage Review: Final Report*, Cm 7432, London: The Stationery Office, 2008, p. 42.

21 Shoshana Zuboff & James Maxmin, *The Support Economy*, London: Allen Lane, 2003, pp. 160-161.

22 For more on continuing-care retirement communities, see 'Planning for Continuing-Care Retirement Communities', *Findings*, York: Joseph Rowntree Foundation, April 2006.

23 **http://www.jrf.org.uk**.

24 Raphael Wittenberg et al., 'Future Demand for Long-Term Care, 2002 to 2041: Projections of Demand for Long-Term Care for Older People in England', PSSRU Discussion Paper 2330, March 2006, p. 22.

25 For a fuller discussion of incremental measures that could be adopted, see Donald Hirsch, *Facing the Cost of Long-Term Care: Towards a Sustainable Funding System*, York: Joseph Rowntree Foundation, 2005.

26 The main options for funding long-term care in England are reviewed by Derek Wanless, *Securing Good Care for Older People*, London: Kings Fund, 2006, pp. 221-246.

27 'Variations persist in life expectancy by social class', ONS Press Release, 24 October 2007.

WILL THE OLDEST OLD HAVE A BETTER LIFE?
WHAT MIGHT BE THE IMPLICATIONS?

- Life will get better for the oldest old
- There will be two particular challenges
- The oldest old will be a huge market for business
- Tomorrow's oldest old will be a 'bridge generation'
- How will the oldest old be viewed?

Life will get better for the oldest old over the next 20 years, especially those with middle or high incomes.

- *Their life spans will be longer.* Indeed, life expectancy may lengthen by more than the government expects.
- *Most of the extra years will be reasonably healthy,* with some increase likely in minor ailments but a decrease in severe disorders (including dementia as brain sciences advance).
- *Quality of life will improve.* Very old people will generally have higher incomes, be less lonely and be treated with greater respect.
- *New forms of care will spread,* allowing the elderly to live independently for longer.
- *A crisis of care is unlikely* over the next quarter of a century, though the outlook beyond is uncertain.

But there will be two challenges that somewhat cloud this good-news story. *The rising costs of healthcare will be the first.* Individuals tend to demand more health services the older they get. So growing numbers of people aged 85 and over will ratchet up pressures on the NHS.

If minor conditions increase faster than serious ones, there will be increasing demands on GPs and other forms of primary care. To reduce serious ill-health, more preventative medicine will also be needed.[1] Early screening may be required to control some cancers, for example.

The 2002 Wanless Final Report reckoned that if the NHS were to have a reasonable chance of meeting future health needs, government health spending would have to rise faster than economic growth until at least 2017–18, and even – unless the report's most optimistic assumptions were met – till 2022–23.[2]

To make room for this, either expenditure in other areas, such as infrastructure, will have to be squeezed or else the tax burden will have to grow. Might the UK become less friendly for business?

Secondly, the government will face a clash of priorities – between persuading more older workers to stay in employment and encouraging families to keep caring for the oldest old.

Caregivers are often adult children who are still at work, not infrequently in full-time jobs. The numbers in this position are set to climb when the state pension age for women goes up after 2010. As well as this, the government will encourage people to keep working till their pension age and even beyond, so that there will be more workers to support those who have retired.

> **'Can raising employment be squared with boosting family care?**

Yet someone in full-time work will have less time to care for a dependent elderly relative. If more people keep working, more care may have to be provided by the state. The government, needless to say, is eager to avoid this: a shift from family to state care would put pressure on taxes.

Can raising employment be squared with boosting family care? Might business be caught in the middle as government seeks to balance the two?

For example, might the government strengthen the right of older employees to request flexible work in order to look after an ageing relative? With tougher laws, employers might be required to grant such a request. If this happened, would employers find older workers a less attractive proposition?

The oldest old will be a huge market for business. There will be more of them and they will have more money to spend than previous generations. In particular, the expansion of the 'health economy', which will be a major trend over the next quarter of a century, will focus on the heaviest users of care – the very old.

Opportunities will grow for the following types of company:

- *Those companies traditionally part of the health sector* – from pharmaceutical firms to providers of residential care. New openings will emerge within the NHS, as the government (at least in England) moves toward greater reliance on private provision.
- *Small players in healthcare at the moment*, such as the manufacturers and suppliers of devices to assist independent living. Innovations over the next two decades could make these companies a major force.

■ *Businesses not currently in health*, but who find this sector an increasing part of their activities. For instance, in neighbourhoods where there is a critical mass of elderly people, why shouldn't Sainsbury's Local or Tesco Express develop bundles of services for the housebound – from gardening to home-delivered groceries, or even forms of care?

With health tourism just beginning, a travel company might partner healthcare providers to offer hip operations in South Africa, for example, where patients could recuperate in the sun. The package could be combined with aftercare back in England. Might many more elderly people be able to afford this if personal budgets were extended to all forms of healthcare?

Highly significant could be what happens to the market for financial products geared towards the oldest old, such as equity release schemes that free up capital in a person's home.

A major expansion of equity release would cut a big hole in the next generation's inheritance. Purchasing power would shift from children to their parents. Might the 'oldest old' market become larger than expected?

What will the oldest old value? Most of those who reach 85 over the next two decades will have grown up under the Poor Law, the depression of the 1930s, and rationing during and after the Second World War. Their experiences will have been very different to someone born in 1950 (who will be 85 in 2035).

The younger person will have been a child in the Macmillan 'never had it so good' era, a teenager in the 1960s freedom decade and an adult at the peak of consumerism, all within the framework of the post-war Welfare State. Will the very old, as some think, be more undemanding and grateful than the generation coming up behind?[3]

It would be a mistake to push this contrast too far. The 85s-plus will have spent over half their lives within the consumer society. Values pioneered by baby boomers in the 1960s, such as greater tolerance and anti-discrimination, will have floated upwards to the older age group. Consumerist children will help their elderly parents in some of their purchasing decisions.

Tomorrow's very old people will be a 'bridge generation' between today's oldest old, many of whom have passively accepted what they have been offered, and baby boomers who – as they turn 85 from 2030 on – will be more demanding and less easily satisfied.

This will affect how brands speak to the very old. Marketers will be addressing an age group who by and large will see their children regularly, will increasingly

> 'The very old will have some values formed by austerity and others by affluence'

contact them online and in time by video conference, and will be heavily influenced by their views. Brands will need to connect with a subtle blend of values, some formed by austerity and others by affluence.

How will the oldest old be viewed? Today's negative view of ageing has developed partly because some very old people *have* often been poor, suffered considerably, looked 'worn and torn' and lost much of their dignity.

This picture will not disappear over the next 20 years, but it will continue to be painted over. Many of the very old will be less poor compared with the rest of the population, new drugs will ease their suffering, new lines in clothing and cosmetics will improve their appearance and personalised services will treat them with greater respect.

We shall be on the way to a very different experience of later life. By the middle of the century, new drugs and greater access to plastic surgery will have dramatically improved how the over-85s look. The genetics revolution will have spawned therapies that massively reduce suffering in very old age.

Life expectancy will have lengthened significantly by this point. This is a controversial area – at one extreme is the Cambridge University geneticist Aubrey de Grey, who in all seriousness has suggested that the first person to live till they are 1,000 years old (yes, 1,000!) may be 60 already.[4]

He argues that if ageing humans can be patched up for up to 30 years now, at the current increasing rate of advance science will develop incredibly quickly to make further repairs yet more effective. Constantly repairing your body could postpone death almost indefinitely!

> 'It has been suggested that the first person to live till they are 1,000 years old may be 60 already

The great majority of experts strongly disagree. They doubt that the body will be as easily repaired as de Grey thinks. There may be a biological ceiling to how long you can live. Many hoped-for breakthroughs could prove disappointing and have unexpected side effects. It can take a long time to develop, test and market new treatments.

Even so, may we be on the way to a very different experience of extreme old age? Will being very old start later in life? Will our longer lives also be far more healthy as serious conditions are much better controlled and the treatment of minor ailments greatly improves?

When you do become seriously ill, will care be of a higher standard and enable you to remain living at home for longer? Will the process of dying be managed with greater dignity and with more effective pain relief?

These are long-term trends, whose beginnings can be observed today. Will they bring a revolution in how old age is viewed? Instead of being seen as decline, will retirement be regarded as a golden age for most people, with a concluding phase that contains far less to fear? If this revolution is going to occur, the next two decades could prepare the ground for it.

1 The government's commitment to preventive care was reaffirmed in *High Quality Care for All: NHS Next Stage Review: Final Report*, Cm 7432, London: The Stationery Office, 2008, pp. 33–38.

2 Derek Wanless, *Securing our Future Health: Taking a Long-Term View: Final Report*, London: HM Treasury, 2002, pp. 75–95.

3 For example, Ray Jones, 'A Journey through the Years: Ageing and Social Care', *Ageing Horizons*, 6, 2007, p. 43.

4 Quoted by Paul Miller & James Wilsdon, 'The Man Who Wants to Live Forever', in Paul Miller & James Wilsdon (eds.), *Better Humans? The Politics of Human Enhancement and Life Expectancy*, London: Demos, 2006, pp. 51–52.

CHAPTER 9
MANAGING COMPLEX LIVES

What themes do the seven stages of life we have examined have in common? We highlight three:

- the growing complexity of people's life journeys and the role of guidance;
- the need for a new approach to savings, so that individuals have financial support at critical points of their lives;
- the ageing of society, and sensible ways to manage it.

NAVIGATING THE JOURNEY

People's lives will continue to become more individualised, fluid and complex over the next 20 years. Trends already in place will persist.

Not least, as more people go to university and witness different values, and as mounting prosperity brings new opportunities, individuals will increasingly be 'unboxed' from their backgrounds. They will be aware of more alternatives, and will have greater confidence in making their own decisions.

Although social background will remain a huge influence, instead of life trajectories being given to them by their birth and upbringing, people will – to a significant extent – create their own biographies.

Making the right choices will become an even greater focus of everyday life than it is today.

For people in the mainstream, the key decisions will remain much as they are now – whether to go university, which one, what career path to take, how to get on the housing ladder, who to settle down with, whether and when to have children, what school to send them to – and so on.

But many of these decisions will become more complicated. There will be more possibilities – for example:

- Should I go to university in this country or abroad?
- Should I get management experience in Asia?
- Should I opt out of the 'personal accounts' pension scheme so that I can save more for a house?

- Should I look for a school that will equip my child to sit the International Baccalaureate?
- Should I take six months out from work now that the children have left home?
- Should I plan to work till my late 60s or even early 70s, so that I don't have to save quite so much each year for a pension?

As now, poor people will have fewer choices. Many young people from disadvantaged backgrounds will continue to live in a fantasy world of celebrity and success, but find it difficult to engage with the real world and make the most of their limited opportunities.

Making the right choices will not be easy. An ever-widening range of options will be just one of the problems.

Even more than today, tomorrow's decision-making will be complicated by a surfeit of information. In 2002 alone, the world produced an estimated five exabytes of new information – equivalent to 37,000 libraries the size of Washington's Library of Congress, or 30 feet of books per person in the world! What's more, the amount of new information is growing exponentially.

Alongside this swirling mass of data will be the question of trust. Who can I trust to give me good advice? Marketers know that the people we turn to for advice are friends and family. We know them and so we trust them.

But these confidants don't always score well on knowledge. If Bill says 'It's worth postponing the state pension if you work beyond 65', this doesn't necessarily mean that he has checked the figures himself, and what makes sense for him may not make sense for you.

The need for trusted advice will grow in every part of our lives. 'Choice managers' – a generic term covering any expert who assists you in making a decision, from shopping advisers to personal coaches – will increasingly help individuals to cope with everyday life.

The idea of lifelong guidance will gain ground, almost certainly. Rather than advice being sporadic, crisis-related and available only if you are lucky, the view is likely to emerge that guidance spanning all stages and aspects of our lives should be available whenever and wherever we need it.

This expanded form of guidance would be:

- *Continuous* – it would be available throughout your life, which would help to build trust. You would get to know your guide and your guide would get to know you.
- *Comprehensive*, covering family, work and other parts of your life. Your guide would have an overview of your life and draw in specialists as required.
- *Available in different formats* whenever you needed it – face to face, by phone or online, for example.
- *Impartial* – advice would be tailored specifically to your needs.

Your guide would be a bit like a personal coach, but would have a much wider view of your life. The quality of advice would be better because the guide knew you so well.

As well as being a sounding board, your guide would put you in touch with experts who could advise on particular aspects of your life, such as job moves, personal finances, parenting, health and fitness, or how to develop an interest or hobby. You would trust these experts because your guide recommended them.

Might this guidance first emerge among the rich and the poor? For affluent people, it would be a next step from personal trainers, life coaches and other forms of support currently available. 'It's great to pay someone who can see my life in the round, and who can put me in touch with experts I can trust!'

For disadvantaged people it would be a significant pulling together of the various forms of support the government is seeking to put in place – such as (in England):

- family nurses working with vulnerable young parents;
- learning mentors who help school children and college students address barriers to learning;
- the Connexions Service offering young people information and advice on how to get to where they want to be in life;
- job brokers helping the unemployed, ex-offenders and disabled people into or back to work.

Integrated and continuous support would ensure that advice was available when it was needed. It would be a new form of safety net, one fit for the twenty-first century.

Whereas the twentieth-century welfare state often created dependency, this new safety net would be designed to encourage independence. Individuals wouldn't be told what to do: they would be equipped to make their own decisions.

To make this support attractive to people from disadvantaged backgrounds, various possibilities would need to be tried. Different approaches may work in different areas.

Significant benefits are likely from getting a coherent approach to guidance right. There are potential gains to the individual, to organisations working with disadvantaged people (whose work might be more effective) and to society, which would be enriched if more people were able to flourish.

The limited evidence from research on careers advice suggests that guidance can be highly effective. An Australian study found that with even a modest amount of careers counselling, a very disadvantaged group of unemployed people increased their participation in learning significantly.

'Life profiles' could play a significant part. Alongside continuous advice, a 'life profile' would be a place for individuals to put together a coherent account of the journey they had made so far. They would have in one place a constantly updated record of, for example:

- prior learning and experience;
- credentials and qualifications;
- references;
- career plans and targets;
- hobbies and interests;
- family milestones;
- pension forecasts and financial records;
- health records.

This voluntary record would be a statement: 'This is who I am.' It could take many forms – on paper, a secure computer file or a privacy-protected feature of a social networking site, such as Facebook – and would be the property of the person concerned.

The balance of content might change at different stages of life, and sensitive data would be encrypted. Various levels of security might be possible, with different price tags.

The profile might be used for online social and professional networking. It would also be available at individuals' discretion to their advisers and potential employers, and would provide a focus for discussing future plans and directions in life. Information and advice could be given in the context of this wider framework.

A SAVINGS RUCKSACK

We have argued that government should adopt a new approach to savings (see chapter 7). The current approach, which focuses largely on pensions, suffers from several weaknesses:

- *It is too long term* for many young people, who often live for today. A pension in 40 years' time seems miles away – far too distant to motivate them to save.
- *It is too inflexible.* The 'personal accounts' pension scheme, to be introduced in 2012, will allow you to put in money only for a pension. Contributions will then be locked away for up to 40 years or more. This rigidity flies in the

face of today's widespread desire not to be tied down – to keep one's options open.

- *Proposed changes could be unwise.* Government plans that workers will be automatically enrolled in personal accounts unless they opt out. But this may encourage some people on modest earnings to save for a pension when they would have been better advised to repay their existing debts and rely instead on the means-tested Pension Credit to increase their retirement income.

We have suggested an alternative approach – a Lifelong Savings Account with the following features:

- *It would be built round the whole life course* rather than retirement alone. Individuals could save up to buy assets that they required now, but which would also boost their incomes in old age.

  These assets would consist of learning (such as paying off a student loan), housing (saving for a deposit or repaying a mortgage) and pensions. As individuals travelled through life, they could put money into their savings rucksack and draw funds out.

- *Savers could choose from a wide range of schemes,* including an adapted version of the new personal accounts. Their savings would be channelled through a single designated bank account.

  Individuals would receive an annual forecast of what their savings would be worth when they retired, based on clearly stated assumptions, and this would be a regular reminder to plan for retirement.

- *Employers and government would make contributions,* as well as individuals, along the lines envisaged for the personal accounts. This would give individuals a good incentive to save.

Such an approach would avoid some of the difficulties in the government's proposed personal accounts scheme.

Savings would be more relevant to people who think short term. They would be able to save for immediate purposes, but in ways that would also bring benefits later in life. Savings would be more flexible.

Might these advantages, together with employer and government contributions, reduce the need for automatic enrolment? Individuals would have a strong enough incentive to save without requiring the inertia effect of being enrolled automatically.

Dropping automatic enrolment would reduce the risk of misleadingly encouraging savings among people who would have little to gain.

The basic ingredients of this 'life journey' approach to savings already exist. What is needed is some joined-up thinking.

For example, all new babies are now entitled to a Child Trust Fund, which is kicked off with a government payment of £250 (and a further payment when the child is aged seven). Parents, family and friends can contribute to the fund, which can grow and earn interest tax-free. Children can spend the money when they are 18.

It would be a small step for the government to limit use of the Fund to repaying a student loan or saving to buy a home. The way would then be open for the Child Trust Fund to become the foundation stage of our proposed Lifelong Savings Account.

The Savings Gateway will be introduced nationally in 2010. It will be a cash savings account for people on lower incomes. The government will match the amount each individual puts into the account to provide a strong incentive to save.

Why not integrate the Savings Gateway with our Lifelong Savings Account? Government would make extra payments into the Lifelong Account to match the contributions of people on low incomes, making the Lifelong Account more attractive to them.

Might Independent Savings Accounts (ISAs) be combined with Lifelong Accounts, too? The tax exemption on contributions would be converted into a government payment (as proposed for pensions). Rolling government support for savings into one flexible scheme would help the public to know what is available. *Personal accounts could provide the nucleus of a lifelong scheme.* The government intends that a national scheme of personal accounts will bring economies of scale, which will cut the cost to individuals of saving for a pension.

Workers will be able to take their savings account with them when they move from one employer to another. They will have a choice of savings funds if they wish.

Why shouldn't these personal accounts become the default option for the Lifelong Savings Account? They would be the option most ordinary people would choose, though individuals wanting to use different savings vehicles would be free to do so. *A revised version of independent learning accounts is under consideration.* These accounts, essentially vouchers to encourage adults back to learning, were withdrawn in 2001 because of difficulties with their delivery. Despite this, parts of the education establishment believe that these vouchers still have potential.

> 'Fragmented government schemes would be brought together to enhance their effect'

To entice adults with few qualifications to start a formal course of study would probably require a distinct scheme. But why shouldn't universal encouragement for learning underpin such a scheme? A Lifelong Savings Account, with the facility to save for learning, could provide that support.

What we are suggesting is a more integrated approach to savings. Fragmented government schemes would be brought together to enhance their effect. Savings would be more relevant to different stages of the life journey. Might putting money aside become more attractive?

MANAGING AN AGEING SOCIETY

Britain's population is about to age rapidly. The chart below shows the latest population projection from the Government Actuary's Department. Though figures are given for England, the pattern basically holds for the UK as a whole.

The chart shows that after two decades of relative stability, the proportion of over-60s in the population is beginning to increase significantly. Whereas they currently represent about 20% of the population, by the mid twenty-first century they will be closer to 30%.

The proportion of over-75s, who make the heaviest demands on services such as healthcare, will increase even more rapidly.

Projected percentage age distribution, England

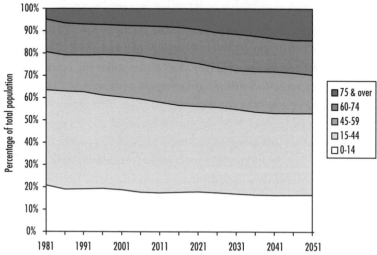

Source: Data drawn from both 'Projection Database', 2006-based principal population projections, Government Actuary's Department, **http://www.gad.gov.uk;** and *Population Trends,* 132, 2008, table 1.4, **http://www.statistics.gov.uk**.

Note: The 15 to 44 age group is so wide ranging because separate statistics were not available for the 15 to 29 and 30 to 44 age groups. It contains twice as many ages as the other age groups in the chart.

An older population is good news because it means that people are generally healthier and living for longer. But it will also be a problem if, as the chart above suggests, the proportion of older people to the working-age population goes up.

On current trends, those in work will have to meet the costs of pensions and healthcare for an ever-growing number of older people. Will workers be willing to foot a lengthening bill?

Three 'simple' answers could each play a part, although they are not an absolute solution.

The first is that higher labour productivity could increase income per worker, making it easier to support an older population.

It is conceivable that new technologies could lift productivity significantly. But in Britain the overall gradual trend of productivity growth has been pretty constant for many years, despite technological advances. There is little sign of a step change.

Might raising the birth rate be a way through? As we saw in chapter 2, too few children are currently being born to replace their parents' generation when they die. If we could increase the number of births, some think, we would eventually have more people of working age to support those who are old.

But there are some real problems with this:

- Even if you increased the birth rate today, it would be more than 20 years before this fed through to a larger workforce.
- Though some countries, like France, give financial incentives to have children, it is not clear how big an incentive is needed to make a difference. The government could waste a lot of money offering incentives that were too small to have an effect – or unnecessarily large.
- Some people think that the population in Britain is already big enough. The Optimum Population Trust, for example, calculates that if the population continues to grow at its current rate, the UK will have over 100 million people by the end of the century (compared to about 60 million today). 'Where would we put them all?' it asks.

Increasing immigration has been another suggestion. Migrants enlarge the workforce so that there are more people to support the dependent population.

But as a solution to population ageing, this runs up against the same overcrowding problem as trying to raise the birth rate. How many more people can Britain fit in?

A greater difficulty is that immigrants grow old, too. As today's migrants age, along with others in the population, even more working-age people would be needed to support them. The need for more workers would increase exponentially.

An early 2000s estimate suggested that using immigration to preserve the current ratio of elderly people to the national workforce would double the UK population to 120 million by 2050, and push it up to 312 million by 2100. This would not be much less than the 2003 population of the whole EU!

Overseas workers can certainly plug short-term skill gaps, but they would not be a panacea for managing the 'greying' of the UK population.

Other ways forward will be needed to support our ageing population. Three possibilities exist, though none will be easy. Each involves increasing the size of the working population so that supporting the elderly can be shared more widely. *The first would be to increase the number of young workers.* It has become taken for granted that we should invest more heavily in the training and education of young people. As we saw in chapter 4, plans in the pipeline will boost this investment substantially.

One result of this, though, will be to reduce the number of teenagers and young adults who are available for permanent, full-time employment. They will take part-time and casual work while they train and learn, but the hours worked will be far fewer than in full-time jobs.

This loss of working hours would be a price worth paying if we could be sure that the extra training and education was necessary. But we have seen that there are good reasons to doubt this.

■ *The UK has too many qualified workers but not enough skilled ones.* As we saw in chapter 4, there are more people with formal qualifications than there are jobs that require these qualifications as an entry requirement. Adding to the numbers with formal qualifications will simply compound this excess supply. At the same time, employers find that many 'qualified' workers don't have necessary skills in numeracy, literacy, IT and relating to other people. These basic skills should be acquired before people leave school. As the government has recognised, more investment is needed earlier in children's lives, so that they don't fall behind and miss out on these skills.

■ *The extra training the government plans may be poor quality.* It is by no means certain that new apprenticeships will lead to permanent jobs, while the new Diplomas may well have little market value, especially at lower levels. This is because employers may not be convinced that people who have a Diploma also have the basic skills mentioned above. Indeed, if low-level Diplomas can be awarded to individuals with few skills, the Diplomas will be a sign to employers that these are precisely the workers they should seek to avoid.

■ *Compulsory education or training to 18 may wreck the youth labour market.* Employers who currently offer full-time jobs to under-18s may stop doing so because of the extra work involved. They would have to make sure their young workers had off-the-job training, as required by the government's proposals. They may recruit 18s and over, perhaps from abroad, instead.

Though this is an unfashionable view, might the government be wiser to invest less in post-16 training and more heavily in special needs and other support for learners who are struggling early in their school years?

This would reduce the number of 16-year-olds who don't have basic literacy and numeracy skills. These teenagers would then be more attractive to employers whom, experience shows, will provide whatever job-specific training is required. Having more teenagers in employment would be one way of enlarging the working population.

Might more people be drawn in from the edge of the labour market? In 2004–07 (before the downturn) over a fifth of working-age men were either unemployed (and looking for work), or not working and not looking for work. The figure for women was even higher.[1] Many came from disadvantaged backgrounds and had a history of unstable employment.

Encouraging adults not in employment back to work has become a priority across the political spectrum. There is a growing recognition that factors making it hard to get a job can build up over a lifetime.

You may be born into a disadvantaged family with hardly a book in sight, for example. By the time you get to school, your reading may be behind others in the class. You may feel discouraged, which reduces your desire to learn.

If this pattern becomes ingrained, you may leave school with poor literacy and numeracy, making it difficult to get a decent job. You may fall in and out of employment for much of your life. As you get older, after a lifetime in poverty you are more likely to be seriously ill, which will reduce your job prospects still further.

Policy-makers are now mostly agreed on the need for interventions throughout a person's life to help break the journey from one misfortune to another. These interventions increasingly include:

- *A focus on high-risk families and individuals,* mainly in highly disadvantaged areas, who are most in need of support.
- *Support in the early years,* especially for parents, who can protect their children from some of the damage caused by poverty.
- *More rigorous phonics-based approaches to learning to read,* which seems to be paying off.
- *Increasing remedial support for children at school,* and at an earlier age, so that those who are struggling have less chance of being left behind and becoming discouraged. Gordon Brown has promised that any primary-school child who falls behind will have a guaranteed right to catch-up tuition.[2]
- *More support for school-leavers* with poor formal qualifications, to help them acquire key skills in literacy, numeracy and IT.
- *A stronger 'carrot and stick' approach to the unemployed,* so that remaining jobless becomes a less desirable option.
- *Earlier intervention when ill-health leads to unemployment,* to make it more likely that individuals will return to work.

Is it time to take a further step, and address the geographical mismatch between unemployment and job vacancies?

In areas where unemployment is high, children may be discouraged from doing well at school, and adults from retraining, because it all seems so pointless. 'There are no jobs round here. Why bother?' Helping people back to work is extremely difficult if there are few openings nearby.

Stronger encouragement for unemployed people to move to where jobs are plentiful might well be controversial, but would it be unreasonable?

There is a long tradition of people 'upping sticks' to where jobs are being created – think of the Industrial Revolution. Nowadays, text and email allow you to stay closely in touch with friends and family, making it emotionally easier to move. As we saw in chapter 5, 'convoys' of friends who travel with you through life, and who would visit you in a new place, are likely to be more common in future.

The critical need is for practical support for people who are willing to move to find a job. Starting with school leavers in selected high unemployment spots, might government pay for generous packages of support?

These packages, which would have a strong focus on quality so that they earn a good reputation, might include:

- *some choice of place* for the jobseeker when moving;
- *temporary accommodation,* and help in finding somewhere permanent;
- *assistance in finding a job,* if necessary including training and mentoring to help the person adapt to the job;
- *financial support,* and a dedicated mentor to help the person make the transition.

If such a scheme was rolled out gradually, might it help to expand the working population?

Extending the length of working lives is an obvious third way of expanding the working population, so that more people can support the growing numbers of 'oldest old'.

The government plans to raise the state pension age to 67 by the middle of the century, encouraging people to work for two extra years. But if life expectancy continues to lengthen by more than official projections, this may not be enough.

Raising the pension age still further, however, could meet stiff resistance from workers who fear that their right to retirement is being eroded.

Might there be ways to overcome this opposition? Possibilities include further encouragement for employers to introduce phased and flexible approaches to retirement. If workers wanted to stay in employment for financial or other reasons, they would find it easier to do so.

Additionally, in chapter 7 we suggested that changes to the state pension age should occur automatically as expectations about life expectancy evolve. An independent body might make the adjustment.

Might such a body emerge from a national debate about the proportion of the average person's life that should be spent in retirement? Debate might be aided by a Commission to enquire into what is reasonable, and might help people to be realistic about what they can sensibly expect.

CHANGING LIVES?

In many ways our lives will continue to unfold in the same way as before – a familiar progression through various stages, each with its own characteristics.

But we cannot ignore the changes that are gradually transforming the journey through life, making it more fluid, individualised and diverse. These have been accompanied – and to some extent caused – by a combination of increasing globalisation and radically new communication technologies.

For many people, these new life journeys, and the myriad new choices within them, offer great potential for personal fulfilment. But they also make everyday life more complicated and pose a range of challenges.

As a society we need to recognise the scale of the changes taking place both now and on the horizon, and we need to help individuals – whether as citizens, workers or consumers – to make the most of their opportunities as they travel through life. Can we escape from past ways of thinking to develop new approaches that fit the life journeys starting to emerge?

---

1 For figures on unemployment and inactivity rates see ONS Labour Market Statistics – Integrated FR LFS TIME PERIODS, tables YBTJ, YBTM, YBTN.
2 Speech made to Labour Party Conference, 23 September 2008.

GLIMPSES of tomorrow *is the Tomorrow Project's online database describing emerging social, economic and demographic trends. GLIMPSES, at* **www.tomorrowproject.net***, provides a 'map' of recent trends to help people answer three questions: Where have we come from? Where are we going? What do we need to think about?*

INDEX